Raspberry Pi Assembly Language Programming

ARM Processor Coding

Stephen Smith

Apress®

Raspberry Pi Assembly Language Programming: ARM Processor Coding

Stephen Smith
Gibsons, BC, Canada

ISBN-13 (pbk): 978-1-4842-5286-4   ISBN-13 (electronic): 978-1-4842-5287-1
https://doi.org/10.1007/978-1-4842-5287-1

Copyright © 2019 by Stephen Smith

Managing Director, Apress Media LLC: Welmoed Spahr
Acquisitions Editor: Aaron Black
Development Editor: James Markham
Coordinating Editor: Jessica Vakili

Cover designed by eStudioCalamar

Cover image designed by Freepik (www.freepik.com)

Distributed to the book trade worldwide by Springer Science+Business Media New York, 233 Spring Street, 6th Floor, New York, NY 10013. Phone 1-800-SPRINGER, fax (201) 348-4505, e-mail orders-ny@springer-sbm.com, or visit www.springeronline.com. Apress Media, LLC is a California LLC and the sole member (owner) is Springer Science + Business Media Finance Inc (SSBM Finance Inc). SSBM Finance Inc is a **Delaware** corporation.

For information on translations, please e-mail rights@apress.com, or visit http://www.apress.com/rights-permissions.

Apress titles may be purchased in bulk for academic, corporate, or promotional use. eBook versions and licenses are also available for most titles. For more information, reference our Print and eBook Bulk Sales web page at http://www.apress.com/bulk-sales.

Any source code or other supplementary material referenced by the author in this book is available to readers on GitHub via the book's product page, located at www.apress.com/978-1-4842-5286-4. For more detailed information, please visit http://www.apress.com/source-code.

Printed on acid-free paper

This book is dedicated to my beloved wife and editor Cathalynn Labonté-Smith.

Table of Contents

About the Author .... **xv**

About the Technical Reviewer .... **xvii**

Acknowledgments .... **xix**

Introduction .... **xxi**

Chapter 1: Getting Started 1

About the ARM Processor 2

What You Will Learn 3

Why Use Assembly..4

Tools You Need...7

Computers and Numbers 8

ARM Assembly Instructions 11

    CPU Registers...12

    ARM Instruction Format..13

    Raspberry Pi Memory 15

About the GCC Assembler 16

Hello World...17

    About the Starting Comment 20

    Where to Start 20

    Assembly Instructions 21

    Data 22

Calling Linux 22

Reverse Engineering Our Program 23

Summary..26

Chapter 2: Loading and Adding 27

Negative Numbers 27

About Two's Complement 27

About Gnome Programmer's Calculator 29

About One's Complement...30

Big vs. Little-endian 30

About Bi-endian..32

Pros of Little-endian 32

Shifting and Rotating 33

About Carry Flag...33

About the Barrel Shifter..34

Basics of Shifting and Rotating 35

MOV/MVN...36

About MOVT 36

Register to Register MOV..37

The Dreaded Flexible Operand2 37

MVN 40

MOV Examples..41

ADD/ADC 45

Add with Carry..47

Summary..51

Chapter 3: Tooling Up..**53**

GNU Make 53

    Rebuilding a File...54

    A Rule for Building .s files 54

    Defining Variables...55

GDB 56

    Preparing to Debug...56

    Beginning GDB..58

Source Control and Build Servers 63

    Git 63

    Jenkins 64

Summary...65

Chapter 4: Controlling Program Flow **67**

Unconditional Branch..67

About the CPSR...68

Branch on Condition..70

About the CMP Instruction 71

Loops 71

    FOR Loops 72

    While Loops 73

If/Then/Else..74

Logical Operators..75

    AND...75

    EOR...76

    ORR...76

    BIC 76

Design Patterns...77

Converting Integers to ASCII 78

    Using Expressions in Immediate Constants...82

    Storing a Register to Memory..82

    Why Not Print in Decimal?...83

Performance of Branch Instructions 83

More Comparison Instructions 84

Summary..85

Chapter 5: Thanks for the Memories 87

Defining Memory Contents 88

Loading a Register 92

    PC Relative Addressing..92

    Loading from Memory 95

    Indexing Through Memory...96

Storing a Register 107

Double Registers 108

Summary..108

Chapter 6: Functions and the Stack 109

Stacks on Raspbian 110

Branch with Link..111

Nesting Function Calls 112

Function Parameters and Return Values...114

Managing the Registers 114

Summary of the Function Call Algorithm 115

Uppercase Revisited 116

Stack Frames 121

    Stack Frame Example..123

Macros 125

    Include Directive..128

    Macro Definition 128

    Labels 129

    Why Macros?...129

  Summary..130

Chapter 7: Linux Operating System Services 131

  So Many Services 131

  Calling Convention 132

    Structures..133

  Wrappers...134

  Converting a File to Uppercase 135

    Opening a File..140

    Error Checking...140

    Looping..142

  Summary..143

Chapter 8: Programming GPIO Pins.....................................145

  GPIO Overview 145

  In Linux, Everything Is a File 146

  Flashing LEDs 148

  Moving Closer to the Metal 152

  Virtual Memory...153

    About Raspberry Pi 4 RAM 154

  In Devices, Everything Is Memory...154

  Registers in Bits...155

    GPIO Function Select Registers 156

    GPIO Output Set and Clear Registers..158

More Flashing LEDs 158

    Root Access 164

    Table Driven.. 164

    Setting Pin Direction... 165

    Setting and Clearing Pins 166

Summary... 167

Chapter 9: Interacting with C and Python 169

Calling C Routines.. 169

    Printing Debug Information 170

    Adding with Carry Revisited 173

Calling Assembly Routines from C 175

Packaging Our Code... 178

    Static Library 178

    Shared Library 179

Embedding Assembly Code Inside C Code.. 182

Calling Assembly from Python 185

Summary... 187

Chapter 10: Multiply, Divide, and Accumulate...................189

Multiplication 189

    Examples 191

Division 194

    Example.. 195

Multiply and Accumulate... 197

    Vectors and Matrices.. 198

    Accumulate Instructions... 199

    Example 1 201

    Example 2 206

Summary... 210

Chapter 11: Floating-Point Operations **211**

   About Floating-Point Numbers...212

      Normalization and NaNs..212

      Rounding Errors...213

   Defining Floating-Point Numbers...214

   FPU Registers...214

   Function Call Protocol 216

   About Building...217

   Loading and Saving FPU Registers 217

   Basic Arithmetic...218

   Distance Between Points 220

   Floating-Point Conversions 224

      Floating-Point Comparison 225

      Example...227

   Summary..231

Chapter 12: NEON Coprocessor **233**

   The NEON Registers...234

   Stay in Your Lane 236

   Arithmetic Operations 237

   4D Vector Distance...238

   3x3 Matrix Multiplication 243

   Summary..248

Chapter 13: Conditional Instructions and Optimizing Code.............**249**

   Reasons Not to Use Conditional Instructions 250

      No Conditional Instructions in 64 Bits 250

      Improved Pipeline..250

   About Conditional Code...251

Optimizing the Uppercase Routine..251

    Simplifying the Range Comparison 252

    Using a Conditional Instruction..255

    Restricting the Problem Domain...256

    Using Parallelism with SIMD 259

Summary...263

Chapter 14: Reading and Understanding Code 265

Raspbian and GCC...265

    Division Revisited 267

Code Created by GCC 271

Reverse Engineering and Ghidra..275

Summary...279

Chapter 15: Thumb Code 281

16-Bit Instruction Format...282

Calling Thumb Code 283

Thumb-2 Is More than 16 Bits 285

IT Blocks 285

Uppercase in Thumb-2...286

Use the C Compiler 293

Summary...295

Chapter 16: 64 Bits...297

Ubuntu MATE...297

About 64 Bits..298

More and Bigger Registers 299

    SP and Zero Register 300

Function Call Interface 301

    Push and Pop Are Gone 302

Calling Linux Services...303

Porting from 32 Bits to 64 Bits..303

Porting Uppercase to 64 Bits 304

Conditional Instructions 308

    Example with CSEL..309

FPU and the NEON Coprocessors..311

    Registers 311

    Instructions..312

    Comparisons...313

    Example Using NEON..313

Summary..315

Appendix A: The ARM Instruction Set...317

Appendix B: Linux System Calls 327

Linux System Call Numbers 327

Linux System Call Error Codes...342

Appendix C: Binary Formats 347

Integers..347

Floating-Point..348

Addresses 349

64 Bits...349

Appendix D: Assembler Directives...351

Appendix E: ASCII Character Set 353

References..365

Index...367

About the Author

Stephen Smith is a retired software architect, located in Gibsons, BC, Canada. He's been developing software since high school, or way too many years to record. He worked on the Sage 300 line of accounting products for 23 years. Since retiring, he has pursued artificial intelligence, earned his advanced ham radio license, and enjoys mountain biking, hiking, and nature photography. He continues to write his popular technology blog at smist08.wordpress. com and has written two science fiction novels in a series, *Influence*, available on Amazon.com.

About the Technical Reviewer

Stewart Watkiss is a keen maker, programmer, and author of *Learn Electronics with Raspberry Pi*. He studied at the University of Hull, where he earned a master's degree in electronic engineering, and more recently at Georgia Institute of Technology, where he earned a master's degree in computer science.

Stewart also volunteers as a STEM Ambassador, helping teach programming and physical computer to school children and at Raspberry Pi events. He has created a number of resources using Pygame Zero, which he makes available on his web site (www.penguintutor.com).

Acknowledgments

No book is ever written in isolation. I want to especially thank my wife Cathalynn Labonté-Smith for her support, encouragement, and expert editing.

I want to thank all the good folks at Apress who made the whole process easy and enjoyable. A special shout-out to Jessica Vakili, my coordinating editor, who kept the whole project moving quickly and smoothly. Thanks to Aaron Black, the senior editor, who recruited me and got the project started. Thanks to Stewart Watkiss, my technical reviewer, who helped make this a far better book. Thanks to James Markham, my development editor, for all his good work keeping me to standards.

Introduction

If you really want to learn how a computer works, learning Assembly language is a great way to get into the nitty-gritty details. The popularity and low cost of the Raspberry Pi provide an ideal platform to learn advanced concepts in computing.

Even though the Raspberry Pi is inexpensive and credit card sized, it is still a sophisticated computer with a quad-core processor, a floating-point coprocessor, and a NEON parallel processing unit. What you learn about the Raspberry Pi is directly relevant to any device with an ARM processor, which includes nearly every cell phone and tablet. In fact, by volume, the ARM processor is the number one processor today.

In this book, we will cover how you program the Raspberry Pi at the lowest level; you will be operating as close to the hardware as possible. We will teach the format of the instructions, how to put them together into programs as well as details on the binary data formats they operate on. We will cover how to program the floating-point processor as well as the NEON parallel processor. We cover how to program the GPIO ports to interface to custom hardware, so you can experiment with electronics connected to your Raspberry Pi.

All you need is a Raspberry Pi running Raspbian. This will provide all the tools you need to learn Assembly programming. This is the low cost of entry of running open source software like Raspbian Linux and the GNU Assembler. The last chapter covers 64-bit programming, where you will need to run Ubuntu MATE on your Pi.

This book contains many working programs that you can play with, use as a starting point, or study. The only way to learn programming is by doing; don't be afraid to experiment, as it is the only way you will learn.

Even if you don't use Assembly programming in your day-to-day life, knowing how the processor works at the Assembly level and knowing the low-level binary data structures will make you a better programmer in all other areas. Knowing how the processor works will let you write more efficient C code, and can even help you with your Python programming.

The book is designed to be followed in sequence, but there are chapters that can be skipped or skimmed, for instance, if you aren't interested in interfacing to hardware, you can pass on Chapter 8, "Programming GPIO Pins," or Chapter 11, "Floating-Point Operations" if you will never do numerical computing.

I hope you enjoy your introduction to Assembly language. Learning it for one processor family will help you with any other processor architectures you encounter through your career.

CHAPTER 1

Getting Started

The Raspberry Pi is a credit card–sized computer that costs only US$35. It was originally developed to provide low-cost computers to schools and children, who couldn't afford regular PCs or Macs. Since its release, the Raspberry Pi has been incredibly successful—as of this writing, selling over 25 million units. The Raspberry Pi has become the basis of a whole DIY movement with diverse applications, including home automation control systems, acting as the brain for robots, or linked together to build a personal supercomputer. The Pi is also a great educational tool.

This book will leverage the Raspberry Pi to assist you in learning Assembly language. Programming in Assembly language is programming your computer at the lowest bits and bytes level. People usually program computers in high-level programming languages, like Python, C, Java, C#, or JavaScript. The tools that accompany these languages convert your program to Assembly language, whether they do it all at once or as they run.

Assembly language is specific to the computer processor used. Since we are learning for the Raspberry Pi, we will learn Assembly language for the Advanced RISC Machine (ARM) processor. We will use the Raspbian operating system, a 32-bit operating system based on Debian Linux, so we will learn 32-bit Assembly on the Raspberry Pi's ARM processor.

The Raspberry Pi 3 has an ARM processor that can operate in 64-bit mode, but Raspbian doesn't do that. We will highlight some important differences between 32-bit and 64-bit Assembly, but all our sample programs will be in 32-bit ARM Assembler and will be compiled to run under Raspbian.

© Stephen Smith 2019
S. Smith, *Raspberry Pi Assembly Language Programming*,
https://doi.org/10.1007/978-1-4842-5287-1_1

About the ARM Processor

The ARM processor was originally developed by a group in Great Britain, who wanted to build a successor to the BBC Microcomputer used for educational purposes. The BBC Microcomputer used the 6502 processor, which was a simple processor with a simple instruction set. The problem was there was no successor to the 6502. They weren't happy with the microprocessors that were around at the time, since they were much more complicated than the 6502 and they didn't want to make another IBM PC clone. They took the bold move to design their own. They developed the Acorn computer that used it and tried to position it as the successor to the BBC Microcomputer. The idea was to use Reduced Instruction Set Computer (RISC) technology as opposed to Complex Instruction Set Computer (CISC) as championed by Intel and Motorola. We talk at length about what these terms really mean later.

Developing silicon chips is an expensive proposition, and unless you can get a good volume going, manufacturing is expensive. The ARM processor probably wouldn't have gone anywhere except that Apple came calling looking for a processor for a new device they had under development—the iPod. The key selling point for Apple was that, as the ARM processor was RISC, it used less silicon than CISC processors and as a result used far less power. This meant it was possible to build a device that ran for a long time on a single battery charge.

Unlike Intel, ARM doesn't manufacture chips; it just licenses the designs for others to optimize and manufacture. With Apple onboard, suddenly there was a lot of interest in ARM, and several big manufacturers started producing chips. With the advent of smartphones, the ARM chip really took off and now is used in pretty much every phone and tablet. ARM processors even power some Chromebooks. The ARM processor is the number one processor in the computer market.

What You Will Learn

You will learn Assembly language programming for the ARM processor on the Raspberry Pi, but everything you learn is directly applicable to all these other devices. Learning Assembly language for one processor gives you the tools to learn it for another processor, perhaps, the forthcoming RISC-V.

The chip that is the brains of the Raspberry Pi isn't just a processor, it is also a system on a chip. This means that most of the computer is all on one chip. This chip contains an ARM quad-core processor, meaning that it can process instructions for four programs running at once. It also contains several coprocessors for things like floating-point calculations, a graphics processing unit (GPU) and specialized multimedia support.

ARM does a good job at supporting coprocessors and allowing manufacturers to build their chips in a modular manner incorporating the elements they need. All Raspberry Pi include a floating-point coprocessor (**FPU**). Newer Raspberry Pi have advanced capabilities such as NEON parallel processors. Table 1-1 gives an overview of the units we will be programming and which Raspberry Pi support them. In Table 1-1, **SoC** is system on a chip and contains the Broadcom part number for the unit incorporated.

Table 1-1. *Common Raspberry Pi models and their capabilities relevant to this book*

Model	SoC	Memory	Divide instruction	FPU	NEON coprocessor	64-Bit support
Pi A+	BCM2835	256 MB		v2		
Pi B	BCM2835	512 MB		v2		
Pi Zero	BCM2835	512 MB		v2		
Pi 2	BCM2836	1 GB	Yes	v3	Yes	Yes
Pi 3	BCM2837	1 GB	Yes	v4	Yes	Yes
Pi 3+	BCM2837B0	1 GB	Yes	v4	Yes	Yes
Pi 4	BCM2711	1, 2, or 4 GB	Yes	v4	Yes	Yes

Why Use Assembly

Most programmers today write in a high-level programming language like Python, C#, Java, JavaScript, Go, Julia, Scratch, Ruby, Swift, or C. These are highly productive languages that are used to write major programs from the Linux operating system to web sites like Facebook to productivity software like LibreOffice. If you learn to be a good programmer in a couple of these, you can find a well-paying interesting job and write some great programs. If you create a program in one of these languages, you can easily get it working on multiple operating systems on multiple hardware architectures. You never have to learn the details of all the bits and bytes, and these can remain safely under the covers.

When you program in Assembly language, you are tightly coupled to a given CPU, and moving your program to another requires a complete rewrite of your program. Each Assembly language instruction does only a fraction of the amount of work, so to do anything takes a lot of Assembly statements. Therefore, to do the same work as, say, a Python program, takes an order of magnitude larger amount of effort, for the programmer. Writing in Assembly is harder, as you must solve problems with memory addressing and CPU registers that is all handled transparently by high-level languages. So why would you ever want to learn Assembly language programming? Here are ten reasons people learn and use Assembly language:

1. Even if you don't write Assembly language code, knowing how the computer works internally allows you to write more efficient code. You can make your data structures easier to access and write code in a style that allows the compiler to generate more efficient code. You can make better use of computer resources like coprocessors and use the given computer to its fullest potential.

2. To write your own operating system. The very core of the operating system that initializes the CPU handles hardware security and multi-threading/multi-tasking requires Assembly code.

3. To create a new programming language. If it is a compiled language, then you need to generate the Assembly code to execute. The quality and speed of your language is largely dependent on the quality and speed of the Assembly language code it generates.

4. You want to make the Raspberry Pi faster. The best way to make Raspbian faster is to improve the GNU C compiler. If you improve the ARM 32-bit Assembly code produced by GNU C, then every Linux program compiled for the Pi benefits.

5. You might be interfacing your Pi to a hardware device, either through USB or the GPIO ports, and the speed of data transfer is highly sensitive to how fast your program can process the data. Perhaps there are a lot of bit-level manipulations that are easier to program in Assembly.

6. To do faster machine learning or 3D graphics programming. Both applications rely on fast matrix mathematics. If you can make this faster with Assembly and/or using the coprocessors, then you can make your AI-based robot or video game that much better.

7. Most large programs have components written in different languages. If your program is 99% C++, the other 1% could be Assembly, perhaps giving your program a performance boost or some other competitive advantage.

8. Perhaps you work for a hardware company that makes a single board computer competitor to the Raspberry Pi. These boards have some Assembly language code to manage peripherals included with the board. This code is usually called a BIOS (basic input/output system).

9. To look for security vulnerabilities in a program or piece of hardware. You usually need to look at the Assembly code to do this; otherwise, you may not know what is really going on, and hence where holes might exist.

10.   To look for Easter eggs in programs. These are hidden messages, images, or inside jokes that programmers hide in their programs. They are usually enabled by finding a secret keyboard combination to pop them up. Finding them requires reverse engineering the program and reading Assembly language.

Tools You Need

This book is designed so that all you need is a Raspberry Pi that runs the Raspbian operating system. Raspbian is based on Debian Linux, so anything you know about Linux is directly useful. There are other operating systems for the Pi, but we will only cover Raspbian in this book.

A Raspberry Pi 3, either the B or B+ model, is ideal. Most of what is in this book runs on older models as well, as the differences are largely in the coprocessor units and the amount of memory. We will talk about how to develop programs to run on the compact A models and the Raspberry Pi Zero, but you wouldn't want to develop your programs directly on these.

One of the great things about the Raspbian operating system is that it is intended to teach programming, and as a result has many programming tools preinstalled, including

- GNC Compiler Collection (GCC) that we will use to build our Assembly language programs. We will use GCC for compiling C programs in later chapters.

- GNU Make to build our programs.

- GNU Debugger (GDB) to find and solve problems in our programs.

You will need a text editor to create the source program files. Any text editor can be used. Raspbian includes several by default, both command line and via the GUI. Usually, you learn Assembly language after you've already mastered a high-level language like C or Java. So, chances are you already have a favorite editor and can continue to use it.

We will mention other helpful programs throughout the book that you can optionally use, but aren't required, for example:

- A better programmer's calculator

- A better code analysis tool

All of these are open source and you can install them for free.

Now we are going to switch gears to how computers represent numbers. We always hear that computers only deal in zeros and ones, now we'll look at how they put them together to represent larger numbers.

Computers and Numbers

We typically represent numbers using base 10. The common theory is we do this, because we have 10 fingers to count with. This means a number like 387 is really a representation for

$$387 = 3 * 10^2 + 8 * 10^1 + 7 * 10^0$$
$$= 3 * 100 + 8 * 10 + 7$$
$$= 300 + 80 + 7$$

There is nothing special about using 10 as our base and a fun exercise in math class is to do arithmetic using other bases. In fact, the Mayan culture used base 20, perhaps because we have 20 digits: 10 fingers and 10 toes.

Computers don't have fingers and toes, and in their world, everything is a switch that is either on or off. As a result, it is natural for computers to use base 2 arithmetic. Thus, to a computer a number like 1011 is represented by

$$1011 = 1 * 2^3 + 0 * 2^2 + 1 * 2^1 + 1 * 2^0$$
$$= 1 * 8 + 0 * 4 + 1 * 2 + 1$$
$$= 8 + 0 + 2 + 1$$
$$= 11 \text{ (decimal)}$$

This is great for computers, but we are using 4 digits for the decimal number 11 rather than 2 digits. The big disadvantage for humans is that writing out binary numbers is tiring, because they take up so many digits.

Computers are incredibly structured, so all their numbers are the same size. When designing computers, it doesn't make sense to have all sorts of different sized numbers, so a few common sizes have taken hold and become standard.

A byte is 8 binary bits or digits. In our preceding example with 4 bits, there are 16 possible combinations of 0s and 1s. This means 4 bits can represent the numbers 0 to 15. This means it can be represented by one base 16 digit. Base 16 digits are represented by the numbers 0 to 9 and then the letters A–F for 10–15. We can then represent a byte (8 bits) as two base 16 digits. We refer to base 16 numbers as hexadecimal (Figure 1-1).

Decimal	0 - 9	10	11	12	13	14	15
Hex Digit	0 – 9	A	B	C	D	E	F

Figure 1-1. *Representing hexadecimal digits*

Since a byte holds 8 bits, it can represent 28 (256) numbers. Thus, the byte e6 represents

$$e6 = e * 16^1 + 6 * 16^0$$
$$= 14 * 16 + 6$$
$$= 230 \text{ (decimal)}$$
$$= 1110\ 0110 \text{ (binary)}.$$

We are running the ARM processor in 32-bit mode; we call a 32-bit quantity a word, and it is represented by 4 bytes. You might see a string like B6 A4 44 04 as a representation of 32 bits of memory, or one word of memory, or perhaps the contents of one register.

If this is confusing or scary, don't worry. The tools will do all the conversions for you. It's just a matter of understanding what is presented to you on screen. Also, if you need to specify an exact binary number, usually you do so in hexadecimal, though all the tools accept all the formats.

A handy tool is the Linux Gnome calculator (Figure 1-2). The calculator included with Raspbian can perform math in different bases in its scientific mode, but the Gnome calculator has a nicer Programming Mode which shows a numbers representation in multiple bases at once. To install it, use the command line

```
sudo apt-get install gnome-calculator
```

Run it from the Accessories menu (probably the second calculator there). If you put it in "Programming Mode," you can do the conversions and it shows you numbers in several formats at once.

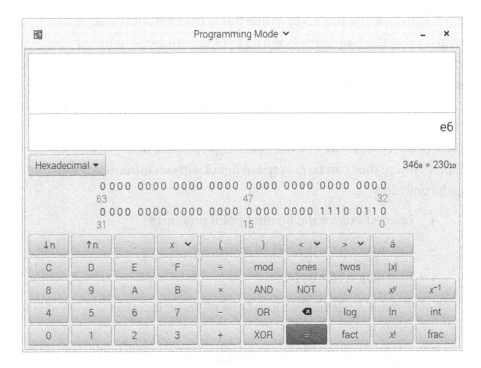

Figure 1-2. *The Gnome calculator*

This is how we represent computer memory. There is a bit more complexity in how signed integers are represented and how arithmetic works. We'll cover that a bit later when we go to do some arithmetic.

In the Assembler we represent hexadecimal numbers (hex for short) with a 0x in front. So 0x1B is how we would specify the hex number 1B.

ARM Assembly Instructions

In this section, we introduce some basic architectural elements of the ARM processor and start to look at the form of its machine code instructions. The ARM is what is called a Reduced Instruction Set Computer (RISC), which theoretically will make learning Assembly easier. There are fewer instructions and each instruction is simpler, so the processor can execute each instruction much quicker. While this is true, the ARM system on a chip used in the Raspberry Pi is a highly sophisticated computer. The core ARM processors handle multiple instruction sets, and then there are theinstruction sets for all the coprocessors.

Our approach to this is to divide and conquer. In the first few chapters of this book, we will cover only the 32-bit standard ARM Assembly instructions. This means that the following topics are deferred to later chapters where they can be covered in detail without introducing too much confusion:

- Instructions for the floating-point processor

- Instructions for the NEON processor

- Instructions for 64 bits

- Thumb mode instructions (special 16-bit compact mode)

In this manner, we just need to attack one topic at a time. Each set of instructions is consistent and easy to understand.

In technical computer topics, there are often chicken and egg problems in presenting the material. The purpose of this section is to introduce all the terms and ideas we will use later. Hopefully, this introduces all the terms, so they are familiar when we cover them in full detail.

CPU Registers

In all computers, data is not operated in the computer's memory; instead, it is loaded into a CPU register, then the data processing or arithmetic operation is performed in the registers. The registers are part of the CPU circuitry allowing instant access, whereas memory is a separate component and there is a transfer time for the CPU to access it.

If you want to add two numbers you might load one into one register, the other into another register, perform the add operation putting the result into a third register, then copy the answer from the result register into memory. As you can see, it takes quite a few instructions to perform simple operations.

A program on an ARM processor in user mode has access to 16 registers:

- **R0** to **R12**: These 13 are general purpose that you can use for anything you like.

- **R13**: The stack pointer.

- **R14**: The link register. **R13** and **R14** are used in the context of calling functions, and we'll explain these in more detail when we cover subroutines.

- **R15**: The program counter. The memory address of the currently executing instruction.

- Current Program Status Register (**CPSR**): This 17th register contains bits of information on the last instruction executed. More on the **CPSR** when we cover branch instructions (if statements).

ARM Instruction Format

Each ARM binary instruction is 32 bits long. Fitting all the information for an instruction into 32 bits is quite an accomplishment requiring using every bit to tell the processor what to do. There are quite a few instruction formats, and we will explain them when we cover that instruction. To give you an idea for data processing instructions, let's consider the format for a common class of instructions that we'll deal with early on. Figure 1-3 shows the format of the instruction and what the bits specify.

31 – 28	27 – 25	24 - 21	20	19 – 16	15 – 12	11 – 0
Condition	Operand type	OpCode	Set Condition Codes	Operand Register	Destination Register	Immediate Operand

Figure 1-3. *Instruction format for data processing instructions*

Let's look at each of these fields:

- **Condition**: Allows the instruction to execute depending on the bits in the CPSR. We'll examine this in detail when we get to branching instructions.

- **Operand type**: Specifies what the operands are in bits 19–0. We could have specified some of these bits, since we used two registers and an immediate operand in this example.

- **Opcode**: Which instruction are we performing, like ADD or MUL.

- **Set condition code**: This is a single bit indicating if this instruction should update the CPSR. If we don't want the result of this instruction to affect following branch instructions, we would set it to 0.

- **Operand register**: One register to use as input.

- **Destination register**: Where to put the result of whatever this instruction does.

- **Immediate operand**: Usually this is a small bit of data that you can specify directly in the instruction. So, if you want to add 1 to a register, you could have this as 1, rather than putting 1 in another register and adding the two registers. The format of this field is quite complicated and requires a larger section to explain all the details, but this is the basic idea.

When things are running well, each instruction executes in one clock cycle. An instruction in isolation takes three clock cycles, namely, one to load the instruction from memory, one to decode the instruction, and then one to execute the instruction. The ARM is smart and works on three instructions at a time, each at a different step in the process, called the instruction pipeline. If you have a linear block of instructions, they all execute on average taking one clock cycle.

Raspberry Pi Memory

Table 1-1 shows the amount of memory each Raspberry Pi contains. Programs are loaded from the Pi's SD card into memory and executed. The memory holds the program, along with any data or variables associated with it. This memory isn't as fast as the CPU registers, but it is much faster than accessing data stored on the SD card or on a device connected to a USB port.

We've talked a lot about 32-bit mode, but what is it? What 32-bit mode really means is that memory addresses are specified using 32 bits and the CPU registers are each 32 bits wide.

Instructions are also 32 bits in size when running in 64-bit mode; the difference is that 64 bits are used to specify a memory address and the registers are 64 bits wide.

If we want to load a register from a known 32-bit memory address, for example, a variable we want to perform arithmetic on. How do we do this? The instruction is only 32 bits in size, and we've already used 4 bits for the opcode, 4 bits for a conditional instruction, 3 bits for the operand type, and 1 bit to say whether we affect the CPSR. We need 4 bits to specify one register, so we have left 16 bits for the memory address (12 bits if we needed to list two registers).

This is a problem that we'll come back to several times, since there are multiple ways to address it. In a CISC computer, this isn't a problem since instructions are typically quite large and variable in length.

You can load from memory by using a register to specify the address to load. This is called indirect memory access. But all we've done is move the problem, since we don't have a way to put the value into that register (in a single instruction).

You could load two registers, each with half the address, then shift the high part, and then add the two. Four instructions to load an address, which seems rather inefficient.

The quick way to load memory that isn't too far away from the program counter (PC) register is to use the load instruction via the PC, since it allows a 12-bit offset from the register. This looks like you can efficiently access memory within 4096 words of the PC, but it's more since a few of the bits specify a shift to give a bigger range. Yuck, how would you write such code? This is where the GNU Assembler comes in. It lets you specify the location symbolically and will figure out the offset/shift for you.

In Chapter 2, "Loading and Adding," we will look at the immediate operand in more detail. We will cover many more ways to specify memory addresses in future chapters, like asking Linux to give us a block of memory, returning the address in a register for us. For now, using the PC with an offset meets our needs.

About the GCC Assembler

Writing Assembler code in binary as 32-bit instructions would be painfully tedious. Enter GNU's Assembler which gives you the power to specify everything that the ARM can do but takes care of getting all the bits in the right place for you. The general way you specify Assembly instructions is

```
label:    opcode    operands
```

The label: is optional and only required if you want the instruction to be the target of a branch instruction.

There are quite a few opcodes, each one is a short mnemonic that is human readable and easy for the Assembler to process. They include

- **ADD** for addition

- **LDR** for load a register

- **B** for branch

There are quite a few different formats for the operands, and we will cover those as we cover the instructions that use them.

Hello World

In almost every programming book, the first program is a simple program to output the string "Hello World". We will do the same with Assembly to demonstrate some of the concepts we've been talking about.

In our favorite text editor, let's create a file "HelloWorld.s" containing that in Listing 1-1.

Listing 1-1. The Hello World program

```
@
@ Assembler program to print "Hello World!"
@ to stdout.
@
@ R0-R2 - parameters to linux function services
@ R7 - linux function number
@

.global _start        @ Provide program starting
@ address to linker

@ Set up the parameters to print hello world
@ and then call Linux to do it.
```

```
_start: mov R0, #1       @ 1 = StdOut
      ldr    R1, =helloworld   @ string to print
      mov    R2, #13      @ length of our string
      mov    R7, #4       @ linux write system call
      svc    0            @ Call linux to print

@ Set up the parameters to exit the program
@ and then call Linux to do it.
        mov      R0, #0  @ Use 0 return code
        mov      R7, #1  @ Service command code 1
                         @ terminates this program
      svc        0       @ Call linux to terminate

.data
helloworld:        .ascii  "Hello World!\n"
```

This is our first look at a complete Assembly language program, so there are a few things to talk about. But first let's compile and run this program.

In our text editor, create a file called "build" that contains

```
as -o HelloWorld.o HelloWorld.s
ld -o HelloWorld HelloWorld.o
```

These are the commands to compile our program. First, we have to make this file executable using the terminal command

```
chmod +x build
```

Now, we can run it by typing **./build**. If the files are correct, we can execute our program by typing **./HelloWorld**. In Figure 1-4, I used **bash -x** (debug mode), so you can see the commands being executed.

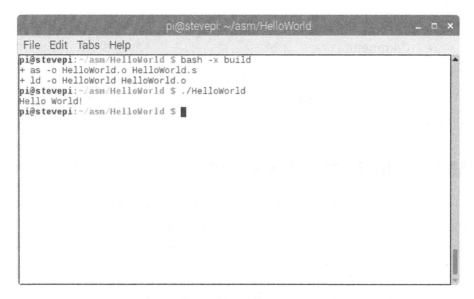

Figure 1-4. *Building and executing HelloWorld*

If we run "ls -l", then the output is

```
-rwxr-xr-x 1 pi pi  62 Jun  6 19:25 build
-rwxr-xr-x 1 pi pi 884 Jun  6 19:25 HelloWorld
-rw-r--r-- 1 pi pi 728 Jun  6 19:25 HelloWorld.o
-rw-r--r-- 1 pi pi 803 Jun  6 19:23 HelloWorld.s
```

Notice how small these files are. The executable is only 884 bytes, not even 1 KB. This is because there is no runtime or any other libraries required to run this program; it is entirely complete in itself. If you want to create very small executables, Assembly language programming is the way to go.

The format for this program is a common convention for Assembly language programs where each line is into these four columns:

- Optional statement label

- Opcode

- Operands

- Comment

These are all separated by tabs, so they line up nicely.

Yay, our first working Assembly language program. Now, let's talk about all the parts.

About the Starting Comment

We start the program with a comment that states what it does. We also document the registers used. Keeping track of which registers are doing what becomes important as our programs get bigger:

- Whenever you see a "@" character in a line, then everything after the "@" is a comment. That means it is there for documentation and is discarded by the GNU Assembler when it processes the file.

- Assembly language is cryptic, so it's important to document what you are doing. Otherwise, you will return to the program after a couple of weeks and have no idea what the program does.

- Each section of the program has a comment stating what it does and then each line of the program has a comment at the end stating what it does. Everything between a /* and */ is also a comment and will be ignored.

Where to Start

Next, we specify the starting point of our program:

- We need to define this as a global symbol, so that the linker (the ld command in our build file) has access to it. The Assembler marks the statement containing **_start** as the program entry point, then the linker can find it because it has been defined as a global variable. All our programs will contain this somewhere.

- Our program can consist of multiple **.s** files, but only one can contain **_start**.

Assembly Instructions

We only use three different Assembly language statements in this example:

1. **MOV** which moves data into a register. In this case, we use an immediate operand, which starts with the "#" sign. So "MOV R1, #4" means move the number 4 into **R1**. In this case, the 4 is in part of the instruction and not stored somewhere else in memory. In the source file, the operands can be upper- or lowercase; I tend to prefer lowercase in my program listings.

2. "LDR R1, =helloworld" statement which loads register 1 with the address of the string we want to print.

3. **SVC 0** command which executes software interrupt number 0. This sends control to the interrupt handler in the Linux kernel, which interprets the parameters we've set in various registers and does the actual work.

Data

Next, we have **.data** which indicates the following instructions are in the data section of the program:

- In this, we have a label "helloworld" followed by an **.ascii** statement and then the string we want to print.

- The **.ascii** statement tells the Assembler just to put our string in the data section and then we can access it via the label as we do in the LDR statement. We'll talk later about how text is represented as numbers, the encoding scheme here being called ASCII.

- The last "\n" character is how we represent a new line. If we don't include this, you must press return to see the text in the terminal window.

Calling Linux

This program makes two Linux system calls to do its work. The first is the Linux write to file command (#4). Normally, we would have to open a file first before using this command, but when Linux runs a program, it opens three files for it:

1. stdin (input from the keyboard)

2. stdout (output to the screen)

3. stderr (also output to the screen)

The Linux shell will redirect these when you ask it to use >, <, and | in your commands. For any Linux system call, you put the parameters in registers **R0–R4** depending on how many parameters are needed. Then a return code is returned in **R0** (which we are bad and not checking). Each system call is specified by putting its function number in **R7**.

The reason we do a software interrupt rather than a branch or subroutine call is so we can call Linux without needing to know where this routine is in memory. This is rather clever and means we don't need to change any addresses in our program as Linux is updated and its routines move around in memory. The software interrupt has another benefit of providing a standard mechanism to switch privilege levels. We'll discuss Linux system calls later in Chapter 7, "Linux Operating System Services."

Reverse Engineering Our Program

We talked about how each Assembly instruction is compiled into a 32-bit word. The Assembler did this for us, but can we see what it did? One way is to use the objdump command-line program

```
objdump -s -d HellowWorld.o
```

which produces Listing 1-2.

Listing 1-2. Disassembly of Hello World

```
HelloWorld.o:      file format elf32-littlearm

Contents of section .text:
 0000 0100a0e3 14109fe5 0d20a0e3 0470a0e3  ......... ...p..
 0010 000000ef 0000a0e3 0170a0e3 000000ef  .........p......
 0020 00000000                             ....
Contents of section .data:
 0000 48656c6c 6f20576f 726c6421 0a        Hello World!.
Contents of section .ARM.attributes:
 0000 41130000 00616561 62690001 09000000  A....aeabi......
 0010 06010801                             ....
```

Disassembly of section .text:

```
00000000 <_start>:
   0: e3a00001    mov     r0, #1
   4: e59f1014    ldr     r1, [pc, #20]      ; 20 <_start+0x20>
   8: e3a0200d    mov     r2, #13
   c: e3a07004    mov     r7, #4
  10: ef000000    svc     0x00000000
  14: e3a00000    mov     r0, #0
  18: e3a07001    mov     r7, #1
  1c: ef000000    svc     0x00000000
  20: 00000000    .word 0x00000000
```

The top part of the output shows the raw data in the file including our eight instructions, then our string to print in the .data section. The second part is a disassembly of the executable .text section.

Let's look at the first **MOV** instruction which compiled to 0xe3a00001 (Figure 1-5):

Hex Digit	e	3	a	0	0	0	0	1
Binary	1110	0011	1100	0000	0000	0000	0000	1

Figure 1-5. *Binary representation of the first MOV instruction*

- Each instruction starts with the hex digit "e" (14 decimal or 1110 binary). This is the condition code, which allows us to conditionally execute an instruction, and now we know "e" means execute the instruction unconditionally.

- The next 3 bits specify 001 which indicates the operand type, which in this case is a register and an immediate operand.

- The next 4 bits are 1110 which is the opcode for the MOV instruction.

- The next bit is 0 which indicates the type of immediate mode parameter, which in this simple case doesn't matter.

- The next 4 bits are the register number which is 0.

- If you look at the other **MOV** instructions, you can see the register number at this location.

- The remaining bits make up our immediate mode number which is 1.

Look at the LDR instruction, it changed from

```
ldr    R1, =helloworld
```

to

```
ldr    r1, [pc, #20]    ; 20 <_start+0x20>
```

This is the Assembler helping you with the ARM processor's obscure mechanism of addressing memory. It lets you specify a symbolic address, namely, "helloworld", and translate that into an offset from the program counter. I'm certainly happy to have a tool do that bit of nastiness for me.

You might notice that the raw instructions in the top part of the output have their bytes reversed, compared to those listed in the disassembly listing. This is because we are using a little-endian encoding, which we will cover in the next chapter.

Feel free to play with the program, for example:

- Change the string but remember to change the length loaded into **R2**.

- Change the return code loaded into **R0** before the second **SVC** call and see what happens.

Tip   You only learn programming by experimenting and writing your own code.

As we progress through each chapter, you will be able to do more and more.

Summary

In this chapter, we introduced the ARM processor and Assembly language programming along with why we want to use Assembly. We covered the tools we will be using. We also saw how computers represent positive integers.

We then looked at in more detail how the ARM CPU represents Assembly instructions along with the registers it contains for processing data. We introduced both the Raspberry Pi's memory and the GNU Assembler that will assist us in writing our Assembly language programs.

Finally, we created a simple complete program to print "Hello World!" in our terminal window.

In Chapter 2, "Loading and Adding," we will look at loading data into the CPU registers and performing basic addition. We'll see how negative numbers are represented and learn new techniques for manipulating binary bits.

CHAPTER 2

Loading and Adding

In this chapter, we will go slowly through the **MOV** and **ADD** instructions to lay the groundwork on how they work, especially in the way they handle parameters (operands). So, in the following chapters, we can proceed at a faster pace, as we encounter the rest of the ARM instruction set.

Before getting into the **MOV** and **ADD** instructions, we will discuss the representation of **negative numbers** and the concepts of **shifting** and **rotating** bits.

Negative Numbers

In the previous chapter, we discussed how computers represent positive integers as binary numbers, called unsigned integers, but what about negative numbers? Our first thought might be to make 1 bit represent whether the number is positive or negative. This is simple, but it turns out it requires extra logic to implement, since now the CPU must look at the sign bits, then decide whether to add or subtract and in which order.

About Two's Complement

The great mathematician John von Neumann, of the Manhattan Project, came up with the idea of the **two's complement** representation for negative numbers, in 1945, when working on the Electronic Discrete Variable Automatic Computer (EDVAC)—one of the earliest electronic computers.

© Stephen Smith 2019
S. Smith, *Raspberry Pi Assembly Language Programming*,
https://doi.org/10.1007/978-1-4842-5287-1_2

Consider a 1-byte hexadecimal number like 01. If we add

$$0x01 + 0xFF = 0x100$$

(all binary ones), we get 0x100.

However, if we are limited to 1-byte numbers, then the 1 is lost and we are left with 00:

$$0x01 + 0xFF = 0x00$$

The mathematical definition of a number's negative is a number that when added to it makes zero; therefore, mathematically, FF is –1. You can get the two's complement form for any number by taking

$$2^N - number$$

In our example, the two's complement of 1 is

$$2^8 - 1 = 256 - 1 = 255 = 0xFF$$

This is why it's called two's complement. An easier way to calculate the two's complement is to change all the 1s to 0s and all the 0s to 1s and then add 1. If we do that to 1, we get

$$0xFE + 1 = 0xFF$$

Two's complement is an interesting mathematical oddity for integers that are limited to having a maximum value of one less than a power of two (which is all computer representations of integers).

Why would we want to represent negative integers this way on computers? As it turns out, addition is simple for the computer to execute. There are no special cases; if you discard the overflow, everything works out. This means less circuitry is required to perform the addition, and as a result it can be performed faster. Besides handling the signs correctly, this also results in the CPU using the same addition logic for signed and unsigned arithmetic, another circuitry saving measure. Consider

$$5 + -3$$

3 in 1 byte is 0x03 or 0000 0011.

Inverting the bits is

1111 1100

Add 1 to get

1111 1101 = 0xFD

Now add

5 + 0xFD = 0x102 = 2

Since we are limited to 1 byte or 8 bits.

About Gnome Programmer's Calculator

Fortunately, we have computers to do the conversions and arithmetic for us, but when we see signed numbers in memory, we need to recognize what they are. The **Gnome programmer's calculator** can calculate two's complement for you. Figure 2-1 shows the Gnome calculator representing –3.

Note   The Gnome programmer's calculator uses 64-bit representations.

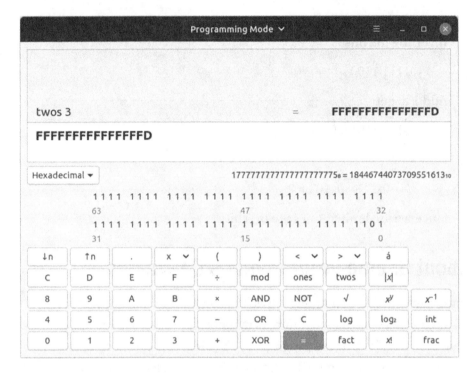

Figure 2-1. *The Gnome calculator calculating the two's complement of 3*

About One's Complement

If we don't add 1 and just change all the 1s to 0s and vice versa, then this is called **one's complement**. There are uses for the one's complement form, and we will encounter it in how some instructions process their operands.

Big vs. Little-endian

At the end of Chapter 1, "Getting Started," we saw that the words of our compiled program had their bytes stored in the reverse order to what we might expect they should be stored as. In fact, if we look at a 32-bit representation of 1 stored in memory, it is

01 00 00 00

rather than

00 00 00 01

Most processors pick one format or the other to store numbers. Motorola and IBM mainframes use what is called big-endian, where numbers are stored in the order of most significant digit to least significant digit, in this case

00 00 00 01

Intel processors use little-endian format and store the numbers in reverse order with the least significant digit first, namely:

01 00 00 00

Figure 2-2 shows how the bytes in integers are copied into memory in both little- and big-endian formats. Notice how the bytes end up in the reverse order to each other.

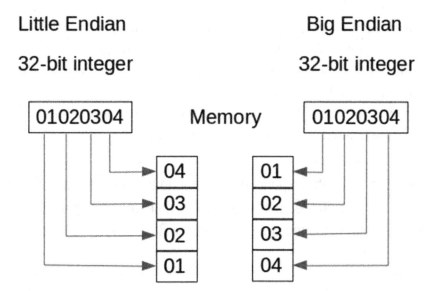

Figure 2-2. *How integers are stored in memory in Little vs. big-endian format*

About Bi-endian

The ARM CPU is called **bi-endian**, because it can do either. There is a program status flag in the **CPSR** that says which endianness to use. We'll look at all the bits in the **CPSR** a bit later. By default, Raspbian and your programs use little-endian like Intel processors. You can change this if you want to. We'll look at an application of changing this flag in a later chapter.

Pros of Little-endian

The advantage of little-endian format is that it makes it easy to change the size of integers, without requiring any address arithmetic. If you want to convert a 4-byte integer to a 1-byte integer, you take the first byte. Assuming the integer is in the range of 0–255, and the other 3 bytes are zero.

For example, if memory contains the 4 byte or word representation for 1, in little-endian, the memory contains

>   01 00 00 00

If we want the 1-byte representation of this number, we take the first byte; for the 16-bit representation, we take the first 2 bytes. The key point is that the memory address we use is the same in call cases, saving us an instruction cycle adjusting it.

When we are in the debugger, we will see more representations, and these will be pointed out again as we run into them.

Note   Even though Raspbian uses little-endian, many protocols like TCP/IP used on the Internet use big-endian and so require a transformation when moving data from the Raspberry Pi to the outside world.

Shifting and Rotating

We have 16 32-bit registers, and much of programming consists of manipulating the bits in these registers. Two extremely useful bit manipulations are shifting and rotating. Mathematically shifting all the bits left one spot is the same as multiplying by 2, and generally shifting n bits is equivalent to multiplying by 2^n. Conversely, shifting bits to the right by n bits is equivalent to dividing by 2^n.

For example, consider shifting the number 3 left by 4 bits:

0000 0011   (the binary representation of the number 3)

Shift the bits left by 4 bits and we get

0011 0000

which is

$$0x30 = 3 * 16 = 3 * 2^4$$

Now if we shift 0x30 right by 4 bits, we undo what we just did and see how it is equivalent to dividing by 24.

About Carry Flag

In the **CPSR**, there is a bit for **carry**. This is normally used to perform addition on larger numbers. If you add two 32-bit numbers and the result is larger than 32 bits, the carry flag is set. We'll see how to use this when we look at addition in detail later in this chapter. When we shift and rotate, it turns out to be useful to include the carry flag. This means we can do a conditional logic based on the last bit shifted out of the register.

About the Barrel Shifter

The ARM processor has circuitry for shifting, called a **barrel shifter**, but there aren't any native instructions for shifting or rotating bits; rather, it is done as a side effect from other instructions like the **MOV** instruction that we are about to cover. The reason for this is that the barrel shifter is outside the **Arithmetic Logic Unit (ALU)** and instead is part of the circuitry that loads the second operand to an instruction. We'll see this in action when we cover **Operand2** for the **MOV** instruction. Figure 2-3 shows the location of the barrel shifter in relation to the ALU.

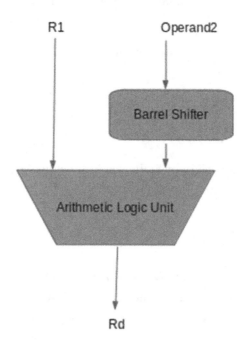

Figure 2-3. *The location of the barrel shifter to perform shifts as part of loading Operand2*

Basics of Shifting and Rotating

We have five cases to cover, as follows:

1. Logical shift left

2. Logical shift right

3. Arithmetic shift right

4. Rotate right

5. Rotate right extend

Logical Shift Left

This is quite straightforward, as we shift the bits left by the indicated number of places, and zeros come in from the right. The last bit shifted out ends up in the carry flag.

Logical Shift Right

Equally easy, here we shift the bits right, zeros come in from the left, and the last bit shifted out ends up in the carry flag.

Arithmetic Shift Right

The problem with logical shift right is, if it is a negative number, having a zero come in from the left suddenly turns the number positive. If we want to preserve the sign bit, use arithmetic shift right. Here a 1 comes in from the left, if the number is negative, and a 0 if it is positive. This is then the correct form if you are shifting signed integers.

Rotate Right

Rotating is like shifting, except the bits don't go off the end; instead, they wrap around and reappear from the other side. So, rotate right shifts right, but the bits that leave on the right, reappear on the left.

Rotate Right Extend

Rotate right extend behaves like rotate right, except it treats the register as a 33-bit register, where the carry flag is the 33rd bit and is to the right of bit 0. This type of rotate is limited to moving 1 bit at a time; therefore, the number of bits is not specified on the instruction.

MOV/MVN

In this section, we are going to look at several forms of the MOV instruction:

1. MOV RD, #imm16

2. MOVT RD, #imm16

3. MOV RD, RS

4. MOV RD, operand2

5. MVN RD, operand2

We've seen examples of the first case, putting a small number into a register. Here the immediate value can be any 16-bit quantity, and it will be placed in the lower 16 bits of the specified register. This form of the **MOV** instruction is as simple as you can get; therefore, we will use it frequently.

About MOVT

The second form answers our question of how to load the full 32 bits of a register. **MOVT**, the move top instruction, loads the 16-bit immediate operand into the upper 16 bits of the register without disturbing the bottom 16 bits. Suppose we want to load register R2 with the hex value 0x4F5D6E3A. We could use

```
MOV    R2, #0x6E3A
MOVT   R2, #0x4F5D
```

Only two instructions, so not too painful, but a bit annoying.

Register to Register MOV

In the next case 3, we have a version that moves one register into another that sounds useful.

The Dreaded Flexible Operand2

All the ARM's data processing instructions have the option of taking a flexible Operand2 as one of their parameters. At this point, it won't be clear why you want some of this functionality, but as we encounter more instructions and start to build small programs, we'll see how they help us. At the bit level, there is a lot of complexity here, but the people who designed the Assembler did a good job of providing syntax to hide a lot of this from us. Still, when doing Assembly programming, it's good to always know what is going on under the covers.

There are two formats for Operand2:

1.   A register and a shift

2.   A small number and a rotation

Operand2 is processed via the barrel shifter, it's just a matter of what is shifted and by how much.

Register and Shift

First, you can specify a register and a shift. For this you specify a register that takes 4 bits and then a shift that is 5 bits (for a total of a full 32-bit shift). For example:

```
MOV   R1, R2, LSL #1      @ Logical shift left
```

is how we specify to take **R2**, logically shift it left by 1 bit, and put the result in **R1**. We can then handle the other shift and rotate scenarios we mentioned earlier with

```
MOV   R1, R2, LSR #1      @ Logical shift right
MOV   R1, R2, ASR #1      @Arithmetic shift right
MOV   R1, R2, ROR #1      @ Rotate right
MOV   R1, R2, RRX         @ Rotate extended right
```

Since shifting and rotating are quite common, the Assembler provides mnemonics for these, so you can specify

```
LSL   R1, R2, #1      @ Logical shift left
LSR   R1, R2, #1      @ Logical shift right
ASR   R1, R2, #1      @Arithmetic shift right
ROR   R1, R2, #1      @ Rotate right
RRX   R1, R2          @ Rotate extended right
```

These assemble to the same byte code. The intent is that it makes the code a little more readable, since it is clear you are doing a shift or rotate operation and not just loading a register.

Small Number and Rotation

Secondly, the other form of operand2 consists of a small number, namely, an 8-bit (1-byte) quantity that can be rotated through an even number of positions, such as **RORs** of 0, 2, 4, 8, …, 30. This uses up the 12 bits we have for operand2, 8 for the number and 4 for the rotation. The values we get are like this:

- 0 - 255 [0 - 0xff]

- 256,260,264,..,1020 [0x100-0x3fc, step 4, 0x40-0xff ror 30]

- 1024,1040,1056,..,4080 [0x400-0xff0, step 16, 0x40-0xff ror 28]

- 4096,4160, 4224,..,16320 [0x1000-0x3fc0, step 64, 0x40-0xff ror 26]

This is quite a clever scheme, as it lets you represent any power of 2 from 0 to 31, so you can set any individual bit in a register. It also lets you set any individual byte in a register. These turn out to be quite frequent scenarios, and you can specify it as part of most data processing instructions.

Fortunately, we don't need to figure this all out. We just specify a number and the Assembler figures out how to represent it. Since there are only 12 bits, not all 32-bit numbers can be represented, so if you specify something that can't be dealt with, then the Assembler gives you an error message. You then need to use a **MOV/MOVT** pair as outlined previously.

MOV has the advantage that it can take an **#imm16** operand, which can usually get us out of trouble. However, other instructions that must specify a third register, like the **ADD** instruction, don't have this luxury.

Frequently, programmers deal with small integers like loop indexes, say to loop from 1 to 10. These simple cases are handled easily, and we don't need to be concerned.

```
@ Too big for #imm16
MOV   R1, #0xAB000000

@ Too big for #imm16 and can't    be represented.
MOV   R1, #0xABCDEF11
```

The second instruction gives the error

```
Error: invalid constant (abcdef11) after fixup
```

when you run your program through the Assembler. This means the Assembler tried all its tricks and failed to represent the number. To load this, you need to use an **MOV/MOVT** pair.

MVN

This is the **Move Not** instruction. It works just like **MOV**, except it reverses all the 1s and 0s as it loads the register. This means it loads the register with the one's complement form of what you specified. Another way to say it is that it applies a **logical NOT** operation to each bit in the word you are loading into the register.

MVT is a distinct opcode and not an alias for another instruction with cryptic parameters. The ARM32 instruction set only has 16 opcodes, so this is an important instruction with three main uses:

1. To calculate the one's complement of something for you. This has its uses, but does it warrant its own opcode?

2. Multiply by –1. We saw that with the shift operations we can multiply or divide by powers of 2. This instruction gets us halfway to multiplying by –1. Remember that the negative of a number is the two's complement of the number or the one's complement plus one. This means we can multiply by –1 by doing this instruction, then add one. Why would we do this rather than use the **Multiply (MUL)** instruction? The same for shifting, why do that rather than using MUL? The answer is that the **MUL** instruction is quite slow and can take

quite a few clock cycles to do its work. Shifting only takes one cycle, and using **MVN** and **ADD**, we can multiply by –1 in only two clock cycles. Multiplying by –1 is very common, and now we can do it quickly.

3. You get twice the number of values due to the extra bit—13 vs. 12. It turns out that all the numbers obtained by using a byte value and even shift are different for **MVN** and **MOV**. This means that if the Assembler sees that the number you specified can't be represented in a **MOV** instruction, then it tries to change it to an **MVN** instruction and vice versa. So, you really have 13 bits of immediate data, rather than 12. NOTE: It still might not be able to represent your number, and you may still need to use a **MOV/MOVT** pair.

MOV Examples

In this section, we will write a short program to exercise all the **MOV** instructions. Create a file called

movexamps.s

containing Listing 2-1.

Listing 2-1. MOV examples

```
@
@ Examples of the MOV instruction.
@
.global _start          @ Provide program starting address

@ Load R2 with 0x4F5D6E3A first using MOV and MOVT
```

```
_start:    MOV   R2, #0x6E3A
       MOVT R2, #0x4F5D

@ Just move R2 into R1
       MOV   R1, R2

@ Now let's see all the shift versions of MOV
       MOV   R1, R2, LSL #1   @ Logical shift left
       MOV   R1, R2, LSR #1   @ Logical shift right
       MOV   R1, R2, ASR #1   @Arithmetic shift right
       MOV   R1, R2, ROR #1   @ Rotate right
       MOV   R1, R2, RRX      @ Rotate extended right

@ Repeat the above shifts using
@       the Assembler mnemonics.

       LSL   R1, R2, #1       @ Logical shift left
       LSR   R1, R2, #1       @ Logical shift right
       ASR   R1, R2, #1       @Arithmetic shift right
       ROR   R1, R2, #1       @ Rotate right
       RRX   R1, R2           @ Rotate extended right

@ Example that works with 8 bit immediate and shift
       MOV   R1, #0xAB000000  @ Too big for #imm16

@ Example that can't be represented and
@       results in an error
@ Uncomment the instruction if you want to
@       see the error
@       MOV   R1, #0xABCDEF11  @ Too big for #imm16

@ Example of MVN
       MVN   R1, #45
```

```
@ Example of a MOV that the Assembler will
@       change to MVN
      MOV    R1, #0xFFFFFFFE  @ (-2)

@ Set up the parameters to exit the program
@ and then call Linux to do it.
      Mov    R0, #0        @ Use 0 return code
      mov    R7, #1        @ Service command code 1
      svc    0             @ Call      Linux to terminate
```

You can compile this program with the build file

```
as -o movexamps.o movexamps.s
ld -o movexamps movexamps.o
```

You can run the program after building it.

Note   This program doesn't do anything besides move various numbers into registers.

We will look at how to see what is going on in Chapter 3, "Tooling Up," when we cover the GNU Debugger (GDB).

If we disassemble the program using

```
objdump -s -d movexamps.o
```

we get Listing 2-2.

Listing 2-2. Disassembly of the MOV examples

```
Disassembly of section .text:

00000000 <_start>:
   0: e3062e3a    movw  r2, #28218  ; 0x6e3a
   4: e3442f5d    movt  r2, #20317  ; 0x4f5d
```

```
 8: e1a01002    mov    r1, r2
 c: e1a01082    lsl    r1, r2, #1
10: e1a010a2    lsr    r1, r2, #1
14: e1a010c2    asr    r1, r2, #1
18: e1a010e2    ror    r1, r2, #1
1c: e1a01062    rrx    r1, r2
20: e1a01082    lsl    r1, r2, #1
24: e1a010a2    lsr    r1, r2, #1
28: e1a010c2    asr    r1, r2, #1
2c: e1a010e2    ror    r1, r2, #1
30: e1a01062    rrx    r1, r2
34: e3a014ab    mov    r1, #-1426063360 ; 0xab000000
38: e3e0102d    mvn    r1, #45      ; 0x2d
3c: e3e01001    mvn    r1, #1
40: e3a00000    mov    r0, #0
44: e3a07001    mov    r7, #1
48: ef000000    svc    0x00000000
```

All the instructions start with

Oxe

that means to always execute the instruction.

Most of the remaining instructions have

0x1a

as their next digits. The first 3 bits are for instruction format and are 0 meaning

- Register

- Register

- Immediate

We then have the 4 bits for the opcode. All the **MOV** instruction variants have this as

1101

the opcode for **MOV**. We see all the shift operations are really **MOV** instructions, and the computer is trying to be helpful by letting us know what the instruction does. The **MVN** instruction has an opcode of

1111

This includes the **MVN** we put in our source file and the **MOV** instruction that the Assembler changed to **MVN** so it could load –2.

The first two instructions that load 16-bit operands are different. Notice that the Assembler changed our first **MOV** into a **Move Wide (MOVW)** instruction. These aren't part of the data processing instructions we are looking at now, and are special cases, but they are handy.

ADD/ADC

We can now put any value we like in a register, so let's start doing some computing. Let's start with addition. The instructions we will cover are

1. ADD{S} Rd, Rs, Operand2

2. ADD{S} Rd, Rs, #imm12

3. ADD{S} Rd, Rs1, Rs2

4. ADC{S} Rd, Rs, Operand2

5. ADC{S} Rd, Rs1, Rs2

These instructions all add their second and third parameters and put the result in their first parameter **Register Destination (Rd).** We already know about the following:

- Registers

- Operand2

- #imm12

Pushing through that stuff with the **MOV** instructions was tough, but it's done. The case with three registers is a special case of Operand2, just with a shift of 0 applied. The registers Rd and **Source Register (Rs)** can be the same. If you just want to add 1 to **R1**, you can specify

```
ADD R1, #1
```

The Assembler compiles this as

```
ADD R1, R1, #1
```

This saves some typing and is a bit clearer. This is a common scenario to increment loop counters.

We haven't developed the code to print out a number yet, as we must first convert the number to an ASCII string. We will get to this after we cover **loops** and **conditional statements**. In the meantime, we can get one number from our program via the program's return code. This is a 1-byte unsigned integer. Let's look at an example of multiplying a number by –1 and see the output. Listing 2-3 is the code to do this.

Listing 2-3. An example of MVN and ADD

```
@
@ Example of the ADD/ADC instructions.
@
.global _start      @ Provide program starting address

@ Multiply 2 by -1 by using MVN and then adding 1
```

```
_start: MVN      R0, #2
     ADD    R0, #1

@ Set up the parameters to exit the program
@ and then call Linux to do it.
@ R0 is the return code and will be what we
@ calculated above.
        mov     R7, #1      @ Service command code 1
        svc     0           @ Call      Linux to terminate
```

Here we use the **MVN** instruction to calculate the one's complement of our number, in this case 2, then we add 1 to get the two's complement form. We use **R0** since this will be the return code returned via the Linux terminate command. To see the return code, type

```
echo $?
```

after running the program and it prints out 254. If you examine the bits, you will see this is the two's complement form for –2 in 1 byte.

Add with Carry

The new concepts in this section are what the {**S**} after the instruction means along with why we have both **ADD** and **ADC**. This will be our first use of the **CPSR**.

Think back to how we learned to add numbers:

```
 17
+78
 95
```

1. We first add 7 + 8 and get 15.

2. We put 5 in our sum and carry the 1 to the tens column.

3. Now we add 1 + 7 + the carry from the ones column, so we add 1+7+1 and get 9 for the tens column.

This is the idea behind the carry flag. When an addition overflows, it sets the carry flag, so we can include that in the sum of the next part. NOTE: A carry is always 0 or 1, so we only need a 1-bit flag for this.

The ARM processor adds 32 bits at a time, so we only need the carry flag if we are dealing with numbers larger than will fit into 32 bits. This means that even though we are in 32-bit mode, we can easily add 64-bit or even larger integers.

In Chapter 1, "Getting Started," we quickly mentioned that bit 20 in the instruction format specifies whether an instruction alters the **CPSR**. So far, we haven't set that bit, so none of the instructions we've written so far will alter the **CPSR**. If we want an instruction to alter the **CPSR**, then we place an "**S**" on the end of the opcode, and the Assembler will set bit 20 when it builds binary version of the instruction. This applies to all instructions, including the **MOV** instructions we just looked at.

```
ADDS R0, #1
```

is just like

```
ADD R0, #1
```

except that it sets various bits in the **CPSR**. We'll cover all the bits when we cover **conditional statements**. For now, we are interested in the carry flag that is designated **C**. If the result of an addition is too large, then the **C** flag is set to 1; otherwise, it is set to 0.

To add two 64-bit integers, use two registers to hold each number. In our example, we'll use registers **R2** and **R3** for the first number, **R4** and **R5** for the second, and then **R0** and **R1** for the result. The code would then be

```
ADDS  R1, R3, R5   @ Lower order word
ADC   R0, R2, R4   @ Higher order word
```

The first **ADDS** adds the lower-order 32 bits and sets the carry flag if needed. It might set other flags in the CPSR, but we'll worry about those later. The second instruction, **ADDC**, adds the higher-order words, plus the carry flag.

The nice thing here is that although we are in 32-bit mode, we can still do a 64-bit addition in only two clock cycles. Let's look at a simple complete example in Listing 2-4.

Listing 2-4. Example of 64-bit addition with ADD and ADC

```
@
@ Example of 64-bit addition with
@     the ADD/ADC instructions.
@
.global _start      @ Provide program starting address

@ Load the registers with some data
@ First 64-bit number is 0x00000003FFFFFFFF
_start:    MOV   R2, #0x00000003
    MOV  R3, #0xFFFFFFFF       @ as      will change to MVN
@ Second 64-bit number is 0x0000000500000001
    MOV  R4, #0x00000005
    MOV  R5, #0x00000001

    ADDS R1, R3, R5      @ Lower order word
    ADC  R0, R2, R4      @ Higher order word
```

```
@ Set up the parameters to exit the program
@ and then call Linux to do it.
@ R0 is the return code and will be what we
@ calculated above.
        mov     R7, #1      @ Service command code 1
        svc     0           @ Call     Linux to terminate
```

Here we are adding

```
00000003 FFFFFFFF
00000005 00000001
00000009 00000000
```

We've rigged this example to demonstrate the carry flag and to produce an answer we can see in the return code. The largest unsigned integer is

0xFFFFFFFF

and adding 1 results in

0x100000000

that doesn't fit in 32 bits, so we get

0x00000000

with a carry. The high-order words add 3 + 5 + carry to yield 9. The high-order word is in R0, so it is the return code when the program exits. If we type

echo $?

we get 9 as expected.

Learning about **MOV** was difficult, because this was the first time; we encountered both shifting and Operand2. With these behind us, learning about **ADD** was much easier. We still have some complicated topics to cover, but as we become more experienced with how to manipulate bits and bytes, the learning should become easier.

Summary

In this chapter, we learned how negative integers are represented in a computer. We went on to discuss big vs. little-endian byte ordering. We then looked at the concept of shifting and rotating the bits in a register.

Next, we looked in detail at the **MOV** instruction that allows us to move data around the CPU registers or load constants from the **MOV** instruction into a register. We discovered the tricks of operand2 on how ARM represents a large range of values, given the limited number of bits it has at its disposal.

Finally, we covered the **ADD** and **ADC** instructions and discussed how to add both 32- and 64-bit numbers.

In Chapter 3, "Tooling Up," we will look at better ways to build our programs and start debugging our programs with the GNU Debugger (**gdb**).

CHAPTER 3

Tooling Up

In this chapter, we will learn a better way to build our programs using
GNU Make. With the GNU Debugger (GDB), we will debug our programs.
And we will quickly introduce the source control system **Git** and the build
server **Jenkins**.

GNU Make

We built our programs using a simple shell script to run the **GNU Assembler**
and then the **Linux linker/loader**. As we move forward, we want a more
sophisticated tool to build our programs. GNU Make is the standard Linux
utility to do this, and it comes preinstalled with Raspbian. In GNU Make

1. Specify the rules for how to build one thing from
   another.

2. GNU Make examines the file date/times to
   determine what needs to be built.

3. GNU Make issues the commands to build the
   components.

Let's look at how to build our HelloWorld program from Chapter 1,
"Getting Started," using **make**. First, create a text file named **makefile**
containing the code in Listing 3-1.

© Stephen Smith 2019
S. Smith, *Raspberry Pi Assembly Language Programming*,
https://doi.org/10.1007/978-1-4842-5287-1_3

Listing 3-1. Simple makefile for HelloWorld

```
HelloWorld: HelloWorld.o
    ld -o HelloWorld HelloWorld.o

HelloWorld.o: HelloWorld.s
    as -o HelloWorld.o HelloWorld.s
```

Note   The command make is particular, and the indented lines must start with a tab, not spaces, or you will get an error.

To build our file, type

```
make
```

Rebuilding a File

If we already built the program, then this won't do anything, since make sees that the executable is older than the **.o** file and that the **.o** file is older than the **.s** file. We can force a rebuild by typing

```
make -B
```

Rather than specify each file separately along with the command to build it, we can define a build rule for say building a **.o** file from an **.s** file.

A Rule for Building .s files

Listing 3-2 shows a more advanced version, where we define a rule for building an **.o** file from an **.s** file. We still need to specify the dependency, but we no longer need the compile rule. As we get more sophisticated and add command-line parameters to the as command, we've now centralized the location to do this.

Listing 3-2. Hello World makefile with a rule

```
%.o : %.s
        as $< -o $@

HelloWorld: HelloWorld.o
        ld -o HelloWorld HelloWorld.o
```

Now make knows how to create a **.o** file from a **.s** file. We've told make to build **HelloWorld** from **HelloWorld.o** and make can look at its list of rules to figure out how to build **HelloWorld.o**. There are some strange symbols in this file, and their meaning is

- **%.s** is like a wildcard, meaning any **.s** file.

- **$<** is a symbol for the source file.

- **$@** is a symbol for the output file.

There is a lot of good documentation on **make**, so we aren't going to go into a lot of detail here.

Defining Variables

Listing 3-3 shows how to define variables. Here we'll do it to centralize the list of files we want to assemble.

Listing 3-3. Adding a variable to the Hello World makefile

```
OBJS = HelloWorld.o

%.o : %.s
        as $< -o $@

HelloWorld: $(OBJS)
        ld -o HelloWorld $(OBJS)
```

With this code, as we add source files, we just add the new file to the **OBJS= line** and **make** takes care of the rest.

This is just an introduction to GNU Make—there is a lot more to this powerful tool. As we go further into the book, we will introduce new elements to our **makefiles** as needed.

GDB

Most high-level languages come with tools to easily output any strings or numbers to the console, a window, or a web page. Often when using these languages, programmers don't bother using the debugger; instead, they rely on libraries that are part of the language.

Later on, we'll look at how to leverage the libraries that are part of other languages, but calling these takes a bit of work. We'll also develop a helpful library to convert numbers to strings, so we can use the techniques, used in Chapter 1's "HelloWorld" to print our work.

When doing Assembly language programming, being proficient with the debugger is critical to success. Not only will this help with your Assembly language programming, but also it is a great tool for you to use with your high-level language programming.

Preparing to Debug

GDB can debug your program as it is, but this isn't the most convenient way to go. For instance, in our HelloWorld program we have the string **helloworld**. If we debug the program as is, the debugger won't know anything about this label, since the Assembler changed it into an address in a .data section. There is a command-line option for the Assembler that includes a table of all our source code labels and symbols, so we can use them in the debugger. This makes our program executable a bit larger.

Often, we set a debug flag while we are developing the program, then remove the debug flag before releasing the program. Unlike some high-level programming languages, the debug flag doesn't affect the machine code generated, so the program behaves exactly the same in both debug and non-debug mode.

We don't want to leave the debug information in our program for release, because besides making the program executable larger, it is a wealth of information for hackers to help them reverse engineer your program. There have been several cases where hackers caused mischief because the program still had debugging information present.

To add debug information to our program, we must assemble it with the **-g** flag. In Listing 3-4 we add a debug flag to our **makefile**. For the first program we'll debug, let's use our examples of the **MOV** statements, since we didn't see the operations working on the various registers.

Listing 3-4. Makefile with a debug flag

```
OBJS = movexamps.o
ifdef DEBUG
DEBUGFLGS = -g
else
DEBUGFLGS =
endif

%.o : %.s
        as $(DEBUGFLGS) $< -o $@

movexamps: $(OBJS)
        ld -o movexamps $(OBJS)
```

This **makefile** sets the debug flag if the variable DEBUG is defined. We can define it on the command line for **make** with

```
make DEBUG=1
```

Or, from the command line, define an environment variable with

```
export DEBUG=1
```

To clear the environment variable, enter

```
export DEBUG=
```

When switching between **DEBUG** and **non-DEBUG**, run make with the **-B** switch to build everything.

Tip   Often, I create to shell scripts **buildd** and **buildr** to call make with and without **DEBUG** defined.

Beginning GDB

To start debugging our **movexamps** program, enter the command

```
gdb movexamps
```

This yields the abbreviated output

```
GNU gdb (Raspbian 7.12-6) 7.12.0.20161007-git
Copyright (C) 2016 Free Software Foundation, Inc.
...
Reading symbols from movexamps...done.
(gdb)
```

- **Gdb** is a command-line program.

- **(gdb)** is the command prompt where you type commands.

- **(hit tab)** for command completion. Enter the first letter or two of a command as a shortcut.

To run the program, type

```
run
```

(or r).

The program runs to completion, as if it ran normally from the command line.

To list our program, type

```
list
```

(or l).

This lists ten lines. Type

```
l
```

for the next ten lines. Type

```
list 1,1000
```

to list our entire program.

Notice that list gives us the source code for our program, including comments. This is a handy way to find line numbers for other commands. If we want to see the raw machine code, we can have gdb disassemble our program with

```
disassemble _start
```

This shows the actual code produced by the Assembler with no comments. We can see whether MOV or MVN was used among other commands this way.

To stop the program, we set a breakpoint. In this case, we want to stop the program at the beginning to single-step through, examining registers as we go. To set a breakpoint, use the **breakpoint** command (or **b**):

```
b _start
```

We can specify a line number or a symbol for our breakpoint. As in this example, now if we run the program, it stops at the breakpoint:

```
(gdb) b _start
Breakpoint 1 at 0x10054: file movexamps.s, line 8.
(gdb) r
Starting program: /home/pi/asm/Chapter 2/movexamps

Breakpoint 1, _start () at movexamps.s:8
8       _start:    MOV   R2, #0x6E3A
(gdb)
```

We can now step through the program with the **step** command (or **s**). As we go, we want to see the values of the registers. We get these with **info registers** (or **i r**):

```
(gdb) s
9               MOVT  R2, #0x4F5D
(gdb) i r
r0              0x0     0
r1              0x0     0
r2              0x6e3a  28218
r3              0x0     0
r4              0x0     0
r5              0x0     0
r6              0x0     0
r7              0x0     0
r8              0x0     0
r9              0x0     0
r10             0x0     0
r11             0x0     0
r12             0x0     0
sp              0x7efff040    0x7efff040
lr              0x0     0
```

```
pc                0x10058      0x10058 <_start+4>
cpsr              0x10   16
(gdb)
```

We see **0x6E3A** put in **R2** as expected.

We can continue stepping or enter **continue** (or **c**) to continue to the next **breakpoint** or to the end of the program. We can set as many breakpoints as we like. We can see them all with the **info breakpoints** (or **i b**) command. We can delete a breakpoint with the **delete** command, specifying the breakpoint number to delete.

```
(gdb) i b
Num     Type           Disp Enb Address    What
1       breakpoint     keep y   0x00010054 movexamps.s:8
        breakpoint already hit 1 time
(gdb) delete 1
(gdb) i b
No breakpoints or watchpoints.
(gdb)
```

We haven't dealt with memory much, but **gdb** has good mechanisms to display memory in different formats. The main command being x. It has the format

```
x /Nfu addr
```

where

- **N** is the number of objects to display

- **f** is the display format where some common ones are

  - t for binary

  - x for hexadecimal

  - d for decimal

- • i for instruction

- • s for string

- **u** is unit size, and is any of

  - • b for bytes

  - • h for halfwords (16 bits)

  - • w for words (32 bits)

  - • g for giant words (64 bits)

Some examples using our code stored at memory location _start, or 0x10054:

```
(gdb) x /4ubft _start
0x10054 <_start>: 00111010 00101110 00000110
                  11100011
(gdb) x /4ubfi _start
=> 0x10054 <_start>:  movw  r2, #28218 ; 0x6e3a
   0x10058 <_start+4>:      movt  r2, #20317 ; 0x4f5d
   0x1005c <_start+8>:      mov   r1, r2
   0x10060 <_start+12>:     lsl   r1, r2, #1
(gdb) x /4ubfx _start
0x10054 <_start>:      0x3a  0x2e  0x06  0xe3
(gdb) x /4ubfd _start
0x10054 <_start>:       58    46    6     -29
```

To exit **gdb**, type **q** (for **quit** or type **control-d**).

Table 3-1 provides a quick reference to the GDB commands we introduced in this chapter. As we learn new things, we'll need to add to our knowledge of **gdb**. It is a powerful tool to help us develop our programs. Assembly language programs are complex and subtle, and **gdb** is great at showing us what is going on with all the bits and bytes.

Table 3-1. *Summary of useful GDB commands*

Command (short form)	Description
break (b) line	Set breakpoint at line
run (r)	Run the program
step (s)	Single-step program
continue (c)	Continue running the program
quit (q or control-d)	Exit gdb
control-c	Interrupt the running program
info registers (i r)	Print out the registers
info break	Print out the breakpoints
delete n	Delete breakpoint n
x /Nuf expression	Show contents of memory

It's worthwhile single-stepping through our three sample programs, and examine the registers at each step to ensure you understand what each instruction is doing.

Even if you don't know of a bug, many programmers like to single-step through their code to look for problems and to convince themselves that their code is good. Often two programmers do this together as part of the pair programming agile methodology.

Source Control and Build Servers
Git

As your program gets larger, consider using a source control system to manage source files. Source control systems keep all the versions of your program. With source control, it's easy to retrieve the files that make up version 1.15 of your program; you can have multiple branches, so you can work on version 1.16 while also working on version 2.1 and keep everything straight.

Once you have a team of programmers working on your project, you need to regulate who is editing what, so people don't overwrite each other's work. **Git** takes this to a new level, where two people can edit the same file, then Git can merge the changes to keep both people's work. Git is a great program for doing this. Git was developed by Linus Torvalds as the source control system for all Linux development. There are cloud versions, like GitHub, that keep your files in the Cloud, and as a result, you don't need to worry about backing them up.

Note   The SD cards the Raspberry Pi uses instead of hard drives or SSDs are not as reliable. They can fail, so you should always have a backup of your work. If you don't back up to the Cloud with a service like Github, back up with one of the following:

- Copy your files to Google Drive.
- Email your files to yourself.
- Copy them to a USB hard drive.

Don't trust the SD card, as it will fail at some point.

Git is a sophisticated system beyond the scope of this book, but worth checking out.

Jenkins

Once you are using GNU Make and Git, you might consider checking out **Jenkins**. Jenkins is a build server that monitors Git, and every time you check in a new version of a program file, it kicks off a build. This is part of a continuous development system that can even deploy your program.

This is especially helpful if you have a team of programmers, where the build takes a long time, or you need the result to automatically be deployed, say to a web server.

If you have a set of automated tests, these are run after each build. Having the automated tests run frequently helps you detect when your program is broken. The cost of fixing a bug tends to be proportional to the time that the bug exists in the code, so finding and fixing bugs quickly is a huge productivity gain.

Summary

In this chapter, we introduced the GNU Make program that we will use to build our programs. This is a powerful tool used to handle all the rules for the various compilers and linkers we need.

We then introduced the GNU Debugger that will allow us to troubleshoot our programs. Unfortunately, programs have bugs and we need a way to single-step through them and examine all the registers and memory as we do so. GDB is a technical tool, but it's indispensable in figuring out what our programs are doing.

Lastly, we mentioned the source control system Git and the build server Jenkins. We won't be using these in this book, but as your needs get more sophisticated, you should check these out.

In Chapter 4, "Controlling Program Flow," we will look at conditionally executing code, branching and looping—the core building blocks of programming logic.

CHAPTER 4

Controlling Program Flow

Now we know a handful of Assembly language instructions and can execute them linearly one after the other. We learned how to start and terminate a program. We built programs and debugged them.

In this chapter, we'll make our programs more interesting by using conditional logic—**if/then/else** statements—in high-level language. We will also introduce loops—**for** and **while** statements—in high-level languages. With these instructions in hand, we will have all the basics for coding program logic.

Unconditional Branch

The simplest branch instruction is

```
B label
```

that is an unconditional branch to a label. The label is interpreted as an offset from the current PC register and has 24 bits in the instruction allowing a range of 8 megawords in either direction or a jump of up to 32 MB in either direction. This instruction is like a goto statement in some high-level languages.

© Stephen Smith 2019
S. Smith, *Raspberry Pi Assembly Language Programming*,
https://doi.org/10.1007/978-1-4842-5287-1_4

If we encode Listing 4-1, the program is in a closed loop and hangs our terminal window until we press **Control + C**.

Listing 4-1. A closed loop branch instruction

```
_start:        MOV R1, #1
                 B _start
```

About the CPSR

We've mentioned the Current Program Status Register (CPSR) several times without really looking at what it contains. We talked about the carry flag when we looked at the ADDS/ADC instructions. In this section, we will look at a few more of the flags in the CPSR.

We'll start by listing all the flags it contains, though many of them won't be discussed until later chapters. In this chapter, we are interested in the group of condition code bits that tell us things about what happens when an instruction executes (Figure 4-1).

31	30	29	28	27	-	24	-	19 – 16	-	9	8	7	6	5	4 – 0
N	Z	C	V	Q		J		GE		E	A	I	F	T	M

Figure 4-1. *The bits in the CPSR*

The condition flags are

- Negative: N is 1 if the signed value is negative and cleared if the result is positive or 0.

- Zero: Is set if the result is 0; this usually denotes an equal result from a comparison. If the result is non-zero, this flag is cleared.

- Carry: For addition type operations, this flag is set if the result produces an overflow. For subtraction type operation, this flag is set if the result requires a borrow. Also, it's used in shifting to hold the last bit that is shifted out.

- OVerflow: For addition and subtraction, this flag is set if a signed overflow occurred. NOTE: Some instructions may specifically set oVerflow to flag an error condition.

The Interrupt flags are

- I: When set, disables IRQ interrupts

- F: When set, disables FIQ interrupts

- A: When set, disables imprecise aborts

The Instruction set flags are

- Thumb: 16-bit compact instructions

- Jazelle: Obsolete mode for directly executing Java bytecodes

The other bits are

- Q: This flag is set to indicate underflow and/or saturation.

- GE: These flags control the Greater than or Equal behavior in SIMD instructions.

- E: Is a flag that controls the "endianness" for data handling.

M is the processor mode such as user or supervisor.

Branch on Condition

The branch instruction, at the beginning of this chapter, can take a modifier that instructs it to only branch if a certain condition flag in the CPSR is set or clear.

The general form of the branch instructions is

B{condition} label

where {condition} is taken from Table 4-1.

Table 4-1. *Condition codes for the branch instruction*

{condition}	Flags	Meaning
EQ	Z set	Equal
NE	Z clear	Not equal
CS or **HS**	C set	Higher or same (unsigned >=)
CC or **LO**	C clear	Lower (unsigned <)
MI	N set	Negative
PL	N clear	Positive or zero
VS	V set	Overflow
VC	V clear	No overflow
HI	C set and Z clear	Higher (unsigned >)
LS	C clear and Z set	Lower or same (unsigned <=)
GE	N and V the same	Signed >=
LT	N and V differ	Signed <
GT	Z clear, N and V the same	Signed >
LE	Z set, N and V differ	Signed <=
AL	Any	Always (same as no suffix)

For example:

```
BEQ _start
```

will branch to _start if the Z flag is set. This seems a bit strange, why isn't the instruction BZ for branch on zero? What is equal here? To answer these questions, we need to look at the CMP instruction.

About the CMP Instruction

The format of the CMP instruction is

```
CMP Rn, Operand2
```

This instruction compares the contents of register **Rn** with **Operand2** by subtracting Operand2 from Rn and updating the status flags accordingly. It behaves exactly like the **SUBS** instruction (which is like the **ADDS** instruction only, it does subtraction rather than addition), except that it only updates the status flags and discards the result. For example, to do a branch only if register **R4** is 45, we might code

```
CMP R4, #45
BEQ _start
```

In this context, we see how the mnemonic BEQ makes sense; since CMP subtracts 45 from **R4,** the result is zero if they are equal and the **Z** flag will be set. If you go back to Table 4-1 and consider the condition codes in this context, then they make sense.

Loops

With branch and comparison instructions in hand, let's look at constructing some loops modelled on what we find in high-level programming languages.

FOR Loops

Suppose we want to do the basic for loop

```
FOR I = 1 to 10
        ... some statements...
NEXT I
```

We can implement this as shown in Listing 4-2.

Listing 4-2. Basic for loop

```
      MOV R2, #1 @ R2 holds I
loop: @ body of the loop goes here.

      @ Most of the logic is at the end
      ADD R2, #1       @ I = I + 1
      CMP R2, #10
      BLE loop         @ IF I <= 10 goto loop
```

If we did this by counting down

```
FOR I = 10 TO 1 STEP -1
        ... some statements...
NEXT I
```

We can implement this as shown in Listing 4-3.

Listing 4-3. Reverse for loop

```
      MOV R2, #10 @R2 holds I
loop: @ body of the loop goes here.

      @ The CMP is redundant since we
      @ are doing SUBS.
      SUBS  R2, #1     @ I = I -1
      BNE   loop       @ branch until I = 0
```

Here we save an instruction, since with the SUBS instruction, we don't need the CMP instruction.

While Loops

Let's code:

```
WHILE X < 5
        ... other statements ....
END WHILE
```

Note   Initializing and changing the variables isn't part of the **while** statement. These are separate statements that appear before and in the body of the loop. In Assembly, we might code as shown in Listing 4-4.

Listing 4-4. While loop

```
@ R4 is X and has been initialized
loop: CMP    R4, #5
      BGE    loopdone
      ... other statements in the loop body ...
      B      loop
loopdone: @program continues
```

Note   A while loop only executes if the statement is initially true, so there is no guarantee that the loop body will ever be executed.

If/Then/Else

In this section, we'll look at coding

```
IF <expression> THEN
      ... statements ...
ELSE
      ... statements ...
END IF
```

In Assembly, we need to evaluate <expression> and have the result end up in a register that we can compare. For now, we'll assume that <expression> is simply of the form

```
register comparison immediate-constant
```

In this way, we can evaluate it with a single CMP instruction. For example, suppose we want to code

```
IF R5 < 10 THEN
      .... if statements ...
ELSE
      ... else statements ...
END IF
```

We can code this as Listing 4-5.

Listing 4-5. If/Then/Else statement

```
CMP R5, #10
    BGE elseclause

    ... if statements ...
```

```
    B endif
elseclause:

    ... else statements ...

endif: @ continue on after the /then/else ...
```

This is fairly simple, but it is still worth putting in comments to be clear which statements are part of the if/then/else and which statements are in the body of the if or else blocks.

Tip   Adding a blank line can make the code much more readable.

Logical Operators

For our upcoming sample program, we need to start manipulating the bits in the registers. The ARM's logical operators provide several tools for us to do this, as follows:

```
AND{S}      Rd, Rs, Operand2
EOR{S}      Rd, Rs, Operand2
ORR{S}      Rd, Rs, Operand2
BIC{S}      Rd, Rs, Operand2
```

These operate on each bit of the registers separately.

AND

AND performs a bitwise logical and operation between each bit in **Rs** and **Operand2**, putting the result in **Rd**. Remember that logical AND is true (1) if both arguments are true (1) and false (0) otherwise, for example.

Let's use AND to mask of a byte of information. Suppose we only want the high-order byte of a register (Listing 4-6).

Listing 4-6. Using AND to mask a byte of information

```
@ mask off the high-order byte
    AND    R6, #0xFF000000

    @ shift the byte down to the
    @ low order position.
    LSR    R6, #24
```

EOR

EOR performs a bitwise exclusive or operation between each bit in **Rs** and **Operand2**, putting the result in **Rd**. Remember that exclusive OR is true (1) if exactly one argument is true (1) and false (0) otherwise.

ORR

ORR performs a bitwise logical or operation between each bit in **Rs** and **Operand2**, putting the result in **Rd**. Remember that logical OR is true (1) if one or both arguments are true (1) and false (0) if both arguments are false (0), for example:

```
    ORR    R6, #0xFF
```

This sets the low-order byte of **R6** to all 1 bits (0xFF) while leaving the three other bytes unaffected.

BIC

BIC (Bit Clear) performs Rs AND NOT Operand2. The reason is that if the bit in **Operand2** is 1, then the resulting bit will be 0. If the bit in **Operand2** is 0, then the corresponding bit in **Rs** will be put in the result **Rd**.

Sometimes the Assembler substitutes this instruction to encode an Operand2 that doesn't work with AND, similar to MOV and MVN, for example:

```
BIC    R6, #0xFF
```

This clears the low-order byte of R6 while leaving the other 3 bytes unaffected (Figure 4-2).

X	Y	X AND Y	X EOR Y	X ORR Y	X BIC Y
0	0	0	0	0	0
0	1	0	1	1	0
1	0	0	1	1	1
1	1	1	0	1	0

Figure 4-2. *What each logical operator does with each pair of bits*

Design Patterns

When writing Assembly language code, there is a great temptation to be creative. For instance, we could do a loop ten times by setting the tenth bit in a register, then shifting it right until the register is zero. This works, but it makes reading your program difficult. If you leave your program and come to it next month, you will be scratching your head as to what the program does.

Design patterns are typical solutions to common programming patterns. If you adopt a few standard design patterns on how to perform loops and other programming constructs, it will make reading your programs much easier.

Design patterns make your programming more productive, since you can just use an example from a collection of tried and true patterns for most situations.

Tip   In Assembly, make sure you document which design pattern you are using, along with documenting the registers used.

Therefore, we implemented loops and if/then/else in the pattern of a high-level language. If we do this, it makes our programs more reliable and quicker to write. Later, we'll look at how to use the macro facility in the Assembler to help with this.

Converting Integers to ASCII

As a first example of a loop, let's convert a 32-bit register to ASCII, so we can display the contents on the console. In our HelloWorld program in Chapter 1, "Getting Started," we used Linux system call number 4 to output our "Hello World!" string. In this program, we will convert the hex digits in the register to ASCII characters digit by digit. ASCII is one way that computers represent all the letters, numbers, and symbols that we read, as numbers that a computer can process. For instance:

- **A** is represented by 65.

- **B** is represented by 66.

- **0** is represented by 48.

- **1** is represented by 49 and so on.

The key point is that the letters A to Z are contiguous as are the numbers 0 to 9. See Appendix E for all 255 characters.

Note   For a single ASCII character that fits in 1 byte, enclose it in single quotes, for example, 'A'. If the ASCII characters are going to comprise a string, use double quotes, for example, "Hello World!".

Here is some high-level language pseudo-code for what we will implement in Assembly language (Listing 4-7).

Listing 4-7. Pseudo-code to print a register

```
outstr = memory where we want the string + 9
     @ (string is form 0x12345678 and we want
     @ the last character)
FOR R5 = 8 TO 1 STEP -1
     digit = R4 AND 0xf
     IF digit < 10 THEN
          asciichar = digit + '0'
     ELSE
          asciichar = digit + 'A' - 10
     END IF
     *outstr = asciichar
     outstr = outstr - 1
NEXT R5
```

Listing 4-8 is the Assembly language program to implement this. It uses what we learned about loops, if/else, and logical statements.

Listing 4-8. Printing a register in ASCII

```
@
@ Assembler program to print a register in hex
@ to stdout.
@
@ R0-R2 - parameters to linux function services
@ R1 - is also address of byte we are writing
@ R4 - register to print
@ R5 - loop index
@ R6 - current character
@ R7 - linux function number
@
```

```
.global _start @ Provide program starting address to linker

_start: MOV R4, #0x12AB @ number to print
      MOVT R4, #0xDE65 @ high bits of number to print
      LDR  R1, =hexstr @ start of string
      ADD  R1, #9       @ start at least sig digit
@ The loop is FOR r5 = 8 TO 1 STEP -1
      MOV  R5, #8        @ 8 digits to print
loop: AND  R6, r4, #0xf @ mask of least sig digit
@ If R6 >= 10 then goto letter
      CMP  R6, #10       @ is 0-9 or A-F
      BGE  letter
@ Else its a number so convert to an ASCII digit
      ADD  R6, #'0'
      B    cont         @ goto to end if
letter: @ handle the digits A to F
      ADD  R6, #('A'-10)
cont: @ end if
      STRB R6, [R1]      @ store ascii digit
      SUB  R1, #1        @ decrement address for next digit
      LSR  R4, #4        @ shift off the digit we just processed

      @ next R5
      SUBS R5, #1        @ step R5 by -2
      BNE  loop          @ another for loop if not done

@ Set up the parameters to print our hex number
@ and then call Linux to do it.
mov    R0, #1           @ 1 = StdOut
      ldr  R1, =hexstr @ string to print
      mov  R2, #11     @ length of our string
      mov  R7, #4      @ linux write system call
      svc  0           @ Call linux to output the string
```

```
@ Set up the parameters to exit the program
@ and then call Linux to do it.
        mov     R0, #0  @ Use 0 return code
        mov     R7, #1  @ Service command code 1 terminates this
        program
        svc     0       @ Call linux to terminate the program

.data
hexstr:         .ascii  "0x12345678\n"
```

If we compile and execute the program, we see

```
pi@stevepi:~/asm/Chapter 4 $ make
as   printword.s -o printword.o
ld -o printword printword.o
pi@stevepi:~/asm/Chapter 4 $ ./printword
0xDE6512AB
pi@stevepi:~/asm/Chapter 4 $
```

as we would expect. The best way to understand this program is to single-step through it in **gdb** and watch how it is using the registers and updating memory.

Make sure you understand why

```
    AND    R6, r4, #0xf
```

masks off the low-order digit; if not, review the "AND" section on logical operators.

Since AND requires both operands to be 1 in order to result in 1, and'ing something with 1s (like 0xf) keeps the other operator as is, whereas and'ing something with 0s always makes the result 0.

In our loop, we shift R4, 4 bits right with

```
    LSR    R4, #4
```

This shifts the next digit into position for processing in the next iteration.

Note   This is destructive to R4, and you will lose your original number during this algorithm.

We've already discussed most of the elements present in this program, but there are a couple of new elements; they are demonstrated in the following.

Using Expressions in Immediate Constants

```
ADD    R6, #('A'-10)
```

This demonstrates a couple of new tricks from the GNU Assembler:

1. We can include ASCII characters in immediate operands by putting them in single quotes.

2. We can place simple expressions in the immediate operands. The GNU Assembler translates 'A' to 65, subtracts 10 to get 55, and uses that as Operand2.

This makes the program more readable, since we can see our intent, rather than if we had just coded 55 here. There is no penalty to the program in doing this, since the work is done when we assemble the program, not when we run it.

Storing a Register to Memory

```
STRB    R6, [R1]
```

The **Store Byte (STRB)** instruction saves the low-order byte of the first register into the memory location contained in R1. The syntax [R1] is to make clear that we are using memory indirection and not just putting the byte into register R1. This is to make the program more readable, so we don't confuse this operation with a corresponding MOV instruction.

Accessing data in memory is the topic of Chapter 5, "Thanks for the Memories," where we will go into far greater detail. The way we are storing the byte could be made more efficient, and we'll look at that then.

Why Not Print in Decimal?

In this example program, we easily convert to a hex string because using AND 0xf is equivalent to getting the remainder when dividing by 16. Similarly shifting the register right 4 bits is equivalent to dividing by 16. If we wanted to convert to a decimal, base 10, string, then we would need to be able to get the remainder from dividing by 10 and later divide by 10.

So far, we haven't seen a divide instruction. This places converting to decimal beyond the scope of this chapter. We could write a loop to implement the long division algorithm we learned in elementary school, but instead we will defer division until *Chapter* 10, "Multiply, Divide, and Accumulate."

Performance of Branch Instructions

In Chapter 1, "Getting Started," we mentioned that the ARM32 instruction set is executed in an instruction pipeline. Individually, an instruction requires three clock cycles to execute, one for each of

1. Load the instruction from memory to the CPU.

2. Decode the instruction.

3. Execute the instruction.

However, the CPU works on three instructions at once, each at a different step, so on average we execute one instruction every clock cycle. But what happens when we branch?

When we execute the branch, we've already decoded the next instruction and loaded the instruction 2 ahead. When we branch, we throw this work away and start over. This means that the instruction after the branch will take three clock cycles to execute.

If you put a lot of branches in your code, you suffer a performance penalty, perhaps slowing your program by a factor of 3. Another problem is that if you program with a lot of branches, this leads to **spaghetti code**—meaning all the lines of code are tangled together like a pot of spaghetti, understandably quite hard to maintain.

When I first learned to program in high school and my undergraduate years before structured programming was available, I used the BASIC and Fortran programming languages to write complex code. I know firsthand that deciphering programs full of branches is a challenge.

Early high-level programming languages relied on the **goto** statement that led to hard to understand code; this led to the structured programming we see in modern high-level languages that don't need a goto statement. We can't entirely do away with branches, since ARM32 doesn't have structured programming constructs, but we need to structure our code along these lines to make it both more efficient and easier to read—another great use for a few good design patterns.

The ARM32 instruction set has a mechanism to deal with this, utilizing the condition code in each instruction. We'll look at this in Chapter 13, "Conditional Instructions and Optimizing Code."

More Comparison Instructions

We looked at the CMP instruction, which is the main comparison instruction; however, there are three more:

- CMNRn, Operand2

- TEQ Rn, Operand2

- TST Rn, Operand2

Remember that the CMP instruction subtracted Operand2 from Rn and set the condition flags in the CPSR accordingly. The result of the subtraction is discarded. These three instructions work the same way, except they use an operation different from subtraction.

The Assembler has the ability to switch between the four comparison instructions to finesse some extra values for Operand2, that otherwise would be impossible. In this book, we'll just use CMP, but you can use these if you find an application, plus it's worth being aware of these in case the Assembler does a substitution. The other three are

- **CMN**: Uses addition instead of subtraction. The N indicates it's the negative (opposite) of CMP.

- **TEQ**: Performs a bitwise exclusive OR between Rn and Operand2. It updates the CPSR based on the result.

- **TST**: Performs a bitwise AND operation between Rn and Operand2. It updates the CPSR based on the result.

Summary

In this chapter, we studied the key instructions for performing program logic with loops and if statements. These included the instructions for comparisons and conditional branching. We discussed several design patterns to code the common constructs from high-level programming languages in Assembly. We looked at the statements for logically working with the bits in a register. We examined how we could output the contents of a register in hexadecimal format.

CHAPTER 5

Thanks for the Memories

In this chapter, we discuss the Raspberry Pi's memory. So far, we've used memory to hold our Assembly instructions; now we will look in detail at how to define data in memory, then how to load memory into registers for processing, and how to write the results back to memory.

The ARM32 uses what is called a **load-store architecture**. This means that the instruction set is divided into two categories: one to load and store values from and to memory and the other to perform arithmetic and logical operations between the registers. We've spent most of our time looking at the arithmetic and logical operations. Now we will look at the other category.

Memory addresses are 32 bits and instructions are 32 bits, so we have the same problems that we experienced in Chapter 2, "Loading and Adding," where we used all sorts of tricks to load 32 bits into a register. In this chapter, we'll use these same tricks for loading addresses, along with a few new ones. The goal is to load a 32-bit address in one instruction in as many cases as we can.

The ARM32 instruction set has some powerful instructions to access memory, including several techniques to access arrays of data structures and to increment pointers in loops while loading or storing data.

© Stephen Smith 2019
S. Smith, *Raspberry Pi Assembly Language Programming*,
https://doi.org/10.1007/978-1-4842-5287-1_5

Defining Memory Contents

Before loading and storing memory, first we need to define some memory to operate on. The GNU Assembler contains several directives to help you define memory to use in your program. These appear in a .data section of your program. We'll look at some examples and then summarize in Table 5-1. Listing 5-1 starts us off by showing us how to define bytes, words, and ASCII strings.

Listing 5-1. Some sample memory directives

```
label: .byte 74, 0112, 0b00101010, 0x4A, 0X4a, 'J', 'H' + 2
       .word  0x1234ABCD, -1434
       .ascii      "Hello World\n"
```

The first line defines 7 bytes all with the same value. We can define our bytes in decimal, octal (base 8), binary, hex, or ASCII. Anywhere we define numbers, we can use expressions that the Assembler will evaluate when it compiles our program.

We start most memory directives with a label, so we can access it from the code. The only exception is if we are defining a larger array of numbers that extends over several lines.

The .byte statement defines 1 or more bytes of memory. Listing 5-1 shows the various formats we can use for the contents of each byte, as follows:

- A decimal integer starts with a non-zero digit and contains decimal digits 0–9.

- An octal integer starts with zero and contains octal digits 0–7.

- A binary integer starts with 0b or 0B and contains binary digits 0–1.

- A hex integer starts with 0x or 0X and contains hex digit 0–F.

- A floating-point number starts with 0f or 0e, followed by a floating-point number.

Note   Be careful not to start decimal numbers with zero (0), since this indicates the constant is an octal (base 8) number.

The example then shows how to define a word and an ASCII string, as we saw in our HelloWorld program in Chapter 1, "Getting Started." There are two prefix operators we can place in front of an integer:

- Negative (-) will take the two's complement of the integer.

- Complement (~) will take the one's complement of the integer.

For example:

```
.byte -0x45, -33, ~0b00111001
```

Table 5-1 lists the various data types we can define this way.

Table 5-1. *The list of memory definition Assembler directives*

Directive	Description
.ascii	A string contained in double quotes
.asciz	A zero-byte terminated ascii string
.byte	1-byte integers
.double	Double-precision floating-point values
.float	Floating-point values
.octa	16-byte integers
.quad	8-byte integers
.short	2-byte integers
.word	4-byte integers

If we want to define a larger set of memory, there are a couple of mechanisms to do this without having to list and count them all, such as:

```
.fill  repeat, size, value
```

This repeats a value of a given size, repeat times, for example:

```
zeros:       .fill  10, 4, 0
```

creates a block of memory with ten 4-byte words all with a value of zero. The following code

```
.rept count
...
.endr
```

repeats the statements between .rept and .endr, count times. This can surround any code in your Assembly, for instance, you can make a loop by repeating your code count times, for example:

```
rpn:    .rept 3
        .byte 0, 1, 2
        .endr
```

is translated to

```
        .byte 0, 1, 2
        .byte 0, 1, 2
        .byte 0, 1, 2
```

In ASCII strings we've seen the special character "\n" for new line. There are a few more for common unprintable characters as well as to give us an ability to put double quotes in our strings. The "\" is called an escape character, which is a metacharacter to define special cases. Table 5-2 lists the escape character sequences supported by the GNU Assembler.

Table 5-2. *ASCII escape character sequence codes*

Escape character sequence	Description
\b	Backspace (ASCII code 8)
\f	Formfeed (ASCII code 12)
\n	New line (ASCII code 10)
\r	Return (ASCII code 13)
\t	Tab (ASCII code 9)
\ddd	An octal ASCII code (ex \123)
\xdd	A hex ASCII code (ex \x4F)
****	The "\" character
\"	The double quote character
\anything-else	anything-else

Loading a Register

In this section, we will look at the **LDR** instruction and its variations. We use LDR to both load an address into a register and to load the data pointed to by that address. There are methods to index through memory, as well as support for all the tricks to get as much as possible out of our 32-bit instructions. We'll go through the cases one by one, including

- PC relative addressing

- Loading from memory

- Indexing through memory

PC Relative Addressing

In Chapter 1, "Getting Started," we introduced the **LDR** instruction to load the address of our "Hello World!" string. We needed to do this to pass the address of what to print to the Linux **write** command. This is a simple example of PC relative addressing. It is convenient, since it doesn't involve any other registers. As long as you keep your data close to your code, it is painless. Remember that when we looked at the disassembly of the LDR instruction

```
LDR    R1, =helloworld
```

was

```
LDR    r1, [pc, #20]
```

Here we are writing an instruction to load the address of our helloworld string into **R1**. The Assembler knows the value of the program counter at this point, so it can provide an offset to the correct memory address. Therefore, it's called PC relative addressing. There is a bit more complexity to this; that we'll get to in a minute.

The offset above takes has 12 bits in the instruction, which gives a range of 0–4095. There is another bit in the instruction to say which direction to offset, so we get a range of ±4095. In this case, we are loading a word, so the address range is ±4095 words.

The general form of this instruction is

```
LDR{type}    Rt, =label
```

where type is one of the types listed in Table 5-3.

Table 5-3. *The data types for the load/store instructions*

Type	Meaning
B	Unsigned byte
SB	Signed byte
H	Unsigned halfword (16 bits)
SH	Signed halfword (16 bits)
–	Omitted for word

In this simple case, where we are only loading the address, the only thing used from the type is the size of the data. If we load a byte, then the offset will be in bytes. This signed part is important when we load and save data, as we'll see shortly.

Note   The offset is ±4095 in the units of the data we are loading.

PC relative addressing has one more trick up its sleeve; it gives us a way to load any 32-bit quantity into a register in only one instruction, for example, consider

```
LDR    R1, =0x1234ABCDF
```

This assembles into

```
ldr    r1, [pc, #8]
.word  0x1234abcd
```

The GNU Assembler is helping us out by putting the constant we want into memory, then creating a PC relative instruction to load it.

In Chapter 2, "Loading and Adding," we performed this with a MOV/ MOVT pair. Here we are doing the same thing in one instruction. Both take the same memory, either two 32-bit instructions or one 32-bit instruction and one 32-bit memory location.

In fact, this is how the Assembler handles all data labels. When we specified

```
LDR    R1, =helloworld
```

the Assembler did the same thing; it created the address of the hellostring in memory and then loaded the contents of that memory location, not the helloworld string. We'll look carefully at this process when we discuss our program to convert strings to uppercase later in this chapter.

These constants the Assembler creates are placed at the end of the **.text** section which is where the Assembly instructions go. Not in the **.data** section. This makes them read-only in normal circumstances, so they can't be modified. Any data that you want to modify should go in a **.data** section.

Why would the Assembler do this? Why not just point the PC relative index directly at the data? There are several reasons for this, not all of them specific to the ARM32 instruction set:

1. An offset of 4096 isn't very large, especially if you have several large strings. This way we can access 4096 objects rather than 4096 words. This helps keep our program equally efficient as it gets larger.

2. All the labels we define go into the object file's symbol table, making this array of addresses essentially our symbol table. This way, it's easy for the linker/loader and operating system to change memory addresses without you needing to recompile your program.

3. If you need any of these variables to be global, you can just make them global (accessible to other files) without changing your program. If we didn't have this level of indirection, making a variable global would require adjustments to the instructions that load and save it.

This is another example of the tools helping us, though at first it may not seem so. In our simple one-line examples, it appears to add a layer of complexity, but in a real program, this is the design pattern that works.

Loading from Memory

In our HelloWorld program, we only needed the address to pass on to Linux, that then used it to print our string. Generally, we like to use these addresses to load data into a register as demonstrated in Listing 5-2.

Listing 5-2. Loading an address and then the value

```
@ load the address of mynumber into R1
      LDR    R1, =mynumber
@ load the word stored at mynumber into R2
      LDR    R2, [R1]              .data

mynumber:    .WORD 0x1234ABCD
```

If you step through this in the debugger, you can watch it load 0x1234ABCD into **R2**.

Note   The square bracket syntax represents indirect memory access. This means load the data stored at the address pointed to by **R1**, not move the contents of **R1** into **R2**.

When we encountered "LDR r1, [pc, #20]", it looked like we were just loading the address of pc+20, but now we know we are actually loading the address stored at pc+20, which is why square brackets are used.

Note   If you want to load a byte from this memory location, you need to add the type to both instructions, or there will be a length mismatch and it won't load the byte you are thinking of.

This works, but you might be dissatisfied that it took us two instructions to load R2 with our value from memory: one to load the address and then one to load the data. This is life programming a RISC processor; each instruction executes very quickly, but performs a small chunk of work. As we develop algorithms, we'll see that we usually load an address once and then use it quite a bit, so most accesses take one instruction once we are going.

Indexing Through Memory

All high-level programming languages have an array construct. They can define an array of objects and then access the individual elements by index. The high-level language will define the array with something like

```
DIM A[10] AS WORD
```

then access the individual elements with statements like those in Listing 5-3.

Listing 5-3. Pseudo-code to loop through an array

```
// Set the 5th element of the array to the value 6
    A[5] = 6
// Set the variable X equal to the 3rd array element
    X = A[3]
// Loop through all 10 elements
    FOR I = 1 TO 10
        // Set element I to I cubed
        A[I] = I ** 3
    NEXT I
```

The ARM32 instruction set gives us support for doing these sorts of operations.

Suppose we have an array of ten words (4 bytes each) defined by

```
arr1: .FILL 10, 4, 0
```

Let's load the array's address into **R1**:

```
    LDR    R1, =arr1
```

We can now access the elements using **LDR** as demonstrated in Listing 5-4 and graphically represented in Figure 5-1.

Listing 5-4. Indexing into an array

```
@ Load the first element
LDR   R2, [R1]
@ Load element 3
@ The elements count from 0, so 2 is
@ the third one. Each word is 4 bytes,
@ so we need to multiply by 4
LDR   R2, [R1, #(2 * 4)]
```

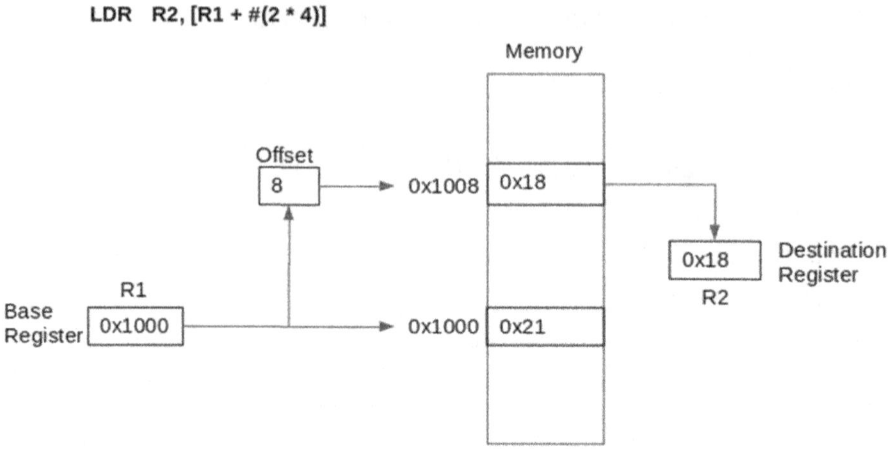

LDR   R2, [R1 + #(2 * 4)]

Figure 5-1. *Graphical view of using R1 and an index to load R2*

This is fine for accessing hard-coded elements, but what about via a variable? We can use a register as demonstrated in Listing 5-5.

Listing 5-5. Using a register as an offset

```
@ The 3rd element is still number 2
    MOV    R3, #(2 * 4)
@ Add the offset in R3 to R1 to get our element.
    LDR    R2, [R1, R3]
```

We can do these shifts in reverse. If **R2** points to the end of the array, we can do

```
    LDR    R2, [R1, #-(2 * 4)]
    LDR    R2, [R1, -R3]
```

With the register as the offset, it is the same as a register and shift type Operand2 which we studied in Chapter 2, "Loading and Adding." For the preceding constants, we could do a * 4 in the immediate instruction, but if it's in a register, we would need to do an additional shift operation and put the result in yet another register. With the register/shift format, we can handle quite a few cases easily. Computing the address of an array of words is demonstrated in Listing 5-6.

Listing 5-6. Multiplying an offset by 4 using a shift operation

```
@ Suppose our array is of WORDs but we only
@ want the low order byte.
MOV   R3, #2
@ Shift R3 left by 2 positions to multiply
@ by 4 to get the correct address.
LDR   R2, [R1, R3, LSL #2]
```

Write Back

When the address is calculated by the adds and shifts, the result is thrown away after we've loaded the register. When performing a loop, it is handy to keep the calculated address. This saves us doing a separate ADD on our index register.

The syntax for this is to put an exclamation mark (**!**) after the instruction, then the Assembler will set the bit in the generated instruction asking the CPU to save the calculated address, thus

```
LDR R2, [R1, R3, LSL #2]!
```

updates **R1** with the value calculated. In the examples we've studied, this isn't that useful, but it becomes much more useful in the next section.

Post-indexed Addressing

The preceding section covers what is called **pre-indexed addressing**. This is because the address is calculated and then the data is retrieved using the calculated address. In **post-indexed addressing,** the data is retrieved first using the base register, then any offset shifting and adding is done. In the context of one instruction, this seems strange, but when we write loops, we will see this is what we want. The calculated address is written back to the base address register, since otherwise there is no point in using this feature, so we don't need the !.

We indicate we want post-indexed addressing by placing the items to add outside the square brackets. In the following examples, LDR will load **R1** with the contents of memory pointed to by **R2** and then update **R2** using the method indicated in each instruction. Listing 5-7 gives some examples of post-indexed addressing.

Listing 5-7. Examples of post-indexed addressing

```
@ Load R1 with the memory pointed to by R2
@ Then do R2 = R2 + R3
LDR    R1, [R2], R3
@ Load R1 with the memory pointed to by R2
@ Then do R2 = R2 + 2
LDR    R1, [R2], #2
@ Load R1 with the memory pointed to by R2
@ Then do R2 = R2 + (R3 shifted 2 left)
LDR    R1, [R2], R3, LSL #2
```

Converting to Uppercase

As an example of how post-indexed addressing helps us write loops, let's consider looping through a string of ASCII bytes. Suppose we want to convert any lowercase characters to uppercase. Listing 5-8 gives pseudo-code to do this.

Listing 5-8. Pseudo-code to convert a string to uppercase

```
i = 0
DO
        char = instr[i]
        IF char >= 'a' AND char <= 'z' THEN
                char = char - ('a' - 'A')
        END IF
        outstr[i] = char
        i = i + 1
UNTIL char == 0
PRINT outstr
```

In this example, we are going to use NULL-terminated strings. These are very common in C programming. Here instead of a string being a length and a sequence of characters, the string is the sequence of characters, followed by a NULL (ASCII code 0 or \0) character. To process the string, we simply loop until we hit the NULL character. This is quite different than the fixed length string we dealt with when printing hex digits in Chapter 4, "Controlling Program Flow."

We've already covered for and while loops. The third common structured programming loop is the **DO/UNTIL** loop that puts the condition at the end of the loop. In this construct, the loop is always executed once. In our case, we want this, since if the string is empty, we still want to copy the NULL character, so the output string will then be empty as well.

Another difference is that we aren't changing the input string. Instead we leave the input string alone and produce a new output string with the uppercase version of the input string.

As is common in Assembly language processing, we reverse the logic to jump around the code in the IF block. Listing 5-9 shows the updated pseudo-code.

Listing 5-9. Pseudo-code on how we will implement the IF statement

```
        IF char < 'a' GOTO continue
        IF char > 'z' GOTO continue
        char = char - ('a' - 'A')
continue: // the rest of the program
```

We don't have the structured programming constructs of a high-level language to help us, and this turns out to be quite efficient in Assembly language.

Listing 5-10 is the Assembly code to convert a string to uppercase.

Listing 5-10. Program to convert a string to uppercase

```
@
@ Assembler program to convert a string to
@ all uppercase.
@
@ R0-R2 - parameters to Linux function services
@ R3 - address of output string
@ R4 - address of input string
@ R5 - current character being processed
@ R7 - Linux function number
@

.global _start @ Provide program starting address

_start: LDR  R4, =instr @ start of input string
        LDR  R3, =outstr @ address of output string
@ The loop is until byte pointed to by R1 is non-zero
@ Load character and increment pointer
loop: LDRB  R5, [R4], #1
@ If R5 > 'z' then goto cont
        CMP    R5, #'z'        @ is letter > 'z'?
        BGT    cont
```

```
@ Else if R5 < 'a' then goto end if
        CMP     R5, #'a'
        BLT     cont  @ goto to end if
@ if we got here then the letter is lower-case,
@ so convert it.
        SUB     R5, #('a'-'A')
cont: @ end if
        STRB    R5, [R3], #1 @ store character to outstr
        CMP     R5, #0       @ stop on hitting a null char
        BNE     loop         @ loop if character isn't null

@ Set up the parameters to print our hex number
@ and then call Linux to do it.
        MOV     R0, #1       @ 1 = StdOut
        LDR     R1, =outstr  @ string to print
@ get the length by subtracting the pointers
        SUB     R2, R3, R1
        MOV     R7, #4       @ linux write system call
        SVC     0            @ Call linux to output the string

@ Set up the parameters to exit the program
@ and then call Linux to do it.
        MOV     R0, #0       @ Use 0 return code
        MOV     R7, #1       @ Service command code 1
        SVC     0            @ Call linux to terminate

.data
instr:  .asciz  "This is our Test String that we will
convert.\n"
outstr:         .fill 255, 1, 0
```

If we compile and run the program, we get the desired output:

```
pi@raspberrypi:~/asm/Chapter 5 $ ./upper
THIS IS OUR TEST STRING THAT WE WILL CONVERT.
pi@raspberrypi:~/asm/Chapter 5 $
```

This program is quite short. Besides all the comments and the code to print the string and exit, there are only 11 Assembly instructions to initialize and execute the loop:

- **Two instructions**: Initialize our pointers for instr and outstr

- **Five instructions**: Make up the if statement

- **Four instructions**: For the loop, including loading a character, saving a character, updating both pointers, checking for a null character, and branching if not null

It would be nice if STRB also set the condition flags, but there is no STRBS version. LDR and STR just load and save; they don't have functionality to examine what they are loading and saving, so they can't set the CPSR. Hence the need for the CMP instruction in the UNTIL part of the loop to test for NULL.

In this example, we use the LDRB and STRB instructions, since we are processing byte by byte. The STRB instruction is the reverse of the LDRB instruction. It saves its first argument to the address built from all its other parameters. By covering LDR in so much detail, we've also covered STR which is the mirror image.

To convert the letter to uppercase, we use

```
SUB    R5, #('a'-'A')
```

The lowercase characters have higher values than the uppercase characters, so we just use an expression that the Assembler will evaluate to get the correct number to subtract.

When we come to print the string, we don't know its length and Linux requires the length. We use the instruction

```
SUB    R2, R3, R1
```

Here we've just loaded R1 with the address of outstr. R3 held the address of outstr in our loop, but because we used post-indexed addressing, it got incremented in each iteration of the loop. As a result, it is now pointing 1 past the end of the string. We then calculate the length by subtracting the address of the start of the string from the address of the end of the string. We could have kept a counter for this in our loop, but in Assembly we are trying to be efficient, so we want as few instructions as possible in our loops.

Let's look at Listing 5-11, a disassembly of our program.

Listing 5-11. Disassembly of the uppercase program

```
 Contents of section .text:

00010074 <_start>:
   10074:    e59f4044    ldr    r4, [pc, #68]      ; 100c0 <cont+0x2c>
   10078:    e59f3044    ldr    r3, [pc, #68]      ; 100c4 <cont+0x30>

0001007c <loop>:
   1007c:    e4d45001    ldrb   r5, [r4], #1
   10080:    e355007a    cmp    r5, #122    ; 0x7a
   10084:    ca000002    bgt    10094 <cont>
   10088:    e3550061    cmp    r5, #97     ; 0x61
   1008c:    ba000000    blt    10094 <cont>
   10090:    e2455020    sub    r5, r5, #32

00010094 <cont>:
   10094:    e4c35001    strb   r5, [r3], #1
   10098:    e3550000    cmp    r5, #0
   1009c:    1afffff6    bne    1007c <loop>
```

```
100a0:    e3a00001    mov    r0, #1
100a4:    e59f1018    ldr    r1, [pc, #24]   ; 100c4 <cont+0x30>
100a8:    e0432001    sub    r2, r3, r1
100ac:    e3a07004    mov    r7, #4
100b0:    ef000000    svc    0x00000000
100b4:    e3a00000    mov    r0, #0
100b8:    e3a07001    mov    r7, #1
100bc:    ef000000    svc    0x00000000
100c0:    000200c8    .word  0x000200c8
100c4:    000200f7    .word  0x000200f7
```

Contents of section .data:

```
200c8 54686973 20697320 6f757220 54657374  This is our Test
200d8 20537472 696e6720 74686174 20776520   String that we
200e8 77696c6c 20636f6e 76657274 2e0a0000  will convert....
200f8 00000000 00000000 00000000 00000000  ................
```

The instruction

```
LDR    R4, =instr
```

has been converted to

```
ldr    r4, [pc, #68]      ; 100c0
```

The comment tells us that pc+68 is the address 0x100c0. We can calculate that ourselves if we take the address of the instruction 2 past this one (the one being loaded as this one executes), which is at 0x1007c, and adding 68 in the Gnome calculator to get the same 0x100c0.

This shows how the Assembler added the literal for the address of the string instr at the end of the code section. When we do the LDR, it accesses this literal and loads it into memory; this gives us the address we need in memory. The other literal added to the code section is the address of outstr.

To see this program in action, it is worthwhile to single-step through it in **gdb**. You can watch the registers with the "i r" (info registers) command. To view instr and oustr as the processing occurs, there are a couple of ways of doing it. From the disassembly we know the address of instr is 0x200c8, so we can enter

```
(gdb) x /2s 0x200c8
0x200c8:    "This is our Test String that we will convert.\n"
0x200f7:    "THI"
(gdb)
```

This is convenient since the x command knows how to format strings, but it doesn't know about labels. We can also enter

```
(gdb) p (char[10]) outstr
$8 = "TH\000\000\000\000\000\000\000"
(gdb)
```

The print (p) command knows about our labels but doesn't know about our data types, and we must cast the label to tell it how to format the output. Gdb handles this better with high-level languages because it knows about the data types of the variables. In Assembly, we are closer to the metal.

Storing a Register

The Store Register **STR** instruction is a mirror of the **LDR** instruction. All the addressing modes we've talked about for LDR work for STR. This is necessary since in a load store architecture, we need to store everything we load after it is processed in the CPU. We've seen the STR instruction a couple of times already in our examples.

If we are using the same registers to load and store the data in a loop, typically the first LDR call will use pre-indexed addressing without writeback and then the STR instruction will use post-indexed addressing with writeback to advance to the next item for the next iteration of the loop.

Double Registers

There are double-word versions of all the LDR and STR instructions we've seen. The LDRD instruction takes two registers to load as parameters and then loads 64 bits of memory into these. Similarly, for the STRD instruction.

For example, Listing 5-12 loads the address of a dword (this is still 32 bits) and then loads the dword into R2 and R3. Then we store R2 and R3 back into the mydword.

Listing 5-12. Example of loading and storing a double-word

```
        LDR    R1, =mydword
        LDRD   R2, R3, [R1]
        STRD   R2, R3, [R1]
.data
mydword:    .DWORD 0x1234567887654321
```

This will be useful when we look at multiplication.

Summary

With this chapter, we can now load data from memory, operate on it in the registers, and then save the result back to memory. We examined how the data load and store instructions help us with arrays of data and how they help us index through data in loops.

In the next chapter, we will look at how to make our code reusable; after all, wouldn't our uppercase program be handy if we could call it whenever we wish?

CHAPTER 6

Functions and the Stack

In this chapter, we will examine how to organize our code into small independent units called **functions**. This allows us to build reusable components that we can call easily from anywhere we wish.

Typically, in software development we start with low-level components, then build on these to create higher and higher level applications. So far, we know how to loop, perform conditional logic, and perform some arithmetic. Now, we examine how to compartmentalize our code into building blocks.

We introduce the **stack**; this is a computer science data structure for storing data. If we are going to build useful reusable functions, we will need a good way to manage register usage, so that all these functions don't clobber each other. In Chapter 5, "Thanks for the Memories," we studied how to store data in a data segment in main memory. The problem with this is that this memory exists for the duration that our program runs. With small functions, like our converting to uppercase program, they run quickly and might need a few memory locations while they run, but when they are done, they don't need this memory anymore. Stacks provide us a tool to manage register usage across function calls and a tool to provide memory to functions for the duration of their invocation.

We introduce a number of low-level concepts first, then we put them all together to effectively create and use functions.

© Stephen Smith 2019
S. Smith, *Raspberry Pi Assembly Language Programming*,
https://doi.org/10.1007/978-1-4842-5287-1_6

Stacks on Raspbian

In computer science, a stack is an area of memory where there are two operations:

- **push**: Adds an element to the area

- **pop**: Returns and removes the element that was most recently added

This behavior is also called a **LIFO** (last in first out) queue.

When Raspbian runs a program, it gives it an 8 MB stack. In Chapter 1, "Getting Started," we mentioned that register **R13** had a special purpose as the Stack Pointer (**SP**). You might have noticed that **R13** is named **SP** in **gdb**, and you might have noticed that when you debugged programs, it had a large value, something like 0x7efff380. This is a pointer to the current stack location.

The ARM32 instruction set has two instructions to manipulate stacks, Load Multiple (**LDM**) and Store Multiple (**STM**). These two instructions have quite a few options. These are to support things like whether the stack grows by increasing addresses or by decreasing addresses—, whether **SP** points to the end of the stack or the next free location on the stack. These options could be useful, if you are creating your own stack, or to match the requirement of a different operating system. But all we want is to work with the stack Raspbian provides us.

Fortunately, the GNU Assembler offers simpler pseudo-instructions that are mapped back to the correct forms of **LDM** and **STM**. These are

```
PUSH    {reglist}
POP     {reglist}
```

The **{reglist}** parameter is a list of registers, containing a comma-separated list of registers and register ranges. A register range is something like **R2–R4,** which means **R2**, **R3**, and **R4**, for example:

```
PUSH    {r0, r5-r12}
POP {r0-r4, r6, r9-r12}
```

The registers are stored on the stack in numerical order, with the lowest register at the lowest address. You shouldn't include **PC** or **SP** in this list. Figure 6-1 shows the process of pushing a register onto the stack and then Figure 6-2 shows the reverse operation of popping that value off the stack.

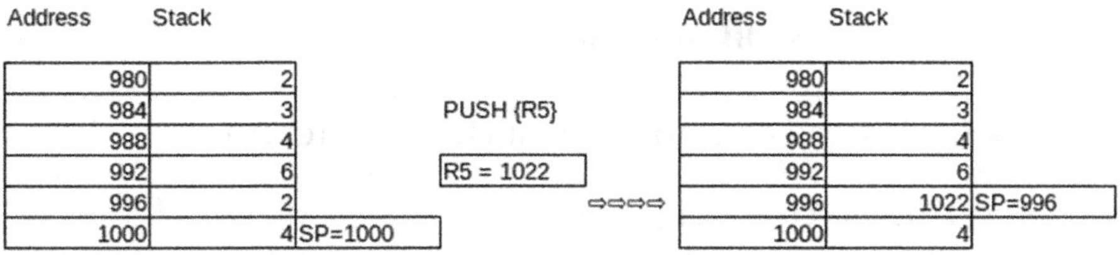

Figure 6-1. *Pushing R5 onto the stack*

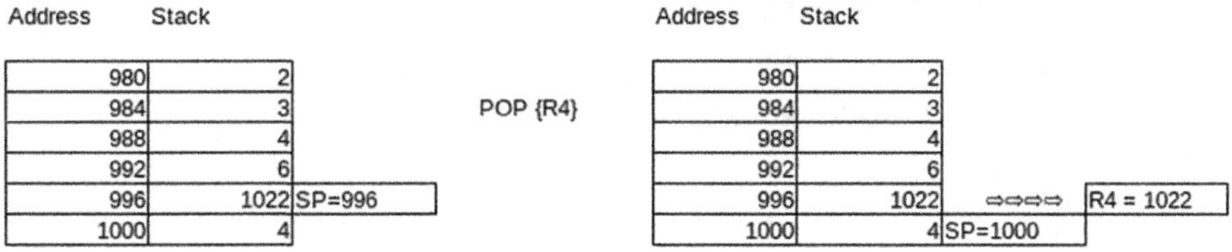

Figure 6-2. *Popping R4 from the stack*

Branch with Link

To call a function, we need to set up the ability for the function to return execution to after the point where we called the function. We do this with the other special register we listed in Chapter 1, "Getting Started," the **Link Register** (**LR**) which is **R14**. To make use of **LR**, we introduce the **Branch with Link** (**BL**) instruction, which is the same as the Branch (**B**) instruction, except it puts the address of the next instruction into **LR** before it performs the branch, giving us a mechanism to return from the function.

To return from our function, we use the **Branch and Exchange** (**BX**) instruction. This branch instruction takes a register as its argument, allowing us to branch to the address stored in **LR** to continue processing after the function completes.

In Listing 6-1, the **BL** instruction stores the address of the following **MOV** instruction into **LR** and then branches to myfunc. Myfunc does the useful work the function was written to do, then returns execution to the caller by having **BX** branch to the location stored in **LR**, which is the **MOV** instruction following the **BL** instruction.

Listing 6-1. Skeleton code to call a function and return

```
@ ... other code ...
BL    myfunc
MOV   R1, #4
@ ... more code ...
-----------------------------
myfunc:      @ do some work
             BX LR
```

Nesting Function Calls

We successfully called and returned from a function, but we never used the stack. Why did we introduce the stack first and then not use it? First think what happens if in the course of its processing myfunc calls another function. We would expect this to be fairly common, as we write code building on the functionality we've previously written. If myfunc executes a **BL** instruction, then **BL** will copy the next address into **LR** overwriting the return address for myfunc and myfunc won't be able to return. What we need is a way to keep a chain of return addresses as we call function after function. Well, not a chain of return addresses, but a stack of return addresses.

If myfunc is going to call other functions, then it needs to push LR onto the stack as the first thing it does and pop it from the stack just before it returns, for example, Listing 6-2 shows this process.

Listing 6-2. Skeleton code for a function that calls another function

```
@ ... other code ...
BL    myfunc
MOV   R1, #4
@ ... more code ...
-----------------------------
myfunc:     PUSH {LR}
            @ do some work ...
            BL    myfunc2
            @ do some more work...
            POP {LR}
            BX LR
myfunc2:    @ do some work ....
            BX LR
```

In this example, we see how convenient the stack is to store data that only needs to exist for the duration of a function call.

If a function, such as myfunc, calls other functions, then it must save **LR**; if it doesn't call other functions, such as myfunc2, then it doesn't need to save **LR**. Programmers often push and pop LR regardless, since if the function is modified later to add a function call and the programmer forgets to add **LR** to the list of saved registers, then the program will fail to return and either go into an infinite loop or crash. The downside is that there is only so much bandwidth between the CPU and memory, so PUSHing and POPing more registers does take extra execution cycles. The trade-off in speed vs. maintainability is a subjective decision depending on the circumstances.

Function Parameters and Return Values

In high-level languages, functions take parameters and return their results. Assembly language programming is no different. We could invent our own mechanisms to do this, but this is counterproductive. Eventually we will want our code to interoperate with code written in other programming languages. We will want to call our new super-fast functions from C code, and we might want to call functions that were written in C.

To facilitate this, there are a set of design patterns for calling functions. If we follow these, our code will work reliably since others have already worked out all the bugs, plus we achieve the goal of writing interoperable code.

The caller passes the first four parameters in **R0**, **R1**, **R2**, and **R3**. If there are additional parameters, then they are pushed onto the stack. If we only have two parameters, then we would only use **R0** and **R1**. This means the first four parameters are already loaded into registers and ready to be processed. Additional parameters need to be popped from the stack before being processed.

To return a value to the caller, place it in **R0** before returning. If you need to return more data, you would have one of the parameters be an address to a memory location where you can place the additional data to be returned. This is the same as C where you return data through call by reference parameters.

Managing the Registers

If you call a function, chances are it was written by a different programmer and you don't know what registers it will use. It would be very inefficient, if you had to reload all your registers every time you call a function. As a result, there are a set of rules to govern which registers a function can use and who is responsible for saving each one:

- **R0–R3**: These are the function parameters. The function can use these for any other purpose modifying them freely. If the calling routine needs them saved, it must save them itself.

- **R4–R12**: These can be used freely by the called routine, but if it is responsible for saving them. That means the calling routine can assume these registers are intact.

- **SP**: This can be freely used by the called routine. The routine must POP the stack the same number of times that it PUSHes, so it is intact for the calling routine.

- **LR**: The called routine must preserve this as we discussed in the last section.

- **CPSR**: Neither routine can make any assumptions about the **CPSR**. As far as the called routine is concerned, all the flags are unknown; similarly, they are unknown to the caller when the function returns.

Summary of the Function Call Algorithm

Calling routine

1. If we need any of **R0–R4**, save them.

2. Move first four parameters into registers **R0–R4**.

3. Push any additional parameters onto the stack.

4. Use **BL** to call the function.

5. Evaluate the return code in **R0**.

6. Restore any of **R0–R4** that we saved.

Called function

1. PUSH **LR** and **R4–R12** onto the stack.

2. Do our work.

3. Put our return code into **R0**.

4. POP **LR** and **R4–R12**.

5. Use the **BX** instruction to return execution to the caller.

Note   We can save ourselves some steps if we just use **R0–R3** for function parameters and return codes and short-term work. Then we never have to save and restore them around function calls.

I specified saving all of **LR** and **R4–R12**, which is the safest and most maintainable practice. However, if we know we don't use some of these registers, we can skip saving them and save some execution time on function entry and exit.

These aren't all the rules. The coprocessors also have registers that might need saving. We'll discuss those rules when we discuss the coprocessors.

Uppercase Revisited

Let's organize our uppercase example from Chapter 5, "Thanks for the Memories," as a proper function. We'll move the function into its own file and modify the makefile to make both the calling program and the uppercase function.

First create a file called main.s containing Listing 6-3 for the driving application.

Listing 6-3. Main program for uppercase example

```
@
@ Assembler program to convert a string to
@ all uppercase by calling a function.
@
@ R0-R2 - parameters to linux function services
@ R1 - address of output string
@ R0 - address of input string
@ R5 - current character being processed
@ R7 - linux function number
@

.global _start     @ Provide program starting address

_start: LDR   R0, =instr @ start of input string
        LDR   R1, =outstr @ address of output string

        BL    toupper

@ Set up the parameters to print our hex number
@ and then call Linux to do it.
        MOV   R2,R0  @ return code is the length of the string

        MOV   R0, #1        @ 1 = StdOut
        LDR   R1, =outstr @ string to print
        MOV   R7, #4        @ linux write system call
        SVC   0            @ Call linux to output the string

@ Set up the parameters to exit the program
@ and then call Linux to do it.
        MOV   R0, #0      @ Use 0 return code
        MOV   R7, #1      @ Command code 1 terminates
        SVC   0          @ Call linux to terminate the program
```

```
.data
instr:  .asciz  "This is our Test String that we will
convert.\n"
outstr:        .fill 255, 1, 0
```

Now create a file called upper.s containing Listing 6-4, the uppercase conversion function.

Listing 6-4. Function to convert strings to all uppercase

```
@
@ Assembler program to convert a string to
@ all uppercase.
@
@ R1 - address of output string
@ R0 - address of input string
@ R4 - original output string for length calc.
@ R5 - current character being processed
@

.global toupper     @ Allow other files to call this routine

toupper:    PUSH    {R4-R5} @ Save the registers we use.
        MOV    R4, R1
@ The loop is until byte pointed to by R1 is non-zero
loop: LDRB  R5, [R0], #1      @ load character and increment
                                 pointer
@ If R5 > 'z' then goto cont
        CMP    R5, #'z'      @ is letter > 'z'?
        BGT    cont
@ Else if R5 < 'a' then goto end if
        CMP    R5, #'a'
        BLT    cont @ goto to end if
```

```
@ if we got here then the letter is lower case, so convert it.
        SUB    R5, #('a'-'A')
cont: @ end if
        STRB   R5, [R1], #1      @ store character to output str
        CMP    R5, #0            @ stop on hitting a null
                                     character
        BNE    loop          @ loop if character isn't null
        SUB    R0, R1, R4    @ get the length by subtracting the
                                 pointers
        POP    {R4-R5}       @ Restore the register we use.
        BX     LR            @ Return to caller
```

To build these, use the makefile in Listing 6-5.

Listing 6-5. Makefile for the uppercase function example

```
UPPEROBJS = main.o upper.o

ifdef DEBUG
DEBUGFLGS = -g
else
DEBUGFLGS =
endif
LSTFLGS =

all: upper

%.o : %.s
        as $(DEBUGFLGS) $(LSTFLGS) $< -o $@

upper: $(UPPEROBJS)
        ld -o upper $(UPPEROBJS)
```

Let's step through the function call and examine the contents of important registers and the stack. We set a breakpoint at _start and single-step through the first couple of instructions and stop at the **BL** instruction. I set **R4** to 12 and **R5** to 13, so we can follow how these are saved to the stack.

r4	0xc	12
r5	0xd	13
sp	0x7efff380	0x7efff380
lr	0x0	0
pc	0x10084	0x10084 < _start+16>

We see the **BL** instruction is at 0x10084. Now let's single-step again to execute the BL instruction. Here are the same registers:

r4	0xc	12
r5	0xd	13
sp	0x7efff380	0x7efff380
lr	0x10088	65672
pc	0x100b0	0x100b0 <toupper>

The **LR** has been set to 0x10088 which is the instruction after the **BL** instruction (0x10084+4). The **PC** is now 0x100b0, pointing to the first instruction in the toupper routine. The first instruction in toupper is the PUSH instruction to save registers R4 and R5. Let's single-step through that instruction and examine the registers again.

r4	0xc	12
r5	0xd	13
sp	0x7efff378	0x7efff378
lr	0x10088	65672
pc	0x100b4	0x100b4 <toupper+4>

We see that the stack pointer (**SP**) has been decremented by 8 bytes (two words) to 0x7efff378. None of the other registers have changed. Pushing registers onto the stack does not affect their values; it only saves them. If we look at location 0x7efff378, we see

```
(gdb) x /4xw 0x7efff378
0x7efff378:    0x0000000c    0x0000000d    0x00000001    0x7efff504
```

We see copies of registers **R4** and **R5** on the stack.

From this little exercise, we can see what type of stack Linux uses, namely, it is a descending stack; the addresses get small as the stack grows. Further **SP** points to the last item saved (and not the next free slot).

Note   The toupper function doesn't call any other functions, so we don't save **LR** along with **R4** and **R5**. If we ever change it to do so, we will need to add **LR** to the list. This version of toupper is intended to be as fast as possible, so I didn't add any extra code for future maintainability and safety.

Most C programmers will object that this function is dangerous. If the input string isn't NULL terminated, then it will overrun the output string buffer, overwriting the memory past the end. The solution is to pass in a third parameter with the buffer lengths and check in the loop that we stop at the end of the buffer if there is no NULL character.

This routine only processes the core ASCII characters. It doesn't handle the localized characters like é; it won't be converted to É.

Stack Frames

In our uppercase function, we didn't need any additional memory, since we could do all our work with the available registers. When we code larger functions, we often require more memory for our variables than fit in the registers. Rather than add clutter to the **.data** section, we store these variables on the stack.

PUSHing these variables on the stack isn't practical, since we usually need to access them in a random order, rather than the strict **LIFO** protocol that PUSH/POP enforce.

To allocate space on the stack, we use a subtract instruction to grow the stack by the amount we need. Suppose we need three variables which are each 32-bit integers, say a, b, and c. Therefore, we need 12 bytes allocated on the stack (3 variables x 4 bytes/word).

```
SUB   SP, #12
```

This moves the stack pointer down by 12 bytes, providing us a region of memory on the stack to place our variables. Suppose a is in **R0**, b in **R1**, and c in **R2**, we can then store these using

```
STR   R0, [SP]          @ Store a
STR   R1, [SP, #4]      @ Store b
STR   R2, [SP, #8]      @ Store c
```

Before the end of the function, we need to execute

```
ADD   SP, #12
```

to release our variables from the stack. Remember, it is the responsibility of a function to restore **SP** to its original state before returning.

This is the simplest way to allocate some variables. However, if we are doing a lot of other things with the stack in our function, it can be hard to keep track of these offsets. The way we alleviate this is with a stack frame. Here we allocate a region on the stack and keep a pointer to this region in another register that we will refer to as the **Frame Pointer (FP)**. You could use any register as the **FP**, but we will follow the C programming convention and use **R11**.

To use a stack frame, we first set our frame pointer to the next free spot on the stack (it grows in descending addresses), then we allocate the space as before:

```
SUB    FP, SP, #4
SUB    SP, #12
```

Now we address our variables using an offset from **FP**.

```
STR    R0, [FP]           @ Store a
STR    R1, [FP, #-4]      @ Store b
STR    R2, [FP, #-8]      @ Store c
```

When we use **FP**, we need to include it in the list of registers we PUSH at the beginning of the function and then POP at the end. Since **R11**, the **FP** is one we are responsible for saving.

In this book, we'll tend to not use **FP**. This saves a couple of cycles on function entry and exit. After all, in Assembly language programming, we want to be efficient.

Stack Frame Example

Listing 6-6 is a simple skeletal example of a function that creates three variables on the stack.

Listing 6-6. Simple skeletal function that demonstrates a stack frame

```
@ Simple function that takes 2 parameters
@ VAR1 and VAR2. The function adds them,
@ storing the result in a variable SUM.
@ The function returns the sum.
@ It is assumed this function does other work,
@ including other functions.

@ Define our variables
        .EQU    VAR1, 0
        .EQU    VAR2, 4
        .EQU    SUM,  8
```

```
SUMFN:      PUSH    {R4-R12, LR}
            SUB     SP, #12     @ room for three 32-bit values
            STR     R0, [SP, #VAR1]    @ save passed in param.
            STR     R1, [SP, #VAR2]    @ save second param.
```

@ Do a bunch of other work, but don't change SP.

```
            LDR     R4, [SP, #VAR1]
            LDR     R5, [SP, #VAR2]
            ADD     R6, R4, R5
            STR     R6, [SP, #SUM]
```

@ Do other work

@ Function Epilog

```
            LDR     R0, [SP, #SUM]     @ load sum to return
            ADD     SP, #12     @ Release local vars
            POP     {R4-R12, PC} @ Restore regs and return
```

Defining Symbols

In this example, we introduce the **.EQU** Assembler directive. This directive allows us to define symbols that will be substituted by the Assembler before generating the compiled code. This way, we can make the code more readable. In this example, keeping track of which variable is which on the stack makes the code hard to read and is error-prone. With the .EQU directive, we can define each variable's offset on the stack once.

Sadly, .EQU only defines numbers, so we can't define the whole "[SP, #4]" type string.

One More Optimization

You might notice that our SUMFN doesn't end in "**BX LR**". This is a little optimization. The **BX** instruction basically moves **LR** into **PC**, so why not just POP **LR** directly into **PC**? Notice this is what the POP instruction at the end of the routine does. If we pushed **LR**, we can save an instruction this way. This works fine as long as the caller is regular ARM32 Assembly code. There is another type of code called Thumb code which we will look at in Chapter 15, "Thumb Code." **BX** lets us return to a caller that is running in Thumb mode, where popping to **PC** won't cause the processor to change how it interprets instructions.

Macros

Another way to make our uppercase loop into a reusable bit of code is to use macros. The GNU Assembler has a powerful macro capability; with macros rather than calling a function, the Assembler creates a copy of the code in each place where it is called, substituting any parameters. Consider this alternate implementation of our uppercase program; the first file is mainmacro.s containing the contents of Listing 6-7.

Listing 6-7. Program to call our toupper macro

```
@
@ Assembler program to convert a string to
@ all uppercase by calling a macro.
@
@ R0-R2 - parameters to linux function services
@ R1 - address of output string
@ R0 - address of input string
@ R7 - linux function number
@

.include "uppermacro.s"

.global _start        @ Provide program starting address

_start:      toupper tststr, buffer
```

```
@ Set up the parameters to print our hex number
@ and then call Linux to do it.
      MOV   R2,R0  @ R0 is the length of the string
      MOV   R0, #1      @ 1 = StdOut
      LDR   R1, =buffer @ string to print
      MOV   R7, #4      @ linux write system call
      SVC   0       @ Call linux to output the string

@ Call it a second time with our second string.
      toupper tststr2, buffer

@ Set up the parameters to print our hex number
@ and then call Linux to do it.
      MOV   R2,R0     @ R0 is the length of the string
      MOV   R0, #1       @ 1 = StdOut
      LDR   R1, =buffer @ string to print
      MOV   R7, #4          @ linux write system call
      SVC   0          @ Call linux to output the string

@ Set up the parameters to exit the program
@ and then call Linux to do it.
      MOV   R0, #0     @ Use 0 return code
      MOV   R7, #1    @ Service command code 1 terminates
                            this program
      SVC   0 @ Call linux to terminate

.data
tststr:  .asciz  "This is our Test String that we will
convert.\n"
tststr2: .asciz     "A second string to uppercase!!\n"
buffer:     .fill 255, 1, 0
```

The macro to uppercase the string is in uppermacro.s containing
Listing 6-8.

Listing 6-8. Macro version of our toupper function

```
@
@ Assembler program to convert a string to
@ all uppercase.
@
@ R1 - address of output string
@ R0 - address of input string
@ R2 - original output string for length calc.
@ R3 - current character being processed
@

@ label 1 = loop
@ label 2 = cont

.MACRO      toupper      instr, outstr
       LDR   R0, =\instr
       LDR   R1, =\outstr
       MOV   R2, R1
@ The loop is until byte pointed to by R1 is non-zero
1:     LDRB  R3, [R0], #1     @ load character and increment
                                 pointer
@ If R5 > 'z' then goto cont
       CMP   R3, #'z'        @ is letter > 'z'?
       BGT   2f
@ Else if R5 < 'a' then goto end if
       CMP   R3, #'a'
       BLT   2f    @ goto to end if
@ if we got here then the letter is lower-case, so convert it.
       SUB   R3, #('a'-'A')
2:     @ end if
       STRB  R3, [R1], #1 @ store character to output str
       CMP   R3, #0         @ stop on hitting a null character
```

```
        BNE    1b                @ loop if character isn't null
        SUB    R0, R1, R2 @ get the length by subtracting the pointers
.ENDM
```

Include Directive

The file uppermacro.s defines our macro to convert a string to uppercase. The macro doesn't generate any code; it just defines the macro for the Assembler to insert wherever it is called from. This file doesn't generate an object (*.o) file; rather, it is included by whichever file needs to use it.

The **.include** directive

```
.include "uppermacro.s"
```

takes the contents of this file and inserts it at this point, so that our source file becomes larger. This is done before any other processing. This is similar to the C **#include** preprocessor directive.

Macro Definition

A macro is defined with the **.MACRO** directive. This gives the name of the macro and lists its parameters. The macro ends at the following **.ENDM** directive. The form of the directive is

```
.MACRO      macroname      parameter1, parameter2, ...
```

Within the macro, you specify the parameters by preceding their name with a backslash, for instance, \parameter1 to place the value of parameter1. Our toupper macro defines two parameters instr and outstr:

```
.MACRO      toupper      instr, outstr
```

You can see how the parameters are used in the code with \instr and \
oustr. These are text substitutions and need to result in correct Assembly
syntax or you will get an error.

Labels

Our labels "loop" and "cont" are replaced with the labels "1" and "2".
This takes away from the readability of the program. The reason we do this
is that if we didn't, we would get an error that a label was defined more
than once, if we use the macro more than once. The trick here is that the
Assembler lets you define numeric labels as many times as you want. Then
to reference them in our code, we used

```
BGT    2f
BNE    1b                 @ loop if character isn't null
```

The **f** after the **2** means the next label **2** in the forward direction. The **1b**
means the next label **1** in the backward direction.

To prove that this works, we call toupper twice in the mainmacro.s file
to show everything works and that we can reuse this macro as many times
as we like.

Why Macros?

Macros substitute a copy of the code at every point they are used. This will
make your executable file larger. If you

```
objdump -d mainmacro
```

you will see the two copies of code inserted. With functions, there is no
extra code generated each time. This is why functions are quite appealing,
even with the extra work of dealing with the stack.

The reason macros get used is performance. Most Raspberry Pi models have a gigabyte or more of memory that is room for a lot of copies of code. Remember that whenever we branch, we have to restart the execution pipeline, making branching an expensive instruction. With macros, we eliminate the **BL** branch to call the function and the **BX** branch to return. We also eliminate the **PUSH** and **POP** instructions to save and restore any registers we use. If a macro is small and we use it a lot, there could be considerable execution time savings.

Note   Notice in the macro implementation of toupper that I only used registers **R0–R3**. This is to try and avoid using any registers important to the caller. There is no standard on how to regulate register usage with macros, like there is with functions, so it is up to you, the programmer, to avoid conflicts and strange bugs.

Summary

In this chapter, we covered the ARM stack and how it is used to help implement functions. We covered how to write and call functions as a first step to creating libraries of reusable code. We learned how to manage register usage, so there aren't any conflicts between our calling programs and our functions. We learned the function calling protocol that will allow us to interoperate with other programming languages. We looked at defining stack-based storage for local variables and how to use this memory.

Finally, we covered the GNU Assembler's macro ability as an alternative to functions in certain performance critical applications.

CHAPTER 7

Linux Operating System Services

In Chapter 1, "Getting Started," we needed the ability to exit our program and to display a string. We used Raspbian Linux to do this, invoking operating system services directly. In all high-level programming languages, there is a runtime library that includes wrappers for calling the operating system. This makes it appear that these services are part of the high-level language. In this chapter, we'll be looking at what these runtime libraries do under the covers to call Linux and what services are available to us.

We will review the syntax for calling the operating system and the error codes returned to us. There is a complete listing of all the services and error codes in Appendix B, "Linux System Calls."

So Many Services

If you look at Appendix B, "Linux System Calls," it looks like there are nearly 400 Linux system services. Why so many? Linux turned 25 years old in 2019. That's quite old for a computer program. These services were added piece by piece over all those years. The problem of this patchwork development arises in software compatibility. If a service call requires a parameter change, then the current service can't be changed without breaking a bunch of programs.

© Stephen Smith 2019
S. Smith, *Raspberry Pi Assembly Language Programming*,
https://doi.org/10.1007/978-1-4842-5287-1_7

The solution to software incompatibility is often to just add a new function. The old function then becomes a thin wrapper that translates the parameters to what the new function requires. Examples of this are any file access routines that take an offset into a file or a size parameter. Originally, 32-bit Linux only supported files 32 bits in length (4 GB). This became too small, and a whole new set of file I/O routines were added that take a 64-bit parameter for file offsets and sizes. All these functions are like the 32-bit versions, but with 64 appended to their names.

Fortunately, the Linux documentation for all these services is quite good. It is oriented entirely to C programmers, so anyone else using it must know enough C to convert the meaning to what is appropriate for the language they are using.

Linux is a powerful operating system—as an application or systems programmer, it certainly will help you learn Linux system programming. There are a lot of services to help you. You don't want to be reinventing all these yourself, unless you are creating a new operating system.

Calling Convention

We've used two system calls: one to write ASCII data to the console and the second to exit our program. The calling convention for system calls is different than that for function. It uses a software interrupt to switch context from our user-level program to the context of the Linux kernel.

The calling convention is

1. **r0–r6**: Input parameters, up to seven parameters for the system call.

2. **r7**: The Linux system call number (see Appendix B, "Linux System Calls").

3. Call software interrupt 0 with "**SVC 0**".

4. **R0**: The return code from the call (see Appendix B, "Linux System Calls").

The software interrupt is a clever way for us to call routines in the Linux kernel without knowing where they are stored in memory. It also provides a mechanism to run at a higher security level while the call executes. Linux will check if you have the correct access rights to perform the requested operation and give back an error code like EACCES (13) if you are denied.

Although it doesn't follow the function calling convention from Chapter 6, "Functions and the Stack," the Linux system call mechanism will preserve all registers not used as parameters or the return code. When system calls require a large block of parameters, they tend to take a pointer to a block of memory as one parameter, which then holds all the data they need. Hence, most system calls don't use that many parameters.

The return code for these functions is usually zero or a positive number for success and a negative number for failure. The negative number is the negative of the error codes in Appendix B, "Linux System Calls." For example, the open call to open a file returns a file descriptor if it is successful. A file descriptor is a small positive number, then a negative number if it fails, where it is the negative of one of the constants in Appendix B, "Linux System Calls."

Structures

Many Linux services take pointers to blocks of memory as their parameters. The contents of these blocks of memory are documented with C structures, so as Assembly programmers, we have to reverse engineer the C and duplicate the memory structure. For instance, the nanosleep service lets your program sleep for a number of nanoseconds; it is defined as

```
int nanosleep(const struct timespec *req, struct timespec *rem);
```

and then the struct timespec is defined as

```
struct timespec {
            time_t tv_sec;        /* seconds */
            long   tv_nsec;       /* nanoseconds */
        };
```

We then must figure out that these are two 32-bit integers, then define in Assembly

```
timespecsec:    .word   0
timespecnano:   .word   100000000
```

To use them, we load their address into the registers for the first two parameters:

```
        ldr         r0, =timespecsec
        ldr         r1, =timespecsec
```

We'll be using the nanosleep function in Chapter 8, "Programming GPIO Pins," but this is typical of what it takes to directly call some Linux services.

Wrappers

Rather than figure out all the registers each time we want to call a Linux service, we will develop a library of routines or macros to make our job easier. The C programming language includes function call wrappers for all the Linux services; we will see how to use these in Chapter 9, "Interacting with C and Python."

Rather than duplicate the work of the C runtime library, we'll develop a library of Linux system calls using the GNU Assembler's macro functionality. We won't develop this for all the functions, just the functions we need. Most programmers do this, then over time their libraries become quite extensive.

A problem with macros is that you often need several variants with different parameter types. For instance, sometimes you might like to call the macro with a register as a parameter and other times with an immediate value.

Converting a File to Uppercase

In this chapter, we present a complete program to convert the contents of a text file to all uppercase. We will use our toupper function from Chapter 6, "Functions and the Stack," and get practice coding loops and if statements.

To start with, we need a library of file I/O routines to read from our input file, then write the uppercased version to another file. If you've done any C programming, these should look familiar, since the C runtime provides a thin layer over these services. We create a file fileio.s containing Listing 7-1 to do this.

Listing 7-1. Macros to help us read and write files

```
@ Various macros to perform file I/O

@ The fd parameter needs to be a register.
@ Uses R0, R1, R7.
@ Return code is in R0.

.include "unistd.s"

.equ  O_RDONLY, 0
.equ  O_WRONLY, 1
.equ  O_CREAT,  0100
.equ  S_RDWR,   0666

.macro  openFile   fileName, flags
        ldr        r0, =\fileName
        mov        r1, #\flags
```

```
          mov        r2, #S_RDWR  @ RW access rights
          mov        r7, #sys_open
          svc        0
.endm
.macro  readFile    fd, buffer, length
          mov        r0, \fd      @ file descriptor
          ldr        r1, =\buffer
          mov        r2, #\length
          mov        r7, #sys_read
          svc        0
.endm
.macro  writeFile   fd, buffer, length
          mov        r0, \fd      @ file descriptor
          ldr        r1, =\buffer
          mov        r2, \length
          mov        r7, #sys_write
          svc        0
.endm
.macro  flushClose  fd
@fsync syscall
          mov        r0, \fd
          mov        r7, #sys_fsync
          svc        0
@close syscall
          mov        r0, \fd
          mov        r7, #sys_close
          svc        0
.endm
```

Now we need a main program to orchestrate the process. We'll call this main.s containing the contents of Listing 7-2.

Listing 7-2. Main program for our case conversion program

```
@
@ Assembler program to convert a string to
@ all uppercase by calling a function.
@
@ R0-R2, R7 - used by macros to call linux
@ R8 - input file descriptor
@ R9 - output file descriptor
@ R10 - number of characters read
@

.include "fileio.s"

.equ  BUFFERLEN, 250

.global _start    @ Provide program starting address

_start:       openFile   inFile, O_RDONLY
      MOVS         R8, R0    @ save file descriptor
      BPL          nxtfil @ pos number file opened ok
      MOV          R1, #1  @ stdout
      LDR          R2, =inpErrsz    @ Error msg
      LDR          R2, [R2]
      writeFile    R1, inpErr, R2 @ print the error
      B            exit

nxtfil: openFile   outFile, O_CREAT+O_WRONLY
      MOVS         R9, R0    @ save file descriptor
      BPL          loop   @ pos number file opened ok
      MOV          R1, #1
      LDR          R2, =outErrsz
      LDR          R2, [R2]
      writeFile    R1, outErr, R2
      B            exit
```

```
@ loop through file until done.
loop: readFile      R8, buffer, BUFFERLEN
      MOV           R10, R0     @ Keep the length read
      MOV           R1, #0      @ Null terminator for string

      @ set up call to toupper and call function
      LDR           R0, =buffer  @ first param for toupper
      STRB          R1, [R0, R10] @ put null at end of string.
      LDR           R1, =outBuf
      BL            toupper

      writeFile     R9, outBuf, R10

      CMP           R10, #BUFFERLEN
      BEQ           loop

      flushClose    R8
      flushClose    R9

@ Set up the parameters to exit the program
@ and then call Linux to do it.
exit: MOV     R0, #0      @ Use 0 return code
      MOV     R7, #1      @ Command code 1 terms
      SVC     0           @ Call linux to terminate

.data
inFile:  .asciz  "main.s"
outFile: .asciz    "upper.txt"
buffer:     .fill  BUFFERLEN + 1, 1, 0
outBuf:     .fill  BUFFERLEN + 1, 1, 0
inpErr: .asciz     "Failed to open input file.\n"
inpErrsz: .word  .-inpErr
outErr:     .asciz      "Failed to open output file.\n"
outErrsz: .word    .-outErr
```

The makefile is contained in Listing 7-3.

Listing 7-3. Makefile for our file conversion program

```
UPPEROBJS = main.o upper.o

ifdef DEBUG
DEBUGFLGS = -g
else
DEBUGFLGS =
endif
LSTFLGS =

all: upper

%.o : %.s
        as $(DEBUGFLGS) $(LSTFLGS) $< -o $@

upper: $(UPPEROBJS)
        ld -o upper $(UPPEROBJS)
```

This program uses the upper.s file from Chapter 6, "Functions and the Stack," that contains the function version of our uppercase logic. The program also uses the unistd.s from Appendix B, "Linux System Calls," that gives meaningful definitions of the Linux service function numbers.

If you build this program, notice that it is only 13 KB in size. This is one of the appeals of pure Assembly language programming. There is nothing extra added to the program—we control every byte—no mysterious libraries or runtimes added.

Note   The files this program operates on are hard-coded in the **.data** section. Feel free to change them, play with them, generate some errors to see what happens. Single-step through the program in **gdb** to ensure you understand how it works.

Opening a File

The Linux open service is typical of a Linux system service. It takes three parameters:

1. **Filename**: The file to open as a NULL-terminated string.

2. **Flags**: To specify whether we're opening it for reading or writing or whether to create the file. We included some **.EQU** directives with the values we need (using the same names as in the C runtime).

3. **Mode**: The access mode for the file when creating the file. We included a couple of defines, but in octal these are the same as the parameters to the **chmod** Linux command.

The return code is either a file descriptor or an error code. Like many Linux services, the call fits this in a single return code by making errors negative and successful results positive.

Error Checking

Books tend to not promote good programming practices for error checking. The sample programs are kept as small as possible, so the main ideas being explained aren't lost in a sea of details. This is the first program where we test any return codes. Partly, we had to develop enough code to be able to do it, and second error checking code tends to not reveal any new concepts.

File open calls are prone to failing. The file might not exist, perhaps because we are in the wrong folder, or we may not have sufficient access rights to the file. Generally, check the return code to every system call, or function you call, but practically programmers are lazy and tend to only check those that are likely to fail. In this program, we check the two file open calls.

First of all, we have to copy the file descriptor to a register that won't be overwritten, so we move it to R8. We do this with a MOVS instruction, so the CPSR will be set.

```
MOVS      R8, R0      @ save file descriptor
```

This means we can test if it's positive and if so go on to the next bit of code.

```
BPL       nxtfil  @ pos number file opened ok
```

If the branch isn't taken, then openFile returned a negative number. Here we use our writeFile routine to write an error message to stdout, then branch to the end of the program to exit.

```
MOV         R1, #1  @ stdout
LDR         R2, =inpErrsz @ Error msg sz
LDR         R2, [R2]
writeFile   R1, inpErr, R2 @ print the error
B           exit
```

In our .data section, we defined the error messages as follows:

```
inpErr: .asciz    "Failed to open input file.\n"
inpErrsz: .word   .-inpErr
```

We've seen **.asciz** and this is standard. For writeFile, we need the length of the string to write to the console. In Chapter 1, "Getting Started," we counted the characters in our string and put the hard-coded number in our code. We could do that here too, but error messages start getting long and counting the characters seems like something the computer should do. We could write a routine like the C library's **strlen()** function to calculate the length of a NULL-terminated string. Instead, we use a little GNU Assembler trickery. We add a .word directive right after the string and initialize it with ".-inpErr". The " . " is a special Assembler variable that contains the current address the Assembler is on as it works. Hence, the current address right after the string minus the address of the start of the string is the length. Now people can revise the wording of the error message to their heart's content without needing to count the characters each time.

Most applications contain an error module, so if a function fails, the error module is called. Then the error module is responsible for reporting and logging the error. This way, error reporting can be made quite sophisticated without cluttering up the rest of the code with error-handling code. Another problem with error-handling code is that it tends to not be tested. Often bad things can happen when an error finally does happen, and problems with the previously untested code manifest.

Looping

In our loop, we

1. Read a block of 250 characters from the input file.

2. Append a NULL terminator.

3. Call toupper.

4. Write the converted characters to the output file.

5. If we aren't done, branch to the top of the loop.

We check if we are done with

```
CMP         R10, #BUFFERLEN
BEQ         loop
```

R10 contains the number of characters returned from the read service call. If it equals the number of characters requested, then we branch to loop. If it doesn't equal exactly, then either we hit end of file, so the number of characters returned is less (and possibly 0), or an error occurred, in which case the number is negative. Either way, we are done and fall through to the program exit.

Summary

In this chapter, we gave an overview of how to call the various Linux system services. We covered the calling convention and how to interpret the return codes. We didn't cover the purpose of each call and referred the user to the Linux documentation instead.

We presented a program to read a file, convert it to uppercase, and write it out to another file. This is our first chance to put together what we learned in Chapters 1–6 to build a full application, with loops, if statements, error messages, and file I/O.

In the next chapter, we will use Linux service calls to manipulate the GPIO pins on the Raspberry Pi board.

CHAPTER 8

Programming GPIO Pins

The Raspberry Pi has a set of General Purpose I/O (**GPIO**) pins that you can use to control homemade electronic projects. Most of the Raspberry Pi starter kits include a breadboard and a few electronic components to play with. In this chapter, we will look at programming GPIO pins from Assembly language.

We will experiment with a breadboard containing a number of LEDs and resistors, so we can write some real code. We will program the GPIO pins two ways, firstly by using the included Linux device driver and secondly by accessing the GPIO controller's registers directly.

GPIO Overview

The original Raspberry Pi 1 has 26 GPIO pins; newer Raspberry Pi expanded this to 40 pins. In this section, we will limit our discussion to the original 26 pins. They either provide power or are generally programmable:

- **Pins 1 and 17**: Provide +3.3V DC power

- **Pins 2 and 4**: Provide +5V DC power

© Stephen Smith 2019
S. Smith, *Raspberry Pi Assembly Language Programming*,
https://doi.org/10.1007/978-1-4842-5287-1_8

- **Pins 6, 9, 14, 20, and 25**: Provide electrical ground

- **Pins 3, 5, 7–8, 10–13, 15, 16, 18, 19, 21–24, and 26**: Are programmable general purpose

For the programmable pins, we can use them for output, where we control whether they output power or not (are binary 1 or 0). We can read them to see if power is provided, for instance, if it is connected to a switch.

However, this isn't all there is to GPIO; besides the functions we've talked about so far, a number of the pins have alternate functions that you can select programmatically. For instance, pins 3 and 5 can support the I2C standard that allows two microchips to talk to each other.

There are pins that can support two serial ports which are handy for connecting to radios or printers. There are pins that support pulse width modulation (PWM) and pulse-position modulation (PPM) that convert digital to analog and are handy for controlling electric motors.

In Linux, Everything Is a File

The model for controlling devices in Linux is to map each device to a file. The file appears under either /dev or /sys and can be manipulated with the same Linux service calls that operate on regular files. The GPIO pins are no different. There is a Linux device driver for them that then controls the pin's operations via application programs opening files then reading and writing data to them.

The files to controlling the GPIO pin all appear under the /sys/class/gpio folder. By writing short text strings to the files here, we control the operation of the pins.

Suppose we want to programmatically control pin 17; the first thing we do is tell the driver we want to do this. We write the string "17" to /sys/class/gpio/export. If this succeeds, then we now control the pin. The driver then creates the following files in a gpio17 folder:

- /sys/class/gpio/gpio17/direction: Used to specify whether the pin is for input or output

- /sys/class/gpio/gpio17/value: Used to set or read the value of the pin

- /sys/class/gpio/gpio17/edge: Used to set an interrupt to detect value changes

- /sys/class/gpio/gpio17/active_low: Used to invert the meaning of 0 and 1

The next thing we do is set the direction for the pin, either use it for input or for output. We either write "in" or "out" to the direction file to do this.

Now we can write to the value file for an output pin or read the value file for an input pin. To turn on a pin, we write "1" to value, and to turn it off, we write "0". When activated, the GPIO pin provides +3.3V.

When we are done with a pin, we should write its pin number to /sys/class/gpio/unexport. However, this will be done automatically when our program terminates.

We can do all this with the macros we created in Chapter 7, "Linux Operating System Services," in fileio.s. In fact, by providing this interface, you can control the GPIO pins via any programming language capable of reading and writing files, that is pretty much every single one. Raspbian includes some special libraries to control the GPIO pins for Python and Scratch to make it easier, but behind the scenes they are just making the file I/O calls we are describing.

Flashing LEDs

To demonstrate programming the GPIO, we will connect some LEDs to a breadboard and then make them flash in sequence.

We will connect each of three LEDs to a GPIO pin (in this case 17, 27, and 22), then to ground through a resistor. We need the resistor because the GPIO is specified to keep the current under 16mA, or you can damage the circuits. Most of the kits come with several 220 Ohm resistors. By Ohm's law, I = V / R, these would cause the current to be 3.3V/220Ω = 15mA, so just right. You need to have a resistor in series with the LED since the LED's resistance is quite low (typically around 13 Ohms and variable).

WARNING: LEDs have a positive and negative side. The positive side needs to connect to the GPIO pin; reversing it could damage the LED.

Figure 8-1 shows how the LEDs and resistors are wired up on a breadboard.

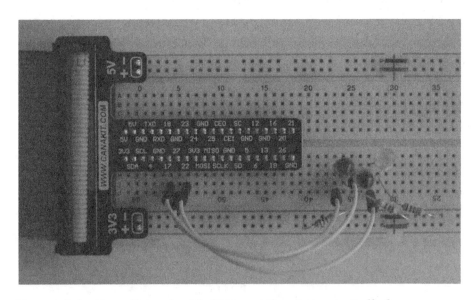

Figure 8-1. *Breadboard with LEDs and resistors installed*

Initially, we'll define a set of macros in gpiomacros.s containing Listing 8-1 that use the macros in fileio.s to perform the various GPIO functions.

Listing 8-1. Macros to control the GPIO pins

```
@ Various macros to access the GPIO pins
@ on the Raspberry Pi.
@
@ R8 - file descriptor.
@

.include "fileio.s"

@ Macro nanoSleep to sleep .1 second
@ Calls Linux nanosleep service which is funct 162.
@ Pass a reference to a timespec in both r0 and r1
@ First is input time to sleep in secs and nanosecs.
@ Second is time left to sleep if interrupted
.macro  nanoSleep
        ldr         r0, =timespecsec
        ldr         r1, =timespecsec
        mov         r7, #sys_nanosleep
        svc         0
.endm
.macro  GPIOExport  pin
        openFile    gpioexp, O_WRONLY
        mov         r8, r0      @ save the file desc
        writeFile   r8, \pin, #2

        flushClose  r8
.endm
.macro  GPIODirectionOut    pin
        @ copy pin into filename pattern
        ldr         r1, =\pin
```

```
        ldr         r2, =gpiopinfile
        add         r2, #20
        ldrb        r3, [r1], #1 @ load pin and post incr
        strb        r3, [r2], #1 @ store to filename and post incr
        ldrb        r3, [r1]
        strb        r3, [r2]
        openFile    gpiopinfile, O_WRONLY
        mov         r8, r0      @ save the file descriptor
        writeFile   r8, outstr, #3
        flushClose  r8
.endm
.macro  GPIOWrite   pin, value
        @ copy pin into filename pattern
        ldr         r1, =\pin
        ldr         r2, =gpiovaluefile
        add         r2, #20
        ldrb        r3, [r1], #1    @ load pin and post increment
        strb        r3, [r2], #1    @ store to filename and
                                        post increment
        ldrb        r3, [r1]
        strb        r3, [r2]
        openFile    gpiovaluefile, O_WRONLY
        mov         r8, r0      @ save the file descriptor
        writeFile   r8, \value, #1
        flushClose  r8
.endm

.data
timespecsec:    .word   0
timespecnano:   .word   100000000
gpioexp:    .asciz  "/sys/class/gpio/export"
gpiopinfile: .asciz "/sys/class/gpio/gpioxx/direction"
```

```
gpiovaluefile: .asciz "/sys/class/gpio/gpioxx/value"
outstr:       .asciz  "out"
              .align  2           @ save users of this file having
                                    to do this.
```

Now we need a controlling program, main.s containing *Listing 8-2*, to orchestrate the process.

Listing 8-2. Main program to flash the LEDs

```
@
@ Assembler program to flash three LEDs connected to
@ the Raspberry Pi GPIO port.
@
@ r6 - loop variable to flash lights 10 times
@
.include "gpiomacros.s"

.global _start              @ Provide program starting
                              address to linker
_start: GPIOExport  pin17
        GPIOExport  pin27
        GPIOExport  pin22
        nanoSleep

        GPIODirectionOut pin17
        GPIODirectionOut pin27
        GPIODirectionOut pin22
        @ set up a loop counter for 10 iterations
        mov         r6, #10

loop:   GPIOWrite   pin17, high
        nanoSleep
        GPIOWrite   pin17, low
```

```
        GPIOWrite    pin27, high
        nanoSleep
        GPIOWrite    pin27, low
        GPIOWrite    pin22, high
        nanoSleep
        GPIOWrite    pin22, low
        @decrement loop counter and see if we loop
   @ Subtract 1 from loop register
   @ setting status register.
        subs    r6, #1
   @ If we haven't counted down to 0 then loop
        bne     loop

_end:   mov     R0, #0  @ Use 0 return code
        mov     R7, #1  @ Command code 1 terminates
        svc     0       @ Linux command to terminate

pin17:      .asciz  "17"
pin27:      .asciz  "27"
pin22:      .asciz  "22"
low:        .asciz  "0"
high:       .asciz  "1"
```

This program is a straightforward application of the Linux system service calls we learned in Chapter 7, "Linux Operating System Services."

Moving Closer to the Metal

For Assembly language programmers, the previous example is not satisfying. When we program in Assembly, we are usually directly manipulating devices for performance reasons or to perform operations that simply can't be done in high-level programming languages. In this section, we will interact with the GPIO controller directly.

WARNING: Make sure you back up your work before running your program, since you may need to power off and power back on again. The GPIO controller controls 54 pins; the Raspberry Pi only exposes either 26 or 40 of them, depending on the Pi model, for external use; many of the others are used by the Raspberry Pi for other important tasks. In the previous section, the device driver provided a level of protection, so we couldn't easily do any damage. Now that we are writing directly to the GPIO controller, we have no such protection; if we make a mistake and manipulate the wrong pins, we may interfere with the Raspberry Pi's operation and cause it to crash or lock up.

Virtual Memory

We looked at how to access memory in Chapter 5, "Thanks for the Memories," and we looked at the memory addresses our instructions are stored at in **gdb**. These memory addresses aren't physical memory addresses; rather, they are virtual memory addresses. As a Linux process, our program is given a 4 GB virtual address space. 3 GB of this is for us and 1 GB is for system things. Within this address space, some of it is mapped to physical memory to store our Assembly instructions, our .data sections, and our 8 MB stack. Furthermore, Linux may swap some of this memory to secondary storage like the SD card as it needs more physical memory for other processes. There is a lot of complexity in the memory management process to allow dozens of processes to run independently of each other, each thinking it has the whole system to itself.

In the next section, we want access to specific physical memory addresses, but when we request that access, Linux returns a virtual memory pointer that is different than the physical address we asked for. This is okay, as we know that behind the scenes the memory management hardware in the Raspberry Pi will be doing the memory translations between virtual and physical memory for us.

About Raspberry Pi 4 RAM

You might wonder why the Raspberry Pi 4 comes with up to 4 GB of RAM, but our process can only access 3 GB of it? However, all this RAM will be used, since each process and the kernel can have up to 3 GB of RAM. In fact, the memory controller in the Raspberry Pi has 40 address pins, so it can address more than 4 GB of physical memory.

In the future, if there is a 16 GB version of the Pi, that memory can be used, even if Raspbian is still 32 bits. Every 32-bit process could map different sections of memory, so even though a 32-bit process can only access 3 GB of memory at a time, it can use more by swapping parts of its virtual address space to different physical regions.

In Devices, Everything Is Memory

The GPIO controller has 41 registers. We can't read or write these like the ARM CPU's registers. The ARM32 instruction set doesn't know anything about the GPIO controller, and there are no special instructions to support it. The way we access these registers is by reading and writing to specific memory locations. There is circuitry in the Raspberry Pi's system on a chip (SoC) that will see these memory reads and writes and redirect them to the GPIO's registers. This is how most hardware communicates. This is the job of the Linux device drivers, to translate these memory register accesses into a standard set of file I/O calls.

The memory address for the GPIO registers on the Raspberry Pi 2, 3, and 4 is 0x3F200000 (for the Raspberry Pi 0 and 1, it is 0x20200000). Sounds easy—we know how to load addresses into registers, then reference the memory stored there. Not so fast, if we tried this, our program would just crash with a memory access error. This is because these memory addresses are outside those assigned to our program, and we are not allowed to use them. Our first job then is to get access.

This leads us back to everything being a file in Linux. There is a file that will give us a pointer that we can use to access these memory locations, as follows:

1. Open the file /dev/mem.

2. Then we ask /dev/mem to map the registers for GPIO into our memory space. We do this with the Linux mmap2 service. Mmap2 takes the following parameters:

    - **R0**: Hint for the virtual address we would like. We don't really care and will use NULL, which gives Linux complete freedom to choose.

    - **R1**: Length of region. Should be a multiple of 4096, the memory page size.

    - **R2**: Memory protection required.

    - **R3**: File descriptor to open /dev/mem.

    - **R4**: Offset into physical memory in 4096-byte pages (we'll use 0x3f200000/4096).

    This call will return a virtual address in **R0** that maps to the physical address we asked for. The original mmap took an offset in bytes for the physical address; this restricted the call to mapping the first 4 GB of memory. The newer mmap2 call takes the address in pages allowing a greater range of physical addresses without the need to go to full 64 bits. This function returns a small negative number if it fails.

Registers in Bits

We will cover just those registers we need to configure our pins for output, then to set the bits to flash the LEDs. If you are interested in the full functionality, then check the Broadcom datasheet for the GPIO controller.

Although we've mapped these registers to memory locations, they don't always act like memory. Some of the registers are write-only, and if we read them, we won't crash, but we'll just read some random bits. Broadcom defines the protocol for interacting with the registers; it's a good idea to follow their documentation exactly. These aren't like CPU registers or real memory. The circuitry is intercepting our memory reads and writes to these locations, but only acting on things that it understands. In the previous sections, the Linux device driver for the GPIO hid all these details from us.

GPIO Function Select Registers

The first thing we need to do is configure the pins we are using for output. There is a bank of six registers to configure all the GPIO pins for input or output. These GPIO Function Select Registers are named GPSEL0–GPSEL5. Each pin gets 3 bits in one of these registers to configure it. These are read-write registers. Since each register is 32 bits, each one can control ten pins, with 2 bits left unused (GPSEL5 only controls four pins). Table 8-1 shows the details of each select register.

Table 8-1. *GPIO Function Select Registers*

No.	Address	Name	Pins
0	0x3f200000	GPSEL0	0–9
1	0x3f200004	GPSEL1	10–19
2	0x3f200008	GPSEL2	20–29
3	0x3f20000c	GPSEL3	30–39
4	0x3f200010	GPSEL4	40–49
5	0x3f200014	GPSEL5	50–53

To use these registers, the protocol is to

1. Read the register.

2. Set the bits for our register.

3. Write the value back.

Note   We must be careful not to affect other bits in the register.

Table 8-2 shows the bits corresponding to each pin in the GPSEL1 register.

Table 8-2. *Pin number and corresponding bits for the GPSEL1 register*

Pin no.	GPSEL1 bits
10	0–2
11	3–5
12	6–8
13	9–11
14	12–14
15	15–17
16	18–20
17	21–23
18	24–26
19	27–29

We store 000 in the 3 bits if we want to input from the pin, and we store 001 in the bits if we want to write to the pin.

GPIO Output Set and Clear Registers

There are two registers for setting pins and then two registers to clear them. The first register controls the first 32 pins and then the second controls the remaining 22 pins that aren't accessible to us. Table 8-3 shows the details of these registers.

Table 8-3. *The GP set and clear pin registers*

No.	Address	Name	Pins
0	0x3f20001c	GPSET0	0–31
1	0x3f200020	GPSET1	32–53
2	0x3f200028	GPCLR0	0–31
3	0x3f20002c	GPCLR1	32–53

These registers are write-only. You should set the bit for the register you want (with all the other bits 0) and write that bit. Reading these registers is meaningless.

The Broadcom datasheet states this as a feature, in that they save you reading the register first, then it's easier to just set a single bit than edit a bit in a sequence of bits. However, it could also be that this saved them some circuitry and reduced the cost of the controller chip.

More Flashing LEDs

We'll now repeat our flashing LEDs program, but this time we'll use mapped memory and access the GPIO's registers directly. First of all, the macros that do the nitty-gritty work from Listing 8-3 go in gpiomem.s.

Listing 8-3. GPIO support macros using mapped memory

```
@ Various macros to access the GPIO pins
@ on the Raspberry Pi.
@
@ R8 - memory map address.
@

.include "fileio.s"

.equ   pagelen, 4096
.equ   setregoffset, 28
.equ   clrregoffset, 40
.equ   PROT_READ, 1
.equ   PROT_WRITE, 2
.equ   MAP_SHARED, 1

@ Macro to map memory for GPIO Registers
.macro mapMem
        openFile    devmem, S_RDWR    @ open /dev/mem
        movs        r4, r0       @ fd for memmap
        @ check for error and print error msg if necessary
        BPL         1f @ pos number file opened ok
        MOV         R1, #1  @ stdout
        LDR         R2, =memOpnsz    @ Error msg
        LDR         R2, [R2]
        writeFile   R1, memOpnErr, R2 @ print the error
        B           _end

@ Set up can call the mmap2 Linux service
1:      ldr         r5, =gpioaddr     @ address we want / 4096
        ldr         r5, [r5]   @ load the address
        mov         r1, #pagelen @ size of mem we want
```

```
@ mem protection options
        mov         r2, #(PROT_READ + PROT_WRITE)
        mov         r3, #MAP_SHARED    @ mem share options
        mov         r0, #0             @ let linux choose a
                                          virtual address
        mov         r7, #sys_mmap2     @ mmap2 service num
        svc         0       @ call service
        movs        r8, r0 @ keep the returned virt addr
        @ check for error and print error msg
        @ if necessary.
        BPL         2f @ pos number file opened ok
        MOV         R1, #1  @ stdout
        LDR         R2, =memMapsz      @ Error msg
        LDR         R2, [R2]
        writeFile   R1, memMapErr, R2 @ print the error
        B           _end
2:
.endm

@ Macro nanoSleep to sleep .1 second
@ Calls Linux nanosleep entry point which is function 162.
@ Pass a reference to a timespec in both r0 and r1
@ First is input time to sleep in seconds and nanoseconds.
@ Second is time left to sleep if interrupted (which we ignore)
.macro  nanoSleep
        ldr         r0, =timespecsec
        ldr         r1, =timespecsec
        mov         r7, #sys_nanosleep
        svc         0
.endm
.macro  GPIODirectionOut   pin
     ldr    r2, =\pin   @ offset of select register
     ldr    r2, [r2]    @ load the value
```

```
        ldr    r1, [r8, r2]  @ address of register
        ldr    r3, =\pin    @ address of pin table
        add    r3, #4 @ load amount to shift from table
        ldr    r3, [r3]        @ load value of shift amt
        mov    r0, #0b111     @ mask to clear 3 bits
        lsl    r0, r3         @ shift into position
        bic    r1, r0         @ clear the three bits
        mov    r0, #1         @ 1 bit to shift into pos
        lsl    r0, r3         @ shift by amount from table
        orr    r1, r0         @ set the bit
        str    r1, [r8, r2]  @ save it to reg to do work
.endm
.macro  GPIOTurnOn    pin, value
        mov    r2, r8       @ address of gpio regs
        add    r2, #setregoffset @ off to set reg
        mov    r0, #1       @ 1 bit to shift into pos
        ldr    r3, =\pin    @ base of pin info table
        add    r3, #8        @ add offset for shift amt
        ldr    r3, [r3]    @ load shift from table
        lsl    r0, r3       @ do the shift
        str    r0, [r2]     @ write to the register
.endm
.macro  GPIOTurnOff    pin, value
        mov    r2, r8       @ address of gpio regs
        add    r2, #clrregoffset @ off set of clr reg
        mov    r0, #1       @ 1 bit to shift into pos
        ldr    r3, =\pin    @ base of pin info table
        add    r3, #8        @ add offset for shift amt
        ldr    r3, [r3]    @ load shift from table
        lsl    r0, r3       @ do the shift
        str    r0, [r2]     @ write to the register
.endm
```

```
.data
timespecsec:    .word   0
timespecnano:   .word   100000000
devmem:         .asciz  "/dev/mem"
memOpnErr:      .asciz  "Failed to open /dev/mem\n"
memOpnsz:       .word   .-memOpnErr
memMapErr:      .asciz  "Failed to map memory\n"
memMapsz:       .word   .-memMapErr
                .align  4 @ realign after strings
@ mem address of gpio register / 4096
gpioaddr: .word   0x3F200
pin17: .word   4    @ offset to select register
       .word   21   @ bit offset in select register
       .word   17   @ bit offset in set & clr register
pin22: .word   8    @ offset to select register
       .word   6    @ bit offset in select register
       .word   22   @ bit offset in set & clr register
pin27: .word   8    @ offset to select register
       .word   21   @ bit offset in select register
       .word   27   @ bit offset in set & clr register

.text
```

Now the driving program mainmem.s contains Listing 8-4 that is quite similar to the last one. The main differences are in the macros.

Listing 8-4. Main program for the memory mapped flashing lights

```
@
@ Assembler program to flash three LEDs connected to the
@ Raspberry Pi GPIO port using direct memory access.
@
@ r6 - loop variable to flash lights 10 times
```

```
@
.include "gpiomem.s"

.global _start                  @ Provide program starting
                                  address to linker
_start: mapMem
        nanoSleep

        GPIODirectionOut pin17
        GPIODirectionOut pin27
        GPIODirectionOut pin22
        @ set up a loop counter for 10 iterations
        mov         r6, #10

loop:   GPIOTurnOn    pin17
        nanoSleep
        GPIOTurnOff   pin17
        GPIOTurnOn    pin27
        nanoSleep
        GPIOTurnOff   pin27
        GPIOTurnOn    pin22
        nanoSleep
brk1:
        GPIOTurnOff   pin22
        @decrement loop counter and see if we loop
        subs    r6, #1
@ If we haven't counted down to 0 then loop
        bne     loop

_end:   mov     R0, #0      @ Use 0 return code
        mov     R7, #1      @ Command code 1 terms
        svc     0           @ Linux command to terminate
```

The main program is the same as the first example, except that it includes a different set of macros.

The first thing we need to do is call the mapMem macro. This opens /dev/mem and sets up and calls the mmap2 service as we described in the section "In Devices, Everything Is Memory." We store the returned address into **R8**, so that it is easily accessible from the rest of the macros. There is error checking on the file open and mmap2 calls since these can fail.

Root Access

To access /dev/mem, you need root access, so run this program with root access via

```
sudo ./flashmem
```

If you don't, then the file open will fail. We didn't have to do this with the last program, because the GPIO device driver keeps everything safe. Accessing /dev/mem is very powerful and gives you access to all memory and all hardware devices.

This is a restricted operation, so we need to be root. Programs that directly access memory are usually implemented as Linux device drivers or kernel loadable modules, but then installing these also requires root access. A virus or other malware would love to have access to all physical memory.

Table Driven

We won't cover multiplication or division until Chapter 10, "Multiply, Divide, and Accumulate"; without these, it's hard to compute the pin offsets inside these registers. Division is a slow operation, and Assembly language programmers tend to avoid it. The common workaround is to use a table of precomputed values, rather than calculating the values as we need them. A table lookup is very fast, and we examined all the features in the ARM instruction set to help us do this in Chapter 5, "Thanks for the Memories."

For each pin, we provide three values in our **.data** section:

1. The offset to the select register (from the base memory address)

2. The bit offset in select register for this pin

3. The bit offset in set and clr register

With these in hand, accessing and manipulating the GPIO control registers is a snap.

Note   We only populate these tables for the three pins we use.

Setting Pin Direction

Start with loading the offset of the selection register for our pin—for pin 17, this is 4.

```
ldr   r2, =\pin     @ offset of select register
ldr   r2, [r2]      @ load the value
```

Now use pre-indexed addressing to load the current contents of the selection register. **r8** is the address, plus the offset we just loaded into **r2**.

```
ldr   r1, [r8, r2]  @ address of register
```

We now load the second item in the table, the shift into the control register for our 3 bits.

```
ldr   r3, =\pin     @ address of pin table
add   r3, #4 @ load amount to shift from table
ldr   r3, [r3]      @ load value of shift amt
```

Clear the 3 bits with a mask of binary 111 that we shift into position, then call bit clear (**bic**) to clear.

```
mov   r0, #0b111    @ mask to clear 3 bits
lsl   r0, r3        @ shift into position
bic   r1, r0        @ clear the three bits
```

We move one into position, so we can set the lower of the 3 bits to 1 using a logical or instruction (**orr**).

```
mov   r0, #1        @ 1 bit to shift into pos
lsl   r0, r3        @ shift by amount from table
orr   r1, r0        @ set the bit
```

Finally, now that we've set our 3 bits, we write the value back to the GPIO control register to execute our command.

```
str   r1, [r8, r2]  @ save it to reg to do work
```

Setting and Clearing Pins

Setting and clearing pins is easier, since we don't need to read the register first. We just need to construct the value to write to it and execute it.

Since all our pins are controlled by one register, we just have its offset defined in a **.EQU** directive. We take the base virtual address and add that offset.

```
mov   r2, r8        @ address of gpio regs
add   r2, #setregoffset @ off to set reg
```

Next, we want to have a register with just a 1 in the correct position. We start with 1 and shift it into position. We look up that shift value as the third item in our pin lookup table.

```
mov   r0, #1        @ 1 bit to shift into pos
ldr   r3, =\pin     @ base of pin info table
```

```
add    r3, #8       @ add offset for shift amt
ldr    r3, [r3]     @ load shift from table
lsl    r0, r3       @ do the shift
```

Now we have **r0** containing a 1 in the correct bit; we write it back to the GPIO set register to turn on the LED.

```
str    r0, [r2]     @ write to the register
```

Clearing the pin is the same, except that we use the clear register rather than the set register.

Summary

In this chapter, we built on everything we've learned so far to write a program to flash a series of LEDs attached to the GPIO ports on our Raspberry Pi. We did this in two ways:

1. Using the GPIO device driver by accessing the files under /sys/class/gpio

2. Using direct memory access by asking the device driver for /dev/mem to give us a virtual block of memory corresponding to the GPIO's control registers

Controlling devices are a key use case for Assembly language programming. Hopefully, this chapter gave you a flavor for what is involved.

In Chapter 9, "Interacting with C and Python," we will learn how to interact with high-level programming languages like C and Python.

CHAPTER 9

Interacting with C and Python

In the early days of microcomputers, like the Apple II, people wrote complete applications in Assembly language, such as the first spreadsheet program VisiCalc. Many video games were written in Assembly to squeeze every bit of performance they could out of the hardware. These days, modern compilers like the GNU C compiler generate fairly good code and microprocessors are much faster; as a result, most applications are written in a collection of programming languages, where each excels at a specific function. If you are writing a video game today, chances are you would write most in C, C++, or even C#, then use Assembly for performance, or to access parts of the video hardware not exposed through the graphics library you are using.

In this chapter, we will look at using components written in other languages from our Assembly language code and look at how other languages can make use of the fast-efficient code we are writing in Assembly.

Calling C Routines

If we want to call C functions, we must restructure our program. The C runtime has a _start label; it expects to be called first and to initialize itself before calling our program, as it does by calling a main function. If we leave our _start label in, we will get an error that _start is defined more

© Stephen Smith 2019
S. Smith, *Raspberry Pi Assembly Language Programming*,
https://doi.org/10.1007/978-1-4842-5287-1_9

than once. Similarly, we won't call the Linux terminate program service anymore; instead, we'll return from main and let the C runtime do that along with any other cleanup it performs.

To include the C runtime, we could add it to the command-line arguments in the **ld** command in our makefile. However, it's easier to compile our program with the GNU C compiler (which includes the GNU Assembler), then it will link in the C runtime automatically. To compile our program, we will use

```
gcc -o myprogram myprogram.s
```

That will call **as** on myprogram.s and then do the **ld** command including the C runtime.

The C runtime gives us a lot of capabilities including wrappers for most of the Linux system services. There is an extensive library for manipulating NULL-terminated strings, routines for memory management, and routines to convert between all the data types.

Printing Debug Information

One handy use of the C runtime is to print out data to trace what our program is doing. We wrote a routine to output the contents of a register in hexadecimal, and we could write more Assembly code to extend this or we could just get the C runtime to do it. After all, if we are printing out trace or debugging information, it doesn't need to be performant, rather just easy to add to our code.

For this example, we'll use the C runtime's printf function to print out the contents of a register in both decimal and hexadecimal format. We'll package this routine as a macro, and we'll preserve all the registers with push and pop instructions. This way, we can call the macro without worrying about register conflicts. The exception is **CPSR** which it can't preserve, so don't put these macros between instructions that set the **CPSR**, then test the **CPSR**. We also provide a macro to print a string for either logging or formatting purposes.

170

The C printf function is mighty; it takes a variable number of arguments depending on the contents of a format string. There is extensive online documentation on printf; so for a fuller understanding, please have a look. We will call our collection of macros debug.s, and it contains the code from Listing 9-1.

Listing 9-1. Debug macros that use the C runtime's printf function

```
@ Various macros to help with debugging

@ These macros preserve all registers.
@ Beware they will change cpsr.

.macro  printReg    reg
        push      {r0-r4, lr} @ save regs
        mov       r2, R\reg    @ for the %d
        mov       r3, R\reg    @ for the %x
        mov       r1, #\reg
        add       r1, #'0'     @ for %c
        ldr       r0, =ptfStr @ printf format str
        bl        printf @ call printf
        pop       {r0-r4, lr} @ restore regs
.endm

.macro     printStr    str
        push      {r0-r4, lr} @ save regs
        ldr       r0, =1f      @ load print str
        bl        printf @ call printf
        pop       {r0-r4, lr} @ restore regs
        b         2f              @ branch around str
1:      .asciz         "\str\n"
        .align         4
2:
.endm
```

```
.data
ptfStr: .asciz    "R%c = %16d, 0x%08x\n"
.align 4
.text
```

Preserving State

First, we push registers **R0–R4** and **LR**; we either use these registers, or printf might change them. They aren't saved as part of the function calling protocol. At the end, we restore these. This makes calling our macros as minimally disruptive to the calling code as possible.

Calling Printf

We call the C function with these arguments:

```
printf("R%c = %16d, 0x%08x\n", reg, Rreg, Rreg);
```

Since there are four parameters, we set them into **R0–R3**. In printf each string that starts with a percentage sign ("%"), it takes the next parameter and formats it according to the next letter:

- **c** for character.
- **d** for decimal.
- **x** for hex.
- **0** means 0 pad.
- A number specifies the length of the field to print.

Note   It is important to move the value of the register to **R2** and **R3** first since populating the other registers might wipe out the passed-in value if we are printing **R0** or **R1**. If our register is **R2** or **R3**, one of the **MOV** instructions does nothing. Luckily, we don't get an error or warning, so we don't need a special case.

Passing a String

In the printStr macro, we pass in a string to print. Assembly doesn't handle strings, so we embed the string in the code with an **.asciz** directive, then branch around it.

There is an **.align** directive right after the string, since Assembly instructions must be word aligned. It is good practice to add an **.align** directive after strings, since other data types will load faster if they are word aligned.

Generally, I don't like adding data to the code section, but for our macro, this is the easiest way. The assumption is that the debug calls will be removed from the final code. If we add too many strings, we could make PC relative offsets too large to be resolved. If this happens, we may need to shorten the strings or remove some.

Adding with Carry Revisited

In Chapter 2, "Loading and Adding," we gave sample code to add two 64-bit numbers using **ADDS** and **ADC** instructions. What was lacking from this example was some way to see the output. Now we'll take addexamp2.s and add some calls to our debug macros, in Listing 9-2, to show it in action.

Listing 9-2. Updated addexamp2.s to print out the inputs and outputs

```
@
@ Example of 64-bit addition with the ADD/ADC
@ instructions.
@

.include "debug.s"

.global main  @ Provide program starting
```

```
@ main routine to be called by C runtime
main:
       push {R4-R12, LR}

@ Load the registers with some data
@ First 64-bit number is 0x00000003FFFFFFFF

       MOV  R2, #0x00000003
       MOV  R3, #0xFFFFFFFF     @Assembler will change to MVN
@ Second 64-bit number is 0x0000000500000001
       MOV  R4, #0x00000005
       MOV  R5, #0x00000001

       printStr "Inputs:"
       printReg 2
       printReg 3
       printReg 4
       printReg 5
       ADDS  R1, R3, R5 @ Lower order word
       ADC   R0, R2, R4 @ Higher order word

       printStr "Outputs:"
       printReg 1
       printReg 0

       mov  r0, #0              @ return code
       @ restore registers and return by popping to PC
       pop  {R4-R12, PC}
```

The makefile, in Listing 9-3, for this is quite simple.

Listing 9-3. Makefile for updated addexamp2.s

```
addexamp2: addexamp2.s debug.s
       gcc -o addexamp2 addexamp2.s
```

If we compile and run the program, we will see:

```
pi@raspberrypi:~/asm/Chapter 9 $ make
gcc -o addexamp2 addexamp2.s
pi@raspberrypi:~/asm/Chapter 9 $ ./addexamp2
Inputs:
R2 =                   3, 0x00000003
R3 =                  -1, 0xffffffff
R4 =                   5, 0x00000005
R5 =                   1, 0x00000001
Outputs:
R1 =                   0, 0x00000000
R0 =                   9, 0x00000009
pi@raspberrypi:~/asm/Chapter 9 $
```

Besides adding the debug statements, notice how the program is restructured as a function. The entry point is main, and it follows the function protocol of saving all the registers. Since this is the main routine and only called once, we save all the registers rather than try to track the registers we are really using. This is the safest, since then we don't have to worry about it as we work on our program.

By just adding the C runtime, we bring a powerful tool chest to save us time as we develop our full Assembly application. On the downside, notice our executable has grown to over 8KB.

Calling Assembly Routines from C

A typical scenario is to write most of our application in C, then call Assembly language routines in specific use cases. If we follow the function calling protocol from Chapter 6, "Functions and the Stack," C won't be able to tell the difference between our functions and any other functions written in C.

As an example, let's call our toupper function from Chapter 6, "Functions and the Stack," and call it from C. Listing 9-4 contains the C code for uppertst.c to call our Assembly function.

Listing 9-4. Main program to show calling our toupper function from C

```
//
// C program to call our Assembly
// toupper routine.
//

#include <stdio.h>

extern int mytoupper( char *, char * );

#define MAX_BUFFSIZE 255
int main()
{
        char *str = "This is a test.";
        char outBuf[MAX_BUFFSIZE];
        int len;

        len = mytoupper( str, outBuf );
        printf("Before str: %s\n", str);
        printf("After str: %s\n", outBuf);
        printf("Str len = %d\n", len);
        return(0);
}
```

The makefile is in Listing 9-5.

Listing 9-5. Makefile for C and our toupper function

```
uppertst: uppertst.c upper.s
    gcc -o uppertst uppertst.c upper.s
```

We had to change the name of our toupper function to mytoupper, since there is already a toupper function in the C runtime, and this led to a multiple definition error. This had to be done in both the C and the Assembly code. Otherwise, the function is the same as in Chapter 6, "Functions and the Stack."

We must define the parameters and return code for our function to the C compiler. We do this with

```
extern int mytoupper( char *, char * );
```

This should be familiar to all C programmers, as you must do this for C functions as well. Usually, you would gather up all these definitions and put them in a header (**.h**) file.

As far as the C code is concerned, there is no difference to using this Assembly function than if we wrote it in C. When we compile and run the program, we get

```
pi@raspberrypi:~/asm/Chapter 9 $ make
gcc -o uppertst uppertst.c upper.s
pi@raspberrypi:~/asm/Chapter 9 $ ./uppertst
Before str: This is a test.
After str: THIS IS A TEST.
Str len = 16
pi@raspberrypi:~/asm/Chapter 9 $
```

The string is in uppercase as we would expect, but the string length appears one greater than we might expect. That is because the length includes the NULL character that isn't the C standard. If we really wanted to use this a lot with C, we should subtract 1, so that our length is consistent with other C runtime routines.

Packaging Our Code

We could leave our Assembly code in individual object (**.o**) files, but it is more convenient for programmers using our library to package them together in a library. This way, the user of our Assembly routines just needs to add one library to get all of our code, rather than possibly dozens of **.o** files. In Linux there are two ways to do this; the first way is to package our code together into a static library that is linked into the program. The second method is to package our code as a shared library that lives outside the calling program and can be shared by several applications.

Static Library

To package our code as a static library, we use the Linux **ar** command. This command will take a number of **.o** files and combine them into a single file by convention lib<ourname>.a, that can then be included into a **gcc** or **ld** command. To do this, we modify our makefile to build this way as demonstrated in Listing 9-6.

Listing 9-6. Makefile to build upper.s into a statically linked library

```
LIBOBJS = upper.o

all: uppertst2

%.o : %.s
        as $(DEBUGFLGS) $(LSTFLGS) $< -o $@

libupper.a: $(LIBOBJS)
        ar -cvq libupper.a upper.o

uppertst2: uppertst.c libupper.a
        gcc -o uppertst2 uppertst.c libupper.a
```

If we build and run this program, we get

```
pi@raspberrypi:~/asm/Chapter 9 $ make
as    upper.s -o upper.o
ar -cvq libupper.a upper.o
a - upper.o
gcc -o uppertst2 uppertst.c libupper.a
pi@raspberrypi:~/asm/Chapter 9 $ ./uppertst2
Before str: This is a test.
After str: THIS IS A TEST.
Str len = 16
pi@raspberrypi:~/asm/Chapter 9 $
```

The only difference to the last example is that we first use **as** to compile upper.s into upper.o and then use **ar** to build a library containing our routine. If we want to distribute our library, we include libupper.a, a header file with the C function definitions, and some documentation. Even if you aren't selling or otherwise distributing your code, building libraries internally can help organizationally to share code among programmers and reduce duplicated work.

Shared Library

Shared libraries are much more technical than statically linked libraries. They place the code in a separate file from the executable and are dynamically loaded by the system as needed. There are a number of issues, but we are only going to touch on them, such as versioning and library placement in the filesystem. If you decide to package your code as a shared library, this section provides a starting point and demonstrates that it applies to Assembly code as much as C code.

The shared library is created with the **gcc** command, giving it the **-shared** command-line parameter to indicate we want to create a shared library and then the **-soname** parameter to name it.

To use a shared library, it must be in a specific place in the filesystem. We can add new places, but we are going to use a place created by the C runtime, namely, /usr/local/lib. After we build our library, we copy it here and create a couple of links to it. These steps are all required as part of shared library versioning control system.

Then to use our shared library libup.so.1, we include -lup on the gcc command to compile uppertst3. The makefile is presented in Listing 9-7.

Listing 9-7. Makefile for building and using a shared library

```
LIBOBJS = upper.o

all: uppertst3

%.o : %.s
        as $(DEBUGFLGS) $(LSTFLGS) $< -o $@

libup.so.1.0: $(LIBOBJS)
        gcc -shared -Wl,-soname,libup.so.1 -o libup.so.1.0 $(LIBOBJS)
        mv libup.so.1.0 /usr/local/lib
        ln -sf /usr/local/lib/libup.so.1.0 /usr/local/lib/libup.so.1
        ln -sf /usr/local/lib/libup.so.1.0 /usr/local/lib/libup.so

uppertst3: libup.so.1.0
        gcc -o uppertst3 -lup uppertst.c
```

If we run this, several commands will fail. To copy the files to /usr/local/lib, we need root access, so use the sudo command. The following is the sequence of commands to build and run the program

```
pi@raspberrypi:~/asm/Chapter 9 $ sudo make -B
as    upper.s -o upper.o
gcc -shared -Wl,-soname,libup.so.1 -o libup.so.1.0 upper.o
```

```
mv libup.so.1.0 /usr/local/lib
ln -sf /usr/local/lib/libup.so.1.0 /usr/local/lib/libup.so.1
ln -sf /usr/local/lib/libup.so.1.0 /usr/local/lib/libup.so
gcc -o uppertst3 -lup uppertst.c
pi@raspberrypi:~/asm/Chapter 9 $ sudo ldconfig
pi@raspberrypi:~/asm/Chapter 9 $ ./uppertst3
Before str: This is a test.
After str: THIS IS A TEST.
Str len = 16
pi@raspberrypi:~/asm/Chapter 9 $
```

Notice there is a call to the following command:

```
sudo ldconfig
```

before we run the program. This causes Linux to search all the folders that hold shared libraries and update its master list. We have to run this once after we successfully compile our library, or Linux won't know it exists.

If you use objdump to look inside uppertst3, you won't find the code for the mytoupper routine; instead, in our main code, you will find

```
 104c0:     ebffffb4 bl     10398 <mytoupper@plt>
```

which calls

```
00010398 <mytoupper@plt>:
   10398:  e28fc600 add     ip, pc, #0, 12
   1039c:  e28cca10 add     ip, ip, #16, 20  ; 0x10000
   103a0:  e5bcfc78 ldr     pc, [ip, #3192]! ; 0xc78
```

Gcc inserted this indirection into our code, so the loader can fix up the address when it dynamically loads the shared library.

Embedding Assembly Code Inside C Code

The GNU C compiler allows Assembly code to be embedded right in the middle of C code. It contains features to interact with C variables and labels and cooperate with the C compiler and optimizer for register usage.

Listing 9-8 is a simple example, where we embed the core algorithm for the toupper function inside the C main program.

Listing 9-8. Embedding our Assembly routine directly in C code

```
//
// C program to embed our Assembly
// toupper routine inline.
//

#include <stdio.h>

extern int mytoupper( char *, char * );

#define MAX_BUFFSIZE 255
int main()
{
        char *str = "This is a test.";
        char outBuf[MAX_BUFFSIZE];
        int len;

        asm
        (
                "MOV R4, %2\n"
                "loop:    LDRB   R5, [%1], #1\n"
                "CMP  R5, #'z'\n"
                "BGT  cont\n"
                "CMP  R5, #'a'\n"
                "BLT  cont\n"
                "SUB  R5, #('a'-'A')\n"
```

```
    "cont:       STRB R5, [%2], #1\n"
    "CMP   R5, #0\n"
    "BNE   loop\n"
    "SUB   %0, %2, R4\n"
    : "=r" (len)
    : "r" (str), "r" (outBuf)
    : "r4", "r5"
);

printf("Before str: %s\n", str);
printf("After str: %s\n", outBuf);
printf("Str len = %d\n", len);
return(0);
}
```

The **asm** statement lets us embed Assembly code directly into our C code. Doing this, we could write an arbitrary mixture of C and Assembly. I stripped out the comments from the Assembly code, so the structure of the C and Assembly is a bit easier to read. The general form of the asm statement is

```
asm asm-qualifiers ( AssemblerTemplate
                : OutputOperands
                [ : InputOperands]
                [ : Clobbers ] ]
                [ : GotoLabels])
```

The parameters are

- AssemblerTemplate: A C string containing the Assembly code. There are macro substitutions that start with **%** to let the C compiler insert the inputs and outputs.

- OutputOperands: A list of variables or registers returned from the code. This is required, since it is expected that the routine does something. In our case this is "=r" (len) where the =r means an output register and that we want it to go into the C variable len.

- InputOperands: A list of input variables or registers used by our routine, in this case "r" (str), "r" (outBuf) meaning we want two registers, one holding str and one holding outBuf. It is fortunate that C string variables hold the address of the string, which is what we want in the register.

- Clobbers: A list of registers that we use and will be clobbered when our code runs, in this case "**r4**" and "**r5**".

- GotoLabelsr: A list of C program labels that our code might want to jump to. Usually, this is an error exit. If you do jump to a C label, you have to warn the compiler with a goto asm-qualifier.

You can label the input and output operands, we didn't, and that means the compiler will assign them names %0, %1, ... as you can see used in the Assembly code.

Since this is a single C file, it is easy to compile with

```
gcc -o uppertst4 uppertst4.c
```

Running the program produces the same output as the last section.

If you disassemble the program, you will find that the C compiler avoids using registers **R4** and **R5** entirely, leaving them to us. You will see it load up our input registers from the variables on the stack, before our code executes and then copies our return value from the assigned register to the variable len on the stack. It doesn't give the same registers we originally used, but that isn't a problem.

This routine is straightforward and doesn't have any side effects. If your Assembly code is modifying things behind the scenes, you need to add a volatile keyword to the asm statement to make the C compile be more conservative on any assumptions it makes about your code.

Calling Assembly from Python

If we write our functions following the Raspbian function calling protocol from Chapter 6, "Functions and the Stack," we can follow the documentation on how to call C functions for any given programming language. Python has a good capability to call C functions in its ctypes module. This module requires we package our routines into a shared library. Since Python is an interpreted language, we can't link static libraries to it, but we can dynamically load and call shared libraries. The techniques we go through here for Python have matching components in many other interpreted languages.

The hard part is already done, we've built the shared library version of our uppercase function; all we must do is call it from Python. Listing 9-9 is the Python code for uppertst5.py.

Listing 9-9. Python code to call mytoupper

```
from ctypes import *

libupper = CDLL("libup.so")

libupper.mytoupper.argtypes = [c_char_p, c_char_p]
libupper.mytoupper.restype = c_int

inStr = create_string_buffer(b"This is a test!")
outStr = create_string_buffer(250)

len = libupper.mytoupper(inStr, outStr)
```

```
print(inStr.value)
print(outStr.value)
print(len)
```

The code is fairly simple; we first import the ctypes module so we can use it. We then load our shared library with the CDLL function. This is an unfortunate name since it refers to Windows DLLs rather than something more operating system neutral. Since we installed our shared library in /usr/local/lib and added it to the Linux shared library cache, Python has no trouble finding and loading it.

The next two lines are optional, but good practice. They define the function parameters and return type to Python, so it can do extra error checking.

In Python, strings are immutable, meaning you can't change them, and they are in Unicode, meaning each character takes up more than 1 byte. We need to provide the strings in regular buffers that we can change, and we need the strings in ASCII rather than Unicode. We can make a string ASCII in Python by putting a "b" in front of the string; that means to make it a byte array using ASCII characters. The create_string_buffer function in the ctypes module creates a string buffer that is compatible with C (and hence Assembly) for us to use.

We then call our function and print the inputs and outputs. Raspbian comes with the Thonny Python IDE preinstalled as shown in Figure 9-1, so we can use that to test the program.

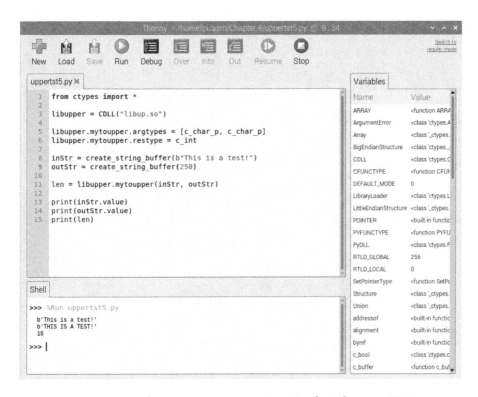

Figure 9-1. *Our Python program running in the Thonny IDE*

Summary

In this chapter, we looked at calling C functions from our Assembly code. We made use of the standard C runtime to develop some debug helper functions to make developing our Assembly code a little easier. We then did the reverse and called our Assembly uppercase function from a C main program.

We learned how to package our code as both static and shared libraries. We discussed how to package our code for consumption. We looked at how to call our uppercase function from Python, which is typical of high-level languages with the ability to call shared libraries.

In the next chapter, Chapter 10, "Multiply, Divide, and Accumulate," we will return to mathematics. We will cover multiplication, division, and multiply with accumulate.

CHAPTER 10

Multiply, Divide, and Accumulate

In this chapter, we return to mathematics. We've covered addition, subtraction, and a collection of bit operations on our 32-bit registers. Now we will cover multiplication and division. The ARM processor has a surplus of multiply instructions, then a dearth of division operations.

We will cover multiply with accumulate instructions. We will provide some background on why the ARM processor has so much circuitry dedicated to performing this operation. This will get us into the mechanics of vector and matrix multiplication.

Multiplication

In Chapter 7, "Linux Operating System Services," we discussed why there are so many Linux service calls and how part of the reason was for compatibility when they needed new functionality; they added a new call, so the old call is preserved. The ARM multiply instructions have a similar history. Multiply has been in the ARM architecture for a long time, but the original instructions were inadequate and new instructions were added while keeping the old instructions for software compatibility.

The original 32-bit instruction is

```
MUL{S}   Rd, Rn, Rm
```

© Stephen Smith 2019
S. Smith, *Raspberry Pi Assembly Language Programming*,
https://doi.org/10.1007/978-1-4842-5287-1_10

This instruction computes Rd = Rn * Rm. It looks good, but people familiar with multiplication might immediately ask "These are all 32-bit registers, so when you multiply two 32-bit numbers, don't you get a 64-bit product?" That is true, and that is the most obvious limitation on this instruction. Here are some notes on this instruction:

- **Rd** is the lower 32 bits of the product. The upper 32 bits are discarded.

- The **MULS** version of the instruction only sets the **N** and **Z** flags; it does not set the **C** or **V** flags, so you don't know if it overflowed.

- There aren't separate signed and unsigned versions; multiplication isn't like addition where the two's complement makes the operations the same.

- All the operands are registers; immediate operands are not allowed.

- **Rd** cannot be the same as **Rn**.

To overcome some of these limitations, later versions of the ARM processor added an abundance of multiply instructions:

- SMULL{S} RdLo, RdHi, Rn, Rm

- UMULL{S} RdLo, RdHi, Rn, Rm

- SMMUL{R} {Rd}, Rn, Rm

- SMUL<x><y> {Rd}, Rn, Rm

- SMULW<y> {Rd}, Rn, Rm

The first **SMULL** instruction will perform signed 32-bit multiplication putting the 64-bit result in two registers. The second **UMULL** instruction is the unsigned version of this. **SMMUL** complements the original **MUL** instruction by providing the upper 32 bits of the product and discarding the lower 32 bits.

Multiplication is an expensive operation, so there is some merit in multiplying small numbers quickly. **SMUL** provides this; it multiplies two 16-bit quantities to provide a 32-bit quantity. The <x> and <y> modifiers specify which 16 bits of the operand registers are used:

- <x> is either B or T. B means use the bottom half (bits [15:0]) of Rn; T means use the top half (bits [31:16]) of Rn.

- <y> is either B or T. B means use the bottom half (bits [15:0]) of Rm; T means use the top half (bits [31:16]) of Rm.

SMULW is an intermediate version that multiplies a 32-bit value by a 16-bit value, then only keeps the upper 32 bits of the 48-bit product. The <y> modifier is the same as for **SMUL**. When I've seen this instruction used, one of the operands has usually been shifted so that the product ends up in the upper 32 bits.

All these instructions have the same performance. The ability to detect when a multiply is done (remaining digits are 0) was added to the ARM processor some time ago, so the need for shorter versions of multiply, in my opinion, doesn't exist anymore. I would recommend always using **SMULL** and **UMULL** as then there are less things to go wrong if your numbers change over time.

Examples

Listing 10-1 is some code to demonstrate all the various multiply instructions. We use our debug.s file from Chapter 9, "Interacting with C and Python," which means our program must be organized with the C runtime in mind.

Listing 10-1. Examples of the various multiply instructions

```
@
@ Example of 16 & 32-bit Multiplication
@

.include "debug.s"

.global main @ Provide program starting address to linker

@ Load the registers with some data
@ Use small positive numbers that will work for all
@ multiply instructions.
main:
        push {R4-R12, LR}
        MOV   R2, #25
        MOV   R3, #4

        printStr "Inputs:"
        printReg 2
        printReg 3

        MUL   R4, R2, R3
        printStr "MUL R4=R2*R3:"
        printReg 4

        SMULL R4, R5, R2, R3
        printStr "SMULL R5, R4=R2*R3:"
        printReg 4
        printReg 5

        UMULL R4, R5, R2, R3
        printStr "UMULL R5, R4=R2*R3:"
        printReg 4
        printReg 5
```

```
        SMMUL  R4, R2, R3
        printStr "SMMUL R4 = top 32 bits of R2*R3:"
        printReg 4

        SMULBB      R4, R2, R3
        printStr "SMULBB R4 = R2*R3:"
        printReg 4

        SMULWB      R4, R2, R3
        printStr "SMULWB R4 = upper 32 bits of R2*R3:"
        printReg 4
        mov    r0, #0           @ return code
        pop    {R4-R12, PC}
```

The makefile is as we would expect. The output is

```
pi@raspberrypi:~/asm/Chapter 10 $ make
gcc -o mulexamp mulexamp.s
pi@raspberrypi:~/asm/Chapter 10 $ ./mulexamp
Inputs:
R2 =                25, 0x00000019
R3 =                 4, 0x00000004
MUL R4=R2*R3:
R4 =               100, 0x00000064
SMULL R5, R4=R2*R3:
R4 =               100, 0x00000064
R5 =                 0, 0x00000000
UMULL R5, R4=R2*R3:
R4 =               100, 0x00000064
R5 =                 0, 0x00000000
SMMUL R4 = top 32 bits of R2*R3:
R4 =                 0, 0x00000000
SMULBB R4 = R2*R3:
R4 =               100, 0x00000064
```

```
SMULWB R4 = upper 32 bits of R2*R3:
R4 =                    0, 0x00000000
pi@raspberrypi:~/asm/Chapter 10 $
```

Multiply is straightforward, especially using **SMULL** and **UMULL**.

Division

Integer division is a much more recent addition to the ARM processor. In fact, the Raspberry Pi 1 and Zero have no integer division instruction. The second generation of the Raspberry Pi 2 uses ARM Cortex-A53 processors, which introduce integer division to the Pi world. The Raspberry Pi 4 includes newer Cortex-A72 processors.

If you are targeting Raspberry Pi Zero or 1, then you will need to either implement your own division algorithm in code, call some C code, or use the floating-point coprocessor. We'll cover the floating-point coprocessor in Chapter 11, "Floating-Point Operations."

The Raspberry Pi 2, 3, and 4's division instructions are

- SDIV {Rd}, Rn, Rm

- UDIV {Rd}, Rn, Rm

where

- **Rd** is the destination register.

- **Rn** is the register holding the numerator.

- **Rm** is a register holding the denominator.

There are a few problems or technical notes on these instructions:

- There is no "S" option of this instruction, as it doesn't set **CPSR** at all.

- Dividing by 0 should throw an exception; with these instructions, it returns 0 which can be very misleading.

- These instructions aren't the inverses of **SMULL** and **UMULL**. For this Rn needs to be a register pair, so the value to be divided can be 64 bits. To divide a 64-bit value, we need to either go to the floating-point processor or roll our own code.

- The instruction only returns the quotient, not the remainder. Many algorithms require the remainder, and you must calculate it as remainder = numerator - (quotient ∗ denominator).

Example

The code to execute the divide instructions is simple; Listing 10-2 is an example like we did for multiplication.

Listing 10-2. Examples of the SDIV and UDIV instructions

```
@
@ Examples of 32-bit Integer Division
@

.include "debug.s"

.global main              @ Provide program starting address to
                            linker

@ Load the registers with some data
@ Perform various division instructions
main:
        push    {R4-R12, LR}
        MOV    R2, #100
        MOV    R3, #4
```

```
printStr "Inputs:"
printReg 2
printReg 3

SDIV  R4, R2, R3
printStr "Outputs:"
printReg 4

UDIV  R4, R2, R3
printStr "Outputs:"
printReg 4

mov   r0, #0            @ return code
pop   {R4-R12, PC}
```

If we try to build this in the same way we did for the multiplication example, we will get the error

```
pi@raspberrypi:~/asm/Chapter 10 $ make -B
gcc -o divexamp divexamp.s
divexamp.s: Assembler messages:
divexamp.s:21: Error: selected processor does not support `sdiv
R4,R2,R3' in ARM mode
make: *** [makefile:15: divexamp] Error 1
pi@raspberrypi:~/asm/Chapter 10 $
```

This is run on a Raspberry Pi 4. Didn't we say it supports the SDIV instruction? The reason is that the Raspberry Pi foundation goes to great pains to ensure all their software runs on all Raspberry Pi no matter how old. The default configuration of the GNU Compiler Collection in Raspbian is to target the lowest common denominator. If we change the makefile to the following

```
divexamp: divexamp.s debug.s
      gcc -march="armv8-a" -o divexamp divexamp.s
```

then the program will compile and run. The -march parameter is for machine architecture, and "arm8-a" is the correct one for the Raspberry Pi 4. We could have used one to match a Raspberry Pi 3, but we'll want to explore some new features in the Pi 4 later.

With this in place, the program runs and we get the expected results:

```
pi@raspberrypi:~/asm/Chapter 10 $ make
gcc -march="armv8-a" -o divexamp divexamp.s
pi@raspberrypi:~/asm/Chapter 10 $ ./divexamp
Inputs:
R2 =               100, 0x00000064
R3 =                 4, 0x00000004
Outputs:
R4 =                25, 0x00000019
Outputs:
R4 =                25, 0x00000019
pi@raspberrypi:~/asm/Chapter 10 $
```

Multiply and Accumulate

The multiply and accumulate operation multiplies two numbers, then adds them to a third. As we go through the next few chapters, we will see this operation reappear again and again. The ARM processor is RISC, if the instruction set is reduced, then why do we find so many instructions, and hence so much circuitry, dedicated to performing multiply and accumulate. The answer goes back to our favorite first year university math course on linear algebra. Most science students are forced to take this course, learn to work with vectors and matrices, then hope they never see these concepts again. Unfortunately, they form the foundation for both graphics and machine learning. Before delving into the ARM instructions for multiply and accumulate, let's review a bit of linear algebra.

Vectors and Matrices

A vector is an ordered list of numbers. For instance, in 3D graphics, it might represent your location in 3D space where [x, y, z] are your coordinates. Vectors have a dimension which is the number of elements they contain. It turns out a useful computation with vectors is something called a dot product. If $A = [a_1, a_2, \ldots, a_n]$ is one vector and $B = [b_1, b_2, \ldots, b_n]$ is another vector, then their dot product is defined as

$$A \cdot B = a_1 * b_1 + a_2 * b_1 + \ldots + a_n * b_n$$

If we want to calculate this dot product, then a loop performing multiply and accumulate instructions should be quite efficient. A matrix is a 2D table of numbers such as

$$\begin{vmatrix} a_{11} & a_{12} \\ a_{21} & a_{22} \end{vmatrix}$$

Matrix multiplication is a complicated process that drives first-year linear algebra students nuts. When you multiply matrix A times matrix B, then each element on the resulting matrix is the dot product of a row of matrix A with a column of matrix B.

$$\begin{vmatrix} a_{11} & a_{12} \\ a_{21} & a_{22} \end{vmatrix} \begin{vmatrix} b_{11} & b_{12} \\ b_{21} & b_{22} \end{vmatrix} = \begin{vmatrix} a_{11}b_{11}+a_{12}b_{21} & a_{11}b_{12}+a_{12}b_{22} \\ a_{21}b_{11}+a_{22}b_{21} & a_{21}b_{12}+a_{22}b_{22} \end{vmatrix}$$

If these were 3x3 matrices, then there would be nine dot products each with nine terms. We can also multiply a matrix by a vector the same way.

$$\begin{vmatrix} a_{11} & a_{12} \\ a_{21} & a_{22} \end{vmatrix} \begin{vmatrix} b_1 \\ b_2 \end{vmatrix} = \begin{vmatrix} a_{11}b_1+a_{12}b_2 \\ a_{21}b_1+a_{22}b_2 \end{vmatrix}$$

In 3D graphics, if we represent a point as a 4D vector [x, y, z, 1], then the affine transformations of scale, rotate, shear, and reflection can be represented as 4x4 matrices. Any number of these transformations can be combined into a single matrix. Thus, to transform an object into a scene requires a matrix multiplication applied to each of the object's vertex points. The faster we can do this, the faster we can render a frame in a video game.

In neural networks, the calculation for each layer of neurons is calculated by a matrix multiplication, followed by the application of a nonlinear function. The bulk of the work is the matrix multiplication. Most neural networks have many layers of neurons, each requiring a matrix multiplication. The matrix size corresponds to the number of variables and the number of neurons; hence, the matrix dimensions are often in the thousands. How quickly we perform object recognition or speech translation is dependent on how fast we can multiply matrices, that is dependent on how fast we can do multiply with accumulate.

These important applications are why the ARM processor dedicates so much silicon to multiply and accumulate. We'll keep returning to how to speed up this process as we explore the Raspberry Pi's FPU and NEON coprocessors in the following chapters.

Accumulate Instructions

As we saw with multiplication, there have been quite a proliferation of multiply with accumulate instructions. Fortunately, we've covered most of the details in the "Multiplication" section. Here they are:

- MLA{S}   Rd, Rn, Rm, Ra

- SMLAL{S}   RdLo, RdHi, Rn, Rm

- SMLA<x><y>   Rd, Rn, Rm, Ra

- SMLAD{X}   Rd, Rn, Rm, Ra

- SMLALD{X}   RdLo, RdHi, Rn, Rm

- SMLAL<x><y>   RdLo, RdHi, Rn, Rm

- SMLAW<y>   Rd, Rn, Rm, Ra

- SMLSD{X}   Rd, Rn, Rm, Ra

- SMLSD{X}   RdLo, RdHi, Rn, Rm

- SMMLA{R}   Rd, Rn, Rm, Ra

- SMMLS{R}   Rd, Rn, Rm, Ra

- SMUAD{X}   {Rd}, Rn, Rm

- UMAAL   RdLo, RdHi, Rn, Rm

- UMLAL{S}   RdLo, RdHi, Rn, Rm

That is a lot of instructions, so we won't cover each in detail, but we can recognize that there is a multiply with accumulate for each regular multiply instruction. Let's look at what leads to a further proliferation of instructions.

If there is an Ra operand, then the calculation is

```
Rd = Rn * Rm + Ra
```

Note   Rd can be the same as Ra for calculating a running sum.

If there isn't an Ra operand, then the calculation is

```
Rd = Rd + Rn * Rm
```

This second form tends to be for instructions with 64-bit results, so the sum needs to be 64 bits, therefore, can't be a single register.

Dual Multiply with Accumulate

The instructions that end in **D** are dual. They do two multiply and accumulates in a single step. They multiply the top 16 bits of Rn and Rm and multiply the bottom 16 bits of Rn and Rm, then add both products to the accumulator.

If there is an S in the instruction instead of an A, then it means it subtracts the two values before adding the result to the accumulator.

```
Rd = Ra + (bottom Rn * bottom Rm - top Rn * top Rm)
```

If the accuracy works for you and you can encode all the data this way, then you can double your throughput using these instructions. We'll look at this in Example 2.

Example 1

We've talked about how multiply and accumulate is ideal for multiplying matrices, so for an example, let's multiply two 3x3 matrices.

The algorithm we are implementing is shown in Listing 10-3.

Listing 10-3. Pseudo-code for our matrix multiplication program

```
FOR row = 1 to 3
    FOR col = 1 to 3
        acum = 0
        FOR i = 1 to 3
            acum = acum + A[row, i]*B[i, col]
        NEXT I
        C[row, col] = acum
    NEXT col
NEXT row
```

Basically, the row and column loops go through each cell of the output matrix and calculate the correct dot product for that cell in the innermost loop.

Listing 10-4 shows our implementation in Assembly.

Listing 10-4. 3x3 matrix multiplication in Assembly

```
@
@ Multiply 2 3x3 integer matrices
@
@ Registers:
@       R1 - Row index
@       R2 - Column index
@       R4 - Address of row
@       R5 - Address of column
@       R7 - 64 bit accumulated sum
@       R8 - 64 bit accumulated sum
@       R9 - Cell of A
@       R10 - Cell of B
@       R11 - Position in C
@       R12 - row in dotloop
@       R6 - col in dotloop

.global main @ Provide program starting address

        .equ  N, 3 @ Matrix dimensions
        .equ  WDSIZE, 4 @ Size of element
main:
        push  {R4-R12, LR}    @ Save required regs

        MOV   R1, #N          @ Row index
        LDR   R4, =A          @ Address of current row
        LDR   R11, =C         @ Addr of results matrix
```

```
rowloop:
      LDR    R5, =B            @ first column in B
      MOV    R2, #N     @ Colindex (will count down)
colloop:
      @ Zero accumulator registers
      MOV    R7, #0
      MOV    R8, #0

      MOV    R0, #N            @ dot product loop counter
      MOV    R12, R4           @ row for dot product
      MOV    R6, R5            @ column for dot product
dotloop:
      @ Do dot product of a row of A with column of B
      LDR    R9, [R12], #WDSIZE @ load A[row, i] and incr
      LDR    R10, [R6], #(N*WDSIZE) @ load B[i, col]
      SMLAL  R7, R8, R9, R10 @ Do multiply and accumulate
      SUBS   R0, #1           @ Dec loop counter
      BNE    dotloop          @ If not zero loop
      STR    R7, [R11], #4    @ C[row, col] = dotprod
      ADD    R5, #WDSIZE      @ Increment current col
      SUBS   R2, #1           @ Dec col loop counter
      BNE    colloop          @ If not zero loop

      ADD    R4, #(N*WDSIZE)  @ Increment to next row
      SUBS   R1, #1           @ Dec row loop counter
      BNE    rowloop          @ If not zero loop
@ Print out matrix C
@ Loop through 3 rows printing 3 cols each time.
      MOV    R5, #3           @ Print 3 rows
      LDR    R11, =C          @ Addr of results matrix
printloop:
```

```
        LDR    R0, =prtstr @ printf format string
        LDR    R1, [R11], #WDSIZE    @ first element in current row
        LDR    R2, [R11], #WDSIZE    @ second element in current row
        LDR    R3, [R11], #WDSIZE    @ third element in current row
        BL     printf               @ Call printf
        SUBS   R5, #1               @ Dec loop counter
        BNE    printloop  @ If not zero loop

        mov    r0, #0               @ return code
        pop    {R4-R12, PC}         @ Restore regs and return
.data
@ First matrix
A:      .word  1, 2, 3
        .word  4, 5, 6
        .word  7, 8, 9
@ Second matrix
B:      .word  9, 8, 7
        .word  6, 5, 4
        .word  3, 2, 1
@ Result matrix
C:      .fill  9, 4, 0

prtstr: .asciz  "%3d  %3d  %3d\n"
```

Compiling and running this program, we get

```
pi@raspberrypi:~/asm/Chapter 10 $ make
gcc -o matrixmult matrixmult.s
pi@raspberrypi:~/asm/Chapter 10 $ ./matrixmult
 30   24   18
 84   69   54
138  114   90
pi@raspberrypi:~/asm/Chapter 10 $
```

Accessing Matrix Elements

We store the three matrices in memory, in row order. They are arranged in the **.word** directives so that you can see the matrix structure. In the pseudo-code, we refer to the matrix elements using 2D arrays. There are no instructions or operand formats to specify 2D array access, so we must do it ourselves. To Assembly, each array is just a nine-word sequence of memory. Now that we know how to multiply, we can do something like

$$A[i, j] = A[i*N + j]$$

where N is the dimension of the array. We don't do this though; in Assembly it pays to notice that we access the array elements in order and can go from one element in a row to the next by adding the size of an element—the size of a word, or four. We can go from an element in a column to the next one by adding the size of a row. Therefore, we use the constant N $*$ WDSIZE so often in the code. This way, we go through the array incrementally and never have to multiply array indexes. Generally, multiplication and division are expensive operations, and we should try to avoid them as much as possible.

We can use post-indexing techniques to access elements increment pointers to the next element. We use post-indexing to store the result of each computation in the array C. We see this in

```
STR    R7, [R11], #4
```

which stores our computed dot product into C, then increments the pointer into C by 4 bytes. We see it again when we print the C matrix at the end.

Multiply with Accumulate

The core of the algorithm relies on the **SMLAL** instruction to multiply an element of A by an element of B and add that to the running sum for the dot product.

```
SMLAL   R7, R8, R9, R10
```

This instruction accumulates a 64-bit sum, but we only take the lower 32 bits in **R7**. We don't check for overflow; if at the end **R8** isn't 0, we are going to give an incorrect result.

Register Usage

We nearly use all the registers; we are lucky we can keep track of all our loop indexes and pointers in registers and don't have to move them in and out of memory. If we needed to do this, we would have allocated space on the stack to hold any needed variables.

Example 2

When we discussed the multiply with accumulate instructions, we mentioned the dual instructions that will do two steps in one instruction. The main problem is packing two numbers that need processing in each 32-bit register. We can create 16-bit integers easily enough using the **.short** Assembler directive. Processing the rows is easy since the cells are next to each other, but for the columns, each element is a row away. How can we easily load two column elements into one 32-bit register?

What we can do is take the transpose of the second matrix. This means making the rows columns and the columns rows, basically switching B[i, j] with B[j, i]. If we do that, then the column elements are next to each other and easy to load into a single 32-bit register.

Listing 10-5 is the code to do this.

Listing 10-5. 3x3 matrix multiplication using a dual multiply/accumulate

```
@
@ Multiply 2 3x3 integer matrices
@ Uses a dual multiply/accumulate instruction
@ so processes two elements in the dot product
@ per loop.
@
@ Registers:
@       R1 - Row index
@       R2 - Column index
@       R4 - Address of row
@       R5 - Address of column
@       R7 - 64 bit accumulated sum
@       R8 - 64 bit accumulated sum
@       R9 - Cell of A
@       R10 - Cell of B
@       R11 - Position in C
@       R12 - row in dotloop
@       R6 - col in dotloop
.global main @ Provide program starting address to linker
        .equ  N, 3  @ Matrix dimensions
        .equ  ELSIZE, 2 @ Size of element
main:
        push  {R4-R12, LR}   @ Save required regs

        MOV   R1, #N         @ Row index
        LDR   R4, =A         @ Address of current row
        LDR   R11, =C        @ Address of results matrix
rowloop:
        LDR   R5, =B         @ first column in B
        MOV   R2, #N         @ Column index (will count down to 0)
```

```
colloop:
        @ Zero accumulator registers
        MOV    R7, #0
        MOV    R8, #0

        MOV    R0, #((N+1)/2)    @ dot product loop counter
        MOV    R12, R4           @ row for dot product
        MOV    R6, R5            @ column for dot product
dotloop:
        @ Do dot product of a row of A with column of B
        LDR    R9, [R12], #(ELSIZE*2) @ load A[row, i] and incr
        LDR    R10, [R6], #(ELSIZE*2) @ load B[i, col]
        SMLAD  R7, R9, R10, R7   @ Do dual multiply and accumulate
        SUBS   R0, #1            @ Dec loop counter
        BNE    dotloop           @ If not zero loop

        STR    R7, [R11], #4     @ C[row, col] = dotprod
        ADD    R5, #((N+1)*ELSIZE)    @ Increment current col
        SUBS   R2, #1            @ Dec col loop counter
        BNE    colloop           @ If not zero loop

        ADD    R4, #((N+1)*ELSIZE)    @ Increment to next row
        SUBS   R1, #1            @ Dec row loop counter
        BNE    rowloop           @ If not zero loop

@ Print out matrix C
@ Loop through 3 rows printing 3 cols each time.
        MOV    R5, #3            @ Print 3 rows
        LDR    R11, =C           @ Addr of results matrix
printloop:

        LDR    R0, =prtstr       @ printf format string
        LDR    R1, [R11], #4     @ first element in current row
        LDR    R2, [R11], #4     @ second element in current row
```

```
LDR   R3, [R11], #4    @ third element in current row
BL    printf           @ Call printf
SUBS  R5, #1           @ Dec loop counter
BNE   printloop  @ If not zero loop
mov   r0, #0           @ return code
pop   {R4-R12, PC}     @ Restore regs and return
```

```
.data
@ First matrix
A:    .short    1, 2, 3, 0
      .short    4, 5, 6, 0
      .short    7, 8, 9, 0
@ Second matrix
B:    .short    9, 6, 3, 0
      .short    8, 5, 2, 0
      .short    7, 4, 1, 0
@ Result matrix
C:    .fill 9, 4, 0

prtstr: .asciz   "%3d  %3d  %3d\n"
```

The saving in instructions is in reducing the inner loop that computes the dot product.

```
MOV   R0, #((N+1)/2)  @ dot product loop counter
```

If our matrix had an even dimension, we would have saved more. For our 3x3 example, the dot product loop still has two elements. But then if we were doing two 4x4 matrices, it would also be two times through this loop. Notice that we had to add a 0 to the end of each row of both matrices, since the dual instruction is going to process an even number of entries.

The real workhorse of this program is

```
SMLAD   R7, R9, R10, R7
```

which multiplies the high part of **R9** by the high part of **R10** and at the same time the low part of **R9** by the low part of **R10**, then adds both to **R7** and puts the new sum into **R7**. Notice it's okay to have **Rd=Ra**, which is what you mostly want.

We still use **LDR** to load the registers from the matrices. This will load 32 bits; since we specified each element to take 16 bits, it will load two at a time enhancing our performance.

Summary

We covered the various forms of the multiply instruction supported in the ARM 32-bit instruction set. We covered the division instructions included in newer versions of the ARM processors, like those in the Raspberry Pi 3 and 4. For older processors we can use the FPU, write our own routine, or call some C code.

We then covered the concept of multiply and accumulate and why these instructions are so important to modern applications in graphics and machine learning. We reviewed the many variations of these instructions and then presented two versions of matrix multiplication to show them in action.

In Chapter 11, "Floating-Point Operations," we will look at more math, but this time in scientific notation allowing fractions and exponents, going beyond integers for the first time.

CHAPTER 11

Floating-Point Operations

The Raspberry Pi is based on a system on a chip. This chip contains the quad-core ARM CPU that we have been studying along with a couple of coprocessors. In this chapter, we'll be looking at what the floating-point unit (FPU) does. Some ARM documentation refers to this as the Vector Floating-Point (VFP) to promote the fact that it can do some limited vector processing. Any vector processing in the FPU is now replaced by the much better parallel processing provided by the NEON coprocessor, which we study in Chapter 12, "NEON Coprocessor." Regardless, the FPU provides several useful instructions for performing floating-point mathematics.

We'll review what floating-point numbers are, how they are represented in memory, and how to insert them into our Assembly programs. We'll look at how to transfer data between the FPU and the ARM's regular registers and memory. We'll look at how to perform basic arithmetic operations, comparisons, and conversions.

© Stephen Smith 2019
S. Smith, *Raspberry Pi Assembly Language Programming*,
https://doi.org/10.1007/978-1-4842-5287-1_11

About Floating-Point Numbers

Floating-point numbers are a way to represent numbers in scientific notation on the computer. Scientific notation represents numbers something like this:

$$1.456354 \times 10^{16}$$

There is a fractional part and an exponent that lets you move the decimal place to the left if it's positive and to the right if it's negative. The Raspberry Pi deals with single-precision floating-point numbers that are 32 bits in size and double-precision floating-point numbers that are 64 bits in size.

The Raspberry Pi uses the IEEE 754 standard for floating-point numbers. Each number contains a sign bit to indicate if it is positive or negative, a field of bits for the exponent, and a string of digits for the fractional part. Table 11-1 lists the number of bits for the parts of each format.

Table 11-1. *Bits of a floating-point number*

Name	Precision	Sign	Fractional	Exponent	Decimal digits
Single	32 bits	1	24	8	7
Double	64 bits	1	53	11	16

The decimal digits column of Table 11-1 is the approximate number of decimal digits that the format can represent, or the decimal precision.

Normalization and NaNs

In the integers we've seen so far, all combinations of the bits provide a valid unique number. No two different patterns of bits produce the same number; however, this isn't the case in floating-point. First of all, we have the concept of not a number or **NaN**. NaNs are produced from illegal operations like dividing by zero or taking the square root of a negative number. These allow the error to quietly propagate through the calculation without crashing a program. In the IEEE 754 specification, a NaN is represented by an exponent of all 1 bits.

A normalized floating-point number means the first digit in the fractional part is non-zero. A problem with floating-point numbers is that numbers can often be represented in multiple ways. For instance, a fractional part of 0 with either sign bit or any exponent is zero. Consider a representation of 1:

$$1E0 = 0.1E1 = 0.01E2 = 0.001E3$$

All of these represent 1, but we call the first one with no leading zeros the normalized form. The ARM FPU tries to keep floating-point numbers in normal form, but will break this rule for small numbers, where the exponent is already as negative as it can go, then to try to avoid underflow errors, the FPU will give up on normalization to represent numbers a bit smaller than it could otherwise.

Rounding Errors

If we take a number like $\frac{1}{3} = 0.33333...$ and represent it in floating-point, then we only keep 7 or so digits for single precision. This introduces rounding errors. If these are a problem, usually going to double precision solves the problems, but some calculations are prone to magnifying rounding errors, such as subtracting two numbers that have a minute difference.

Note   Floating-point numbers are represented in base 2, so the decimal expansions that lead to repeating patterns of digit is different than that of base 10. It comes as a surprise to many people that 0.1 is a repeating binary fraction: 0.00011001100110011..., meaning that adding dollars and cents in floating-point will introduce rounding error over enough calculations.

For financial calculations, most applications use fixed-point arithmetic that is built on integer arithmetic to avoid rounding errors in addition and subtraction.

Defining Floating-Point Numbers

The GNU Assembler has directives for defining storage for both single- and double-precision floating-point numbers. These are **.single** and **.double**, for example:

```
.single    1.343, 4.343e20, -0.4343, -0.4444e-10
.double    -4.24322322332e-10, 3.141592653589793
```

These directives always take base 10 numbers.

FPU Registers

The ARM FPU has its own set of registers. There are 32 single-precision floating-point registers that are referred to as S0, S1, ..., S31. These same registers can also be referred to as 16 double-precision registers D0, ..., D15. Figure 11-1 shows this configuration of registers.

S0-S31   D0-D15

S0	D0
S1	
S2	D1
S3	
S4	D2
S5	
S6	D3
S7	
...	...
S28	D14
S29	
S30	D15
S31	

Figure 11-1. *The ARM's FPU registers (the single-precision registers on the left overlap the double-precision registers on the right)*

Note   Registers **S0** and **S1** take the same space as **D0**. The registers **S2** and **S3** use the same space as **D1** and so on. The FPU just gives an easier syntax to do either single-precision or double-precision operations. It is up to us to keep things straight and not corrupt our registers by accessing the same space incorrectly.

The Raspberry Pi 2, 3, and 4 have 16 additional double-precision registers **D16–D31** which have no single-precision counterparts.

These are a subset of the registers available for the NEON processor, which we will cover in the next chapter. For now, just a warning that there could be a conflict with the NEON processor if we are using that as well.

Function Call Protocol

In Chapter 6, "Functions and the Stack," we gave the protocol for who saves which registers when calling functions. With these floating-point registers, we have to add them to our protocol:

- **Callee saved**: The function is responsible for saving registers **S16–S31** (**D8–D15**) needed to be saved by a function if the function uses them.

- **Caller saved**: All other registers don't need to be saved by a function, so they must be saved by the caller if they are required to be preserved. This includes **S0–S15** (**D0–D7**) and **D16–D31** if they are present. This also applies to any additional registers for the NEON coprocessor.

Note   The double is also our first 64-bit data type. There is an additional rule about placing these in registers, namely, that when passing a 64-bit item, it can go in registers **R0** and **R1** or **R2** and **R3**. It cannot be placed in **R1** and **R2**. And it can't half be in **R3** and half on the stack. We'll see this later calling printf with a double as a parameter.

Here are our first coprocessor instructions:

- **VPUSH**   {reglist}
- **VPOP**   {reglist}

For example:

```
VPUSH   {S16-S31}
VPOP    {S16-S31}
```

You are only allowed one list in these instructions that you can create with either **S** or **D** registers.

Note   The list can't be longer than 16 **D** registers.

About Building

All the examples in this chapter use the C runtime and are built using **gcc**. This works fine in the same manner as the previous chapters. If we want to use the GNU Assembler directly via the **as** command, then we need to modify our makefile with

```
%.o : %.s
     as -mfpu=vfp $(DEBUGFLGS) $(LSTFLGS) $< -o $@
```

Here we specify that we have an FPU. This will give us vfpv2 which works for all Raspberry Pi. We could use vfpv3 or vfpv4 for newer Pi if we need a newer feature. All the floating-point examples in this book work for any Pi and can just use the generic version of the command-line parameter.

Loading and Saving FPU Registers

In Chapter 5, "Thanks for the Memories," we covered the **LDR** and **STR** instructions to load registers from memory, then store them back to memory. The floating-point coprocessor has similar instructions for its registers:

- VLDR   Fd, [Rn{, #offset}]

- VSTR   Fd, [Rn{, #offset}]

We see that both instructions support pre-indexed addressing offsets. The **Fd** register can be either an **S** or **D** register. For example:

```
LDR   R1, =fp1
VLDR  S4, [R1]
VLDR  S4, [R1, #4]
VSTR  S4, [R1]
VSTR  S4, [R1, #4]
...
.data
fp1:  .single    3.14159
fp2:  .single    4.3341
fp3:  .single 0.0
```

There is also a load multiple instruction and store multiple—these are

- VLDM Rn{!}, Registers

- VSTM Rn{!}, Registers

Registers are a range of registers like for the **VPUSH** and **VPOP** instructions. Only one range is allowed, and it can have at most 16 double registers. These will load the number from the address pointed to by **Rn**, and the number of registers and whether they are single or double will determine how much data is loaded. The optional ! will update the pointer in **Rn** after the operation if present.

Basic Arithmetic

The floating-point processor includes the four basic arithmetic operations, along with a few extensions like our favorite multiply and accumulate. There are some specialty functions like square root and quite a few variations that affect the sign—negate versions of functions.

Each of these functions comes in two versions, a 32-bit version that you put .F32 after and a 64-bit version that you place .F64 after. It would be nice if the Assembler just did this for you based on the registers you provide, but if you leave off the size part, the error message is misleading. Here is a selection of the instructions:

- VADD.F32   {Sd}, Sn, Sm

- VADD.F64   {Dd}, Dn, Dm

- VSUB.F32   {Sd}, Sn, Sm

- VSUB.F64   {Dd}, Dn, Dm

- VMUL.F32   {Sd,} Sn, Sm

- VMUL.F64   {Dd,} Dn, Dm

- VDIV.F32   {Sd}, Sn, Sm

- VDIV.F64   {Dd}, Dn, Dm

- VMLA.F32   Sd, Sn, Sm

- VMLA.F64   Dd, Dn, Dm

- VSQRT.F32   Sd, Sm

- VSQRT.F64   Dd, Dm

If the destination register is in curly brackets {}, it is optional, so we can leave it out. This means we apply the second operand to the first, so to add **S1** to **S4**, we simply write

```
VADD.F32    S4, S1
```

These functions are all fairly simple, so let's move on to an example.

Distance Between Points

If we have two points (x_1, y_1) and (x_2, y_2), then the distance between them is given by the formula

$$d = \text{sqrt}(\ (y_2-y_1)^2 + (x_2-x_1)^2\ )$$

Let's write a function to calculate this for any two single-precision floating-point pair of coordinates. We'll use the C runtime's printf function to print out our results. First the distance function from Listing 11-1, in the file distance.s.

Listing 11-1. Function to calculate the distance between two points

```
@
@ Example function to calculate the distance
@ between two points in single precision
@ floating point.
@
@ Inputs:
@     R0 - pointer to the 4 FP numbers
@             they are x1, y1, x2, y2
@ Outputs:
@     R0 - the length (as single precision FP)

.global distance @ Allow function to be called by others

@
distance:
        @ push all registers to be safe, we don't
        @ really need to push so many.
        push  {R4-R12, LR}
        vpush {S16-S31}

        @ load all 4 numbers at once
        vldm  R0, {S0-S3}
```

```
@ calc s4 = x2 - x1
vsub.f32    S4, S2, S0
@ calc s5 = y2 - y1
vsub.f32    S5, S3, S1
@ calc s4 = S4 * S4 (x2-X1)^2
vmul.f32    S4, S4
@ calc s5 = s5 * s5 (Y2-Y1)^2
vmul.f32    S5, S5
@ calc S4 = S4 + S5
vadd.f32    S4, S5
@ calc sqrt(S4)
vsqrt.f32   S4, S4
@ move result to R0 to be returned
vmov   R0, S4

@ restore what we preserved.
vpop   {S16-S31}
pop    {R4-R12, PC}
```

Now we place the code from Listing 11-2 in main.s, which calls distance three times with three different points and prints out the distance for each one.

Listing 11-2. Main program to call the distance function three times

```
@
@ Main program to test our distance function
@
@ r7 - loop counter
@ r8 - address to current set of points

.global main @ Provide program entry point
```

```
@

        .equ   N, 3   @ Number of points.
main:
        push   {R4-R12, LR}

        ldr   r8, =points @ pointer to current points

        mov   r7, #N      @ number of loop iterations

loop: mov   r0, r8      @ move pointer to parameter 1

        bl    distance   @ call distance function
```

@ need to take the single precision return value
@ and convert it to a double, because the C printf
@ function can only print doubles.

```
        vmov  s2, r0            @ move back to fpu for conversion
        vcvt.f64.f32 d0, s2     @ convert single to double
        vmov  r2, r3, d0        @ return double to r2, r3
        ldr   r0, =prtstr       @ load print string
        bl    printf            @ print the distance

        add   r8, #(4*4)        @ 4 points each 4 bytes
        subs  r7, #1            @ decrement loop counter
        bne   loop              @ loop if more points

        mov   r0, #0            @ return code
        pop   {R4-R12, PC}

.data
points:    .single   0.0, 0.0, 3.0, 4.0
        .single    1.3, 5.4, 3.1, -1.5
        .single 1.323e10, -1.2e-4, 34.55, 5454.234
prtstr:    .asciz "Distance = %f\n"
```

The makefile is in Listing 11-3.

Listing 11-3. Makefile for the distance program

```
distance: distance.s main.s
    gcc -o distance distance.s main.s
```

If we build and run the program, we get

```
pi@raspberrypi:~/asm/Chapter 11 $ make
gcc -g -o distance distance.s main.s
pi@raspberrypi:~/asm/Chapter 11 $ ./distance
Distance = 5.000000
Distance = 7.130919
Distance = 13230000128.000000
pi@raspberrypi:~/asm/Chapter 11 $
```

We constructed the data, so the first set of points comprise a 3-4-5 triangle, which is why we get the exact answer of 5 for the first distance.

The distance function is straightforward. It loads all four numbers in one **VLDM** instruction and then calls the various floating-point arithmetic functions to perform the calculation. We don't really need to save any registers, but I included the **VPUSH** and **VPOP** instructions as an example.

The part of the main routine that loops and calls the distance routine is straightforward. The part that calls printf has a couple of new complexities. The problem is that the C printf routine only has support to print doubles. In C this isn't much of a problem, since you can just cast the argument to force a conversion. In Assembly, we need to convert our single-precision sum to a double-precision number, so we can print it.

To do the conversion, we **VMOV** the sum back to the FPU. **VMOV** is a handy instruction to move values between FPU registers and between FPU and CPU registers. We use the strange looking **VCVT.F64.F32** instruction to convert from single to double precision. This function is the topic of the next section. We then **VMOV** the freshly constructed double back to registers **R2** and **R3**.

When we call printf, the first parameter goes in **R0**. We then hit the rule about having to place the next 64-bit parameter in **R2** and **R3**.

Note   If you are debugging the program with **gdb** and you want to see the contents of the FPU registers at any point, use the "**info all-registers**" command that will exhaustively list all the coprocessor registers. We won't see some of these until the next chapter when we cover the NEON coprocessor.

Floating-Point Conversions

In the last example, we had our first look at the conversion instruction **VCVT**. The FPU supports a variety of versions of this function; not only does it support conversions between single- and double-precision floating-point numbers, but it supports conversions to and from integers. It also supports conversion to fixed-point decimal numbers (integers with an implied decimal). It supports several rounding methods as well. The most used versions of this function are

- VCVT.F64.F32   Dd, Sm

- VCVT.F32.F64   Sd, Dm

These convert single to double precision and double to single precision.

To convert from an integer to a floating-point number, we have

- VCVT.F64.S32   Dd, Sm

- VCVT.F32.S32   Sd, Sm

- VCVT.F64.U32   Dd, Sm

- VCVT.F32.U32   Sd, Sm

where the source can be either a signed or unsigned integer.

To convert from floating-point to integer, we have

- VCVTmode.S32.F64 Sd, Dm
- VCVTmode.S32.F32 Sd, Sm
- VCVTmode.U32.F64 Sd, Dm
- VCVTmode.U32.F32 Sd, Sm

In this direction, we have rounding, so we specify the method of rounding we want with mode. Mode must be one of

- **A**: Round to nearest, ties away from zero

- **N**: Round to nearest, ties to even

- **P**: Round toward plus infinity

- **M**: Round toward minus infinity

There are similar versions for fixed point such as

- VCVT.S32.F64   Dd, Dd, #fbits

where #fbits are the number of bits in the fractional part of the fixed-point number.

Note   This form isn't useful for money computations, for those you should multiply by 100, for two decimal places and convert.

Floating-Point Comparison

The floating-point instructions don't affect the **CPSR**. There is a Floating-Point Status Control Register (**FPSCR**) for floating-point operations. It contains **N**, **Z**, **C**, and **V** flags like the **CPSR**. The meaning of these is mostly the same. There are no S versions of the floating-point instructions;

there is only one instruction that updates these flags, namely, the **VCMP** instruction. Here are some of its forms:

- VCMP.F32   Sd, Sm

- VCMP.F32   Sd, #0

- VCMP.F64   Dd, Dm

- VCMP.F64   Dd, #0

It can compare two single-precision registers or two double-precision registers. It allows one immediate value, namely, zero, so it can compare either a single- or double-precision register to zero.

The **VCMP** instruction updates the **FPSCR**, but all our branch-on-condition instructions branch based on flags in the **CPSR**. This forces an extra step to copy the flags from the **FPSCR** to the **CPSR** before using one of our regular instructions to act on the results of the comparison. There is an instruction specifically for this purpose:

- VMRS   APSR_nzcv, FPSCR

VMRS copies just the **N**, **Z**, **C**, and **V** flags from the **FPCR** to the **CPSR**. After the copy, we can use any instruction that reads these flags.

Testing for equality of floating-point numbers is problematic due to rounding error, numbers are often close but not exactly equal. The solution is to decide on a tolerance, then consider numbers equal if they are within the tolerance from each other. For instance, we might define e = 0.000001 and then consider two registers equal if

$$abs(S1 - S2) < e$$

where abs() is a function to calculate the absolute value.

Example

Let's create a routing to test if two floating-point numbers are equal using this technique. We'll first add 100 cents, then test if they exactly equal $1.00 (spoiler alert, they won't). Then we'll compare the sum using our fpcomp routine that tests them within a supplied tolerance (usually referred to as epsilon).

We start with our floating-point comparison routine, placing the contents of Listing 11-4 into fpcomp.s.

Listing 11-4. Routine to compare two floating-point numbers within a tolerance

```
@
@ Function to compare to floating point numbers
@ the parameters are a pointer to the two numbers
@ and an error epsilon.
@
@ Inputs:
@     R0 - pointer to the 3 FP numbers
@            they are x1, x2, e
@ Outputs:
@     R0 - 1 if they are equal, else 0

.global fpcomp @ Allow function to be called by others

@
fpcomp:
      @ push all registers to be safe, we don't really
      @ need to push so many.
      push  {R4-R12, LR}
      vpush {S16-S31}
```

```
    @ load all 3 numbers at once
    vldm  R0, {S0-S2}

    @ calc s3 = x2 - x1
    vsub.f32    S3, S1, S0
    vabs.f32    S3, S3
    vcmp.f32    S3, S2
    vmrs        APSR_nzcv, FPSCR
    BLE         notequal
    MOV         R0, #1
    B           done

notequal:MOV            R0, #0


    @ restore what we preserved.
done: vpop  {S16-S31}
      pop   {R4-R12, PC}
```

Now the main program maincomp.s contains Listing 11-5.

Listing 11-5. Main program to add up 100 cents and compare to $1.00

```
@
@ Main program to test our distance function
@
@ r7 - loop counter
@ r8 - address to current set of points

.global main @ Provide program starting address to linker

    .equ  N, 100    @ Number of additions.
```

```
main:
        push   {R4-R12, LR}

@ Add up one hundred cents and test
@ if they equal $1.00

        mov    r7, #N     @ number of loop iterations

@ load cents, running sum and real sum to FPU
        ldr    r0, =cent
        vldm   r0, {S0-S2}
loop:
        @ add cent to running sum
        vadd.f32    s1, s0
        subs r7, #1      @ decrement loop counter
        bne  loop        @ loop if more points

        @ compare running sum to real sum
        vcmp.f32 s1, s2
        @ copy FPSCR to CPSR
        vmrs        APSR_nzcv, FPSCR
        @ print if the numbers are equal or not
        beq  equal
        ldr  r0, =notequalstr
        bl   printf
        b    next
equal:  ldr       r0, =equalstr
        bl   printf
next:
@ load pointer to running sum, real sum and epsilon
        ldr  r0, =runsum
        vldm r0, {S0-S2}
@ call comparison function
```

```
        bl     fpcomp          @ call comparison function
@ compare return code to 1 and print if the numbers
@ are equal or not (within epsilon).
        cmp    r0, #1
        beq    equal2
        ldr    r0, =notequalstr
        bl     printf
        b      done
equal2: ldr        r0, =equalstr
        bl     printf

done: mov    r0, #0            @ return code
        pop    {R4-R12, PC}
.data
cent: .single   0.01
runsum: .single 0.0
sum:   .single 1.00
epsilon:.single 0.00001
equalstr:   .asciz "equal\n"
notequalstr: .asciz "not equal\n"
```

The makefile, in Listing 11-6, is as we would expect.

Listing 11-6. The makefile for the floating-point comparison example

```
fpcomp: fpcomp.s maincomp.s
     gcc -o fpcomp fpcomp.s maincomp.s
```

If we build and run the program, we get

```
pi@raspberrypi:~/asm/Chapter 11 $ make
gcc -g -o fpcomp fpcomp.s maincomp.s
pi@raspberrypi:~/asm/Chapter 11 $ ./fpcomp
```

```
not equal
equal
pi@raspberrypi:~/asm/Chapter 11 $
```

The program demonstrates how to compare floating-point numbers and how to copy the results to the **CPSR**, so we can branch based on the result.

If we run the program under **gdb**, we can examine the sum of 100 cents. We see

```
S1 = 0x3f7ffff5
S2 = 0x3f80
```

We haven't talked about the bit format of floating-point numbers, but the first bit is zero indicating positive. The next 8 bits are the exponent, which is 7F; the exponent doesn't use two's complement; instead, it's value is what is there minus 127. In this case, the exponent is 0. As S2 has no more bits, but in normalized form, there is an implied 1 after the exponent, so this then gives the value of 1. Then S1 has a value of 0.99999934, showing the rounding error creeping in, even in the small number of additions we performed.

Then we call our fpcomp routine that determines if the numbers are within the provided tolerance and that considers them equal.

It didn't take that many additions to start introducing rounding errors into our sums. You must be careful when using floating-point for this reason.

Summary

In this chapter, we covered what are floating-point numbers and how they are represented. We covered normalization, NaNs, and rounding error. We showed how to create floating-point numbers in our **.data** section and discussed the bank of single- and double-precision floating-point registers and how they overlap. We covered how to load them into the floating-point registers, perform mathematical operations, and save them back to memory.

We looked at how to convert between different floating-point types, how to compare floating-point numbers, and how to copy the result back to the ARM CPU. We looked at the effect rounding error has on these comparisons.

In Chapter 12, "NEON Coprocessor," we'll look at how to perform multiple floating-point operations in parallel.

CHAPTER 12

NEON Coprocessor

In this chapter, we start performing true parallel computing. The NEON coprocessor shares a lot of functionality with the FPU from Chapter 11, "Floating-Point Operations," but can perform several operations at once. For instance, you can perform four 32-bit floating-point operations with one instruction, and these four operations are performed at the same time. The type of parallel processing performed by the NEON coprocessor is Single Instruction Multiple Data (**SIMD**). In SIMD processing, each single instruction you issue executes in parallel on several multiple data items.

Note   The NEON coprocessor was introduced with the Raspberry Pi 2. It is not available on the Raspberry Pi 1 or the Raspberry Pi Zero. The programs in this chapter only run on a Raspberry Pi 2 or later.

The NEON coprocessor shares the same register file we examined in Chapter 11, "Floating-Point Operations," except that it sees a larger set of registers. All the instructions we learned to load and store the FPU registers are the same here, including **VMOV, VLDR, VSTR, VLDM, VSTM, VPUSH,**

© Stephen Smith 2019
S. Smith, *Raspberry Pi Assembly Language Programming*,
https://doi.org/10.1007/978-1-4842-5287-1_12

and **VPOP**. We'll examine how the NEON registers extend the FPU set of registers and how they are intended to be used with NEON.

We'll examine how to arrange data so we can operate on it in parallel and study the instructions that do so. We'll then update our vector distance and 3x3 matrix multiplication programs to use the NEON processor to see how much of the work we can do in parallel.

The NEON Registers

The NEON coprocessor can operate on the 64-bit registers, which we studied in last chapter, and a set of 16 128-bit registers, that are new for this chapter.

Note   All these registers overlap, so care must be taken if you use a combination. See Figure 12-1 for the overlaps.

The NEON coprocessor cannot reference the 32-bit **S** registers that the FPU commonly uses. Any ARM processor with a NEON coprocessor will have all 32 **D** registers.

S0-S31	D0-D15	Q0-Q15
FPU Only	FPU or Neon	Neon Only
S0	D0	Q0
S1		
S2	D1	
S3		
S4	D2	Q1
S5		
S6	D3	
S7		
...	...	
S28	D14	Q7
S29		
S30	D15	
S31		
	D16	Q8
	D17	
	...	...
	D30	Q15
	D31	

Figure 12-1. *The complete set of coprocessor registers for both the FPU and NEON coprocessors*

Having 128-bit registers does not mean the NEON processor performs 128-bit arithmetic. In fact, the NEON processor can't even perform 64-bit floating-point arithmetic. If you remember in Chapter 10, "Multiply, Divide, and Accumulate," in the second example of matrix multiplication, we optimized the program by using a version of the integer multiply instruction that did the multiply as two independent 16-bit operations at the same time. This was our first encounter with SIMD programming. NEON coprocessor takes that idea to a new level, because in one 128-bit register, we can fit four 32-bit single-precision floating-point numbers. If we multiply two such registers, all four 32-bit numbers are multiplied together at the same time.

The NEON coprocessor can operate on both integers and floating-point numbers. However, the sizes are limited to 8, 16, and 32 bits for integers and 16 and 32 bits for floating-point to perform as many operations as possible at once. The greatest parallelism is obtained using 8-bit integers where 16 operations can happen at once.

The NEON coprocessor can operate on 64-bit **D** or 128-bit **Q** registers; of course, if you use 64-bit **D** registers, you only have half the amount of parallelism.

Table 12-1 shows the number of elements that fit in each register type. Next we'll see how we can perform arithmetic on these elements.

Table 12-1. *Number of elements in each register type by size*

	8-bit elements	**16-bit elements**	**32-bit elements**
64-bit D register	8	4	2
128-bit Q register	16	8	4

Stay in Your Lane

The NEON coprocessor uses the concept of lanes for all its computations. When you choose your data type, the processor considers the register divided into the number of lanes—one lane for each data element. If we work on 32-bit integers and use a 128-bit **Q** register, then the register is considered divided into four lanes, one for each integer.

Figure 12-2 shows how the **Q** registers are divided into four lanes, one for each 32-bit number, then how the arithmetic operation is applied to each lane independently. This way, we accomplish four additions in one instruction, and the NEON coprocessor performs them all at the same time—in parallel.

	Lane 1	Lane 2	Lane 3	Lane 4
Q0	4	3	6	7
Q1	2	5	8	9

VADD.I32   Q2, Q0, Q1

Q2	6	8	14	16

Figure 12-2. *Example of the four lanes involved in doing 32-bit addition on the **Q** registers*

Arithmetic Operations

Figure 12-2 shows our first example of a NEON coprocessor instruction. The two forms of the VADD instruction for NEON are

- VADD.datatype   {Qd}, Qn, Qm

- VADD.datatype   {Dd}, Dn, Dm

Datatype must be one of **I8**, **I16**, **I32**, **I64**, or **F32**.

Note   This is very similar to the VADD instruction we saw for the FPU. The Assembler knows the instruction is for the FPU, if you use **S** registers—NEON doesn't support those or if you use the **F64** type— which NEON doesn't support.

The trick to using NEON is arranging your code so that you keep all the lanes doing useful work.

The NEON coprocessor has a great many arithmetic instructions, and there is a lot of similarities to the FPUs. However, there are quite a few differences, such as NEON does not support division, but it does support reciprocal, so you can do division by taking the reciprocal and multiplying. Strangely, NEON doesn't support square root, but it does support reciprocal square root.

Since the NEON processor supports integer operations, it supports all the logical operations like **and**, **bic**, and **orr**. There are also more comparison operations than the FPU supports.

If you look at the list of NEON instructions, there are a lot of specialty instructions provided to help with specific algorithms. For instance, there is direct support for polynomials over the binary ring to support certain classes of cryptographic algorithms.

We will show how to use a few of the instructions in working examples. This will give you enough knowledge to apply the general principles of operations for the NEON coprocessor, then you can peruse all the instructions in the "ARM Instruction Set Reference Guide."

4D Vector Distance

For our first example, let's expand the distance calculation example from Chapter 11, "Floating-Point Operations," to calculate the distance between two 4D vectors. The formula generalizes to any number of dimensions by just adding the extra squares of the differences for the additional dimensions under the square root.

First distance.s, shown in Listing 12-1, using the NEON coprocessor.

Listing 12-1. Routine to calculate the distance between two 4D
vectors using the NEON coprocessor

```
@
@ Example function to calculate the distance
@ between 4D two points in single precision
@ floating point using the NEON Processor
@
@ Inputs:
@     R0 - pointer to the 8 FP numbers
@           they are (x1, x2, x3, x4),
@                     (y1, y2, y3, y4)
@ Outputs:
@     R0 - the length (as single precision FP)

.global distance @ Allow function to be called by others

@
distance:
        @ push all registers to be safe, we don't
        @ really need to push so many.
        push  {R4-R12, LR}
        vpush {S16-S31}

        @ load all 4 numbers at once
        vldm  R0, {Q2-Q3}

        @ calc q1 = q2 - q3
        vsub.f32   Q1, Q2, Q3
        @ calc Q1 = Q1 * Q1 (xi-yi)^2
        vmul.f32   Q1, Q1, Q1
        @ calc S0 = S0 + S1 + S2 + S3
        vpadd.f32  D0, D2, D3
        vadd.f32   S0, S1
```

```
@ calc sqrt(S4)
vsqrt.f32   S4, S0
@ move result to R0 to be returned
vmov R0, S4

@ restore what we preserved.
vpop    {S16-S31}
pop     {R4-R12, PC}
```

Now main.s, shown in Listing 12-2, to test the routine.

Listing 12-2. The main program to test the 4D distance function

```
@
@ Main program to test our distance function
@
@ r7 - loop counter
@ r8 - address to current set of points

.global main @ Provide program starting

        .equ  N, 3    @ Number of points.

main:
        push  {R4-R12, LR}

        ldr   r8, =points @ pointer to current points

        mov   r7, #N      @ number of loop iterations

loop: mov   r0, r8      @ move pointer to parameter 1 (r0)

        bl    distance   @ call distance function

@ need to take the single precision return value
@ and convert it to a double, because the C printf
@ function can only print doubles.
```

```
    vmov  s2, r0        @ move back to fpu for conversion
    vcvt.f64.f32 d0, s2 @ convert single to double
    vmov  r2, r3, d0    @ return double to r2, r3
    ldr   r0, =prtstr   @ load print string
    bl    printf    @ print the distance

    add   r8, #(8*4) @ 8 elements each 4 bytes
    subs  r7, #1     @ decrement loop counter
    bne   loop       @ loop if more points

    mov   r0, #0     @ return code
    pop   {R4-R12, PC}
.data
points:     .single    0.0, 0.0, 0.0, 0.0, 17.0, 4.0, 2.0, 1.0
       .single    1.3, 5.4, 3.1, -1.5, -2.4, 0.323, 3.4, -0.232
       .single 1.323e10, -1.2e-4, 34.55, 5454.234, 10.9, -3.6,
       4.2, 1.3
prtstr:     .asciz "Distance = %f\n"
```

The makefile is in Listing 12-3.

Listing 12-3. The makefile for the distance program

```
distance: distance.s main.s
    gcc -mfpu=neon-vfpv4 -o distance distance.s main.s
```

If we build and run the program, we see

```
pi@raspberrypi:~/asm/Chapter 12 $ make
gcc -mfpu=neon-vfpv4 -g -o distance distance.s main.s
pi@raspberrypi:~/asm/Chapter 12 $ ./distance
Distance = 17.606817
Distance = 6.415898
Distance = 13230000128.000000
pi@raspberrypi:~/asm/Chapter 12 $
```

We load one vector into **Q2** and the other into **Q3**. Each vector consists of four 32-bit floating-point number, so each one can be placed in a 128-bit **Q** register and treated as four lanes. We then subtract all four components at once using a single **VSUB.F32** instruction. We calculate the squares all at once using a **VMUL.F32** instruction. Both instructions operate on all four lanes in parallel.

We want to add up all the sums which are all in **Q1**. This means all the numbers are in different lanes and we can't add them in parallel. This is a common situation to get into; fortunately, the NEON instruction set does give us some help. It won't add up all the lanes in a register, but it will do pairwise additions in parallel. The instruction

```
vpadd.f32    D0, D2, D3
```

will add the two 32-bit numbers in **D2**, put the sum in half of **D0**, and similarly add the two halves of **D3**, putting the sum in the other half of **D0**. The pairwise instruction only operates on **D** registers and only does two 32-bit additions at a time. The numbers to add are all in **Q1**, which is why we select **D2** and **D3** for the instruction, since these are the registers that overlap **Q1**; see Figure 12-1.

This accomplishes two of the additions we need; we then perform the third using the regular FPU **VADD.F32** instruction, noting that **S0** and **S1** overlap **D0**.

Once the numbers are added, we use the FPU's square root instruction to calculate the final distance.

Figure 12-3 shows how these operations flow through the lanes in our registers.

Lane 1	Lane 2	Lane 3	Lane 4
Q2 x1	x2	x3	x4
Q3 y1	y2	y3	y4

vsub.f32 Q1, Q2, Q3

Q1 x1-y1	x2-y2	x3-y3	x4-y4

vmul.f32 Q1, Q1, Q1

Q1=D2, D3 (x1-y1)^2	(x2-y2)^2	(x3-y3)^2	(x4-y4)^2

vpadd.f32 D0, D2, D3

D0=S0, S1 (x1-y1)^2+(x2-y2)^2	(x3-y3)^2+(x4-y4)^2

vadd.f32 S0, S1

S0 (x1-y1)^2+(x2-y2)^2+(x3-y3)^2+(x4-y4)^2

vsqrt.f32 S4, S0

S4 SQRT((x1-y1)^2+(x2-y2)^2+(x3-y3)^2+(x4-y4)^2)

Figure 12-3. *Flow of the calculations through the registers showing the lanes*

This shows a nice feature of having the NEON and FPU sharing registers, in that it allows us to intermix FPU and NEON instructions without needing to move data around.

The only change to the main program is to make the vectors 4D and adjust the loop to use the new vector size.

Notice that the makefile includes the gcc option:

```
-mfpu=neon-vfpv4
```

This tells the GNU C compiler or GNU Assembler that you have a NEON coprocessor and want to generate code for it. If we don't include this, we will get a lot of errors about instructions not being supported on our processor. This is because by default the tools target all Raspberry Pi models, and what we are doing won't work on the Pi 1 or Zero.

3x3 Matrix Multiplication

Let's take the 3x3 matrix multiplication example program from Chapter 10, "Multiply, Divide, and Accumulate," and optimize it use the parallel processing abilities of the NEON coprocessor.

The NEON coprocessor does have a dot product function **VSDOT**, but sadly it only operates on 8-bit integers. This isn't suitable for most matrices, so we won't use it. As we saw in the last example, adding within one register is a problem, and similarly there are problems with just doing multiply with accumulates. The recommended solution is to reverse two of our loops from the previous program. This way, we do the multiply with accumulates as separate instructions, but we do it on three vectors at a time. The result is we eliminate one of our loops from the previous program and achieve some level of parallel operation.

The trick is to notice that one 3x3 matrix multiplication is really three matrices by vector calculations, namely

- Ccol1 = A * Bcol1

- Ccol2 = A * Bcol2

- Ccol3 = A * Bcol3

If we look at one of these matrix times a vector for example

$$\begin{vmatrix} a & b & c \\ d & e & f \\ g & h & i \end{vmatrix} \begin{vmatrix} x \\ y \\ z \end{vmatrix}$$

we see the calculation is

$$\begin{vmatrix} ax + by + cz \\ dx + ey + fz \\ gx + hy + iz \end{vmatrix}$$

If we put a, d, and g in a register in separate lanes and b, e, and h in another register and c, f, and i in a third register in the matching lanes, then we can calculate a column in the results matrix, as shown in Figure 12-4.

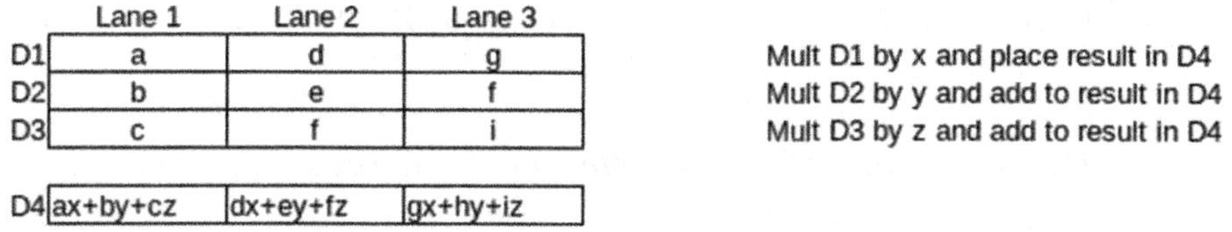

	Lane 1	Lane 2	Lane 3
D1	a	d	g
D2	b	e	f
D3	c	f	i

	Lane 1	Lane 2	Lane 3
D4	ax+by+cz	dx+ey+fz	gx+hy+iz

Mult D1 by x and place result in D4
Mult D2 by y and add to result in D4
Mult D3 by z and add to result in D4

Figure 12-4. *Showing how the calculations flow through the lanes*

This is the recommended algorithm for matrix multiplication on the NEON coprocessor. We will use short integers like we did before, so we can fit a column of any of our matrices in a **D** register.

What we did earlier is for one column of the results matrix; we then need to do this for all the columns. We will place this logic in a macro, so we can repeat the calculation three times. Since the goal is as fast matrix multiplication as possible, it is worth removing the loops, since it saves extra logic. This makes the program look much simpler.

Listing 12-4 is the code for our NEON-enabled matrix multiplication.

Listing 12-4. NEON-enabled 3x3 matrix multiplication example

```
@
@ Multiply 2 3x3 integer matrices
@ Uses the NEON Coprocessor to do
@ some operations in parallel.
@
@ Registers:
@       D0 - first column of matrix A
@       D1 - second column of matrix A
@       D2 - third column of matrix A
@       D3 - first column of matrix B
@       D4 - second column of matrix B
@       D5 - third column of matrix B
@       D6 - first column of matrix C
@       D7 - second column of matrix C
@       D8 - third column of matrix C
```

```
.global main @ Provide program starting address

main:
      push    {R4-R12, LR}   @ Save required regs

@ load matrix A into NEON registers D0, D1, D2
      LDR     R0, =A         @ Address of A
      VLDM    R0, {D0-D2}    @ bulk load the three columns

@ load matrix B into NEON registers D3, D4, D5
      LDR     R0, =B         @ Address of B
      VLDM    R0, {D3-D5}    @ bulk load the three columns

.MACRO mulcol ccol bcol
      VMUL.I16    \ccol, D0, \bcol[0]
      VMLA.I16    \ccol, D1, \bcol[1]
      VMLA.I16    \ccol, D2, \bcol[2]
.ENDM

      mulcol     D6, D3    @ process first column
      mulcol     D7, D4    @ process second column
      mulcol     D8, D5    @ process third column

      LDR    R1, =C        @ Address of C
      VSTM   R1, {D6-D8}   @ store the three columns

@ Print out matrix C
@ Loop through 3 rows printing 3 cols each time.
      MOV    R5, #3         @ Print 3 rows
      LDR    R11, =C        @ Addr of results matrix
printloop:

      LDR    R0, =prtstr    @ printf format string
@ print transpose so matrix is in
@ usual row column order.
@ first ldrh post-indexes by 2 for next row
```

```
@ so second ldrh adds 6, so is ahead
@ by 2+6=8=row size
@ similarly for third ldh ahead
@ by 2+14=16 = 2 x row size
        LDRH    R1, [R11], #2      @ first element in current row
        LDRH    R2, [R11,#6]       @ second element in current row
        LDRH    R3, [R11,#14]      @ third element in current row
        BL      printf             @ Call printf
        SUBS    R5, #1             @ Dec loop counter
        BNE     printloop          @ If not zero loop

        mov     r0, #0             @ return code
        pop     {R4-R12, PC}       @ Restore regs and return

.data
@ First matrix in column major order
A:      .short      1, 4, 7, 0
        .short      2, 5, 8, 0
        .short      3, 6, 9, 0
@ Second matrix in column major order
B:      .short      9, 6, 3, 0
        .short      8, 5, 2, 0
        .short      7, 4, 1, 0
@ Results matrix in column major order
C:      .fill 12, 2, 0

prtstr: .asciz   "%3d  %3d  %3d\n"
```

We store both matrices in column major order, and the C matrix is produced in column major order. This is to make setting up the calculations easier, since everything is aligned properly to bulk load into our NEON registers. We changed the print loop, so that it prints out the results matrix in our usual row order form, basically doing a matrix transpose as it loops through the C matrix.

In the macro, we do the scalar multiplication

```
VMUL.I16   \ccol, D0, \bcol[0]
```

which translates to something like

```
VMUL.I16   D6, D0, D3[0]
```

We don't have access to the S registers to access a single floating-point number, but in many instructions, we can refer to a given lane. Here the **D3[0]** syntax is like an array index into **D3** or can be thought of as **D3** lane 0—counting lanes from zero. When we multiply a register with lanes by a single lane, then **VMUL** will perform a scalar multiplication of the single number by each lane in the first operand—**D3** in this case.

Summary

This chapter was a quick overview of how the NEON coprocessor works and how to write programs for it. We covered how NEON uses lanes to perform parallel computations and a selection of the instructions available for computations. We gave two examples, one to calculate the distance between two 4D vectors and one to perform 3x3 matrix multiplication to demonstrate how you can easily harness the power of the NEON coprocessor.

In Chapter 13, "Conditional Instructions and Optimizing Code," we'll look at what the four condition code bits in each instruction do and how to take advantage of them.

CHAPTER 13

Conditional Instructions and Optimizing Code

In Chapter 4, "Controlling Program Flow," we learned how to branch code conditionally based on flags in the **CPSR**. In this chapter, we will look at how this can be generalized to all instructions.

In Chapter 1, "Getting Started," we looked at the ARM Instruction Format and noted that nearly every instruction contains a 4-bit condition code. So far, we've ignored the purpose of these bits; now we'll look at how to use them and why we want to execute instructions conditionally to reduce the number of branch instructions. We want to minimize the number of branch instructions, because they are expensive to execute, since they interrupt the execution pipeline.

To demonstrate we'll apply conditional instructions to our uppercase program that we talked about in Chapter 4, "Controlling Program Flow," and Chapter 6, "Functions and the Stack." We'll optimize its range comparison to use a single conditional instruction, then look at some other code optimizations we can apply.

© Stephen Smith 2019
S. Smith, *Raspberry Pi Assembly Language Programming*,
https://doi.org/10.1007/978-1-4842-5287-1_13

Reasons Not to Use Conditional Instructions

Before we get into how and why to add condition codes to all our instructions, I want to note a couple of reasons why these are becoming obsolete and not needed today as much as they were in the earlier days of the ARM processor, such as when porting your Assembly code to 64 bits, and the improved pipeline.

No Conditional Instructions in 64 Bits

When the ARM engineers designed the 64-bit instruction set, they kept the instruction length to 32 bits. However, they wanted to double the number of registers and increase the number of opcodes. To do this, they took the 4 bits dedicated to conditional instructions and distributed them for these other purposes.

Hence, in the ARM's 64-bit mode, there are only a handful of branch type instructions that can conditionally execute. If you plan to port your Assembly code to 64 bits one day, it will be a lot less work if it isn't full of conditional instructions.

Improved Pipeline

In this chapter, we promote conditional instructions as a solution to branches causing the instruction pipeline to stall and cause performance to suffer. Won't this cause 64-bit code to be much slower than 32-bit code? The ARM engineers mitigated this problem by making the instruction pipeline more sophisticated. They created a table that keeps a record of where recent branch instructions go, with most loops branching back to the loop 90% of the time and advancing 10%. Knowing this, the instruction pipeline can make an informed guess and continue working as if the branch will take place. This way, the branch will only interrupt the pipeline when it takes its less travelled route. This is called **branch prediction**. There are other improvements to caching and the pipeline to generally speed things up.

The key takeaway is that the conditional instructions presented in this chapter will help code running on older Raspberry Pis more than newer ones.

About Conditional Code

We can add any condition code from Chapter 4's Table 4-1 to nearly any Assembly instruction. The only exceptions include setting a breakpoint, halting the processor and a couple of other instructions. When the condition is not met, then the instruction performs a no operation and executes the next instruction, for example:

```
ADDEQ      R2, R3, R4
```

only performs the addition if the **Z** flag is set. If the **Z** flag isn't set, then this instruction is skipped, but it still takes one instruction cycle.

We can combine this with the S modifier

```
ADDEQS     R2, R3, R4
```

in which case the **CPSR** is updated if the **ADD** instruction is executed. The **S** must come last, or you will confuse the Assembler.

Optimizing the Uppercase Routine

Our original uppercase routine implements the pseudo-code

```
IF (R5 >= 'a') AND (R5 <= 'z') THEN
    R5 = R5 - ('a'-'A')
END IF
```

with the following Assembly code:

```
@ If R5 > 'z' then goto cont
    CMP   R5, #'z'        @ is letter > 'z'?
    BGT   cont
@ Else if R5 < 'a' then goto end if
    CMP   R5, #'a'
    BLT   cont            @ goto to end if
@ if we got here then the letter is lower-case, so convert it.
    SUB   R5, #('a'-'A')
cont: @ end if
```

This code implements the reverse logic of branching around the **SUB** instruction if **R5** < 'a' or **R5** > 'z'. This was fine for a chapter teaching branch instructions, since it demonstrated two of them. In this chapter, we look at eliminating branches entirely, so let's see how we can improve this code one step at a time.

Simplifying the Range Comparison

A common way to simplify range comparisons is to shift the range, so we don't need a lower comparison. If we subtract 'a' from everything, then our pseudo-code becomes

```
R5 = R5 - 'a'
IF (R5 >= 0) AND R5 <= ('z'-'a') THEN
        R5 = R5 + 'A'
END IF
```

If we treat **R5** as an unsigned integer, then the first comparison does nothing, since all unsigned integers are greater than 0. In this case, we simplified our range from two comparisons to one comparison that is **R5** <= ('z'-'a').

This leads us to the first improved version of our upper.s file. This new upper.s is shown in Listing 13-1.

Listing 13-1. Uppercase routine with simplified range comparison

```
@
@ Assembler program to convert a string to
@ all uppercase.
@
@ R1 - address of output string
@ R0 - address of input string
@ R4 - original output string for length calc.
@ R5 - current character being processed
@ R6 - minus 'a' to compare < 26.
@

.global toupper   @ Allow other files to call this routine

toupper:    PUSH  {R4-R6}   @ Save the registers we use.
       MOV   R4, R1
@ The loop is until byte pointed to by R1 is non-zero
loop: LDRB  R5, [R0], #1   @ load character and incr
@ Want to know if 'a' <= R5 <= 'z'
@ First subtract 'a'
       SUB   R6, R5, #'a'
@ Now want to know if R6 <= 25
       CMP   R6, #25        @ chars are 0-25 after shift
       BHI   cont
@ if we got here then the letter is lower case, so convert it.
       SUB   R5, #('a'-'A')
cont: @ end if
       STRB  R5, [R1], #1 @ store character to output str
       CMP   R5, #0     @ stop on hitting a null
```

```
BNE    loop        @ loop if character isn't null
SUB    R0, R1, R4  @ get the length by subtracting the
                     pointers
POP    {R4-R6}     @ Restore the register we use.
BX     LR          @ Return to caller
```

All the examples in this chapter use the same main.s from Listing 6-3, except the third which skips needing a main.s. Listing 13-2 is a makefile for all the code in this chapter. Comment out any programs that you haven't gotten to yet, or you will get a compile error.

Listing 13-2. Makefile for the uppercase routine version in this chapter

```
UPPEROBJS = main.o upper.o
UPPER2OBJS = main.o upper2.o
UPPER3OBJS = upper3.o
UPPER4OBJS = main.o upper4.o

all: upper upper2 upper3 upper4

%.o : %.s
        as -mfpu=neon-vfpv4 $(DEBUGFLGS) $(LSTFLGS) $< -o $@

upper: $(UPPEROBJS)
        ld -o upper $(UPPEROBJS)

upper2: $(UPPER2OBJS)
        ld -o upper2 $(UPPER2OBJS)

upper3: $(UPPER3OBJS)
        ld -o upper3 $(UPPER3OBJS)

upper4: $(UPPER4OBJS)
        ld -o upper4 $(UPPER4OBJS)
```

This is an improvement and a great optimization to use when you need range comparisons. Let's use a conditional instruction to remove another branch.

Using a Conditional Instruction

The obvious instruction to make conditional is the subtraction that does the conversion to uppercase. Listing 13-3 is the upper2.s version of the routine.

Listing 13-3. Uppercase routine using a conditional **SUBLS** instruction

```
@
@ Assembler program to convert a string to
@ all uppercase.
@
@ R1 - address of output string
@ R0 - address of input string
@ R4 - original output string for length calc.
@ R5 - current character being processed
@ R6 - minus 'a' to compare < 26.
@

.global toupper     @ Allow other files to call this routine

toupper:    PUSH   {R4-R6}     @ Save the registers
      MOV   R4, R1
@ The loop is until byte pointed to by R1 is non-zero
loop: LDRB R5, [R0], #1    @ load character and incr
@ Want to know if 'a' <= R5 <= 'z'
@ First subtract 'a'
      SUB   R6, R5, #'a'
@ Now want to know if R6 <= 25
       CMP   R6, #25     @ chars are 0-25 after shift
```

255

```
@ if we got here then the letter is lowercase, so convert it.
      SUBLS R5, #('a'-'A')
      STRB  R5, [R1], #1  @ store character
      CMP   R5, #0     @ stop on hitting a null char
      BNE   loop       @ loop if character isn't null
      SUB   R0, R1, R4 @ get the length by subtracting the
                          pointers
      POP   {R4-R6}          @ Restore the registers
      BX    LR         @ Return to caller
```

We use the **SUBLS** instruction here. **LS** is for lower or same which is the suffix for unsigned <=. The **SUBLS** instruction will only do the subtraction if **R5** is less than or equal to 25 which is where we shifted 'z'. In Listing 13-3, the only branch instruction is for the loop.

Note   If the SUBLS instruction doesn't do anything, it still takes a cycle to execute. This means it only makes sense to use this instead of a branch, if we place the condition on up to three instructions. Otherwise, branching around the code is faster.

Restricting the Problem Domain

When optimizing code, the best optimizations arise from restricting the problem domain. If we are only dealing with alphabetic characters, we can eliminate the range comparison entirely. If we look at Appendix E, "ASCII Character Set," we notice that the only difference between upper- and lowercase letters is that lowercase letters have the 0x20 bit set, whereas uppercase letters do not. This means we can convert a lowercase letter to uppercase by performing a Bit Clear (**BIC**) operation on that bit. If we do this to special characters, it will mess up quite a few of them.

Often in computing, we want our code to be case insensitive, meaning that you can enter any combination of case. The Assembler does this, so it doesn't care if we enter MOV or mov. Similarly, many computer languages are case insensitive, so you can enter variable names in any combination of upper- and lowercase and it means the same thing. AI algorithms that process text always convert them into a standard form, usually throwing away all punctuation and converting them to all one case. Forcing this standardization saves a lot of extra processing later on.

Let's look at an implementation of this for our code—Listing 13-4 goes in upper3.s.

Listing 13-4. Uppercase routine as a macro, using BIC for alphabetic characters only

```
@
@ Assembler program to convert a string to
@ all uppercase. Assumes only alphabetic
@ characters. Uses bit clear blindly without
@ checking if character is alphabetic or not.
@
@ R0 - address of input string
@ R1 - address of output string
@ R2 - original output string for length calc.
@ R3 - current character being processed
@

.global _start     @ Provide program starting address

.MACRO toupper inputstr, outputstr
        LDR   R0, =\inputstr      @ start of input string
        LDR   R1, =\outputstr     @ addr of output string
        MOV   R2, R1
```

```
@ The loop is until byte pointed to by R1 is non-zero
loop: LDRB  R3, [R0], #1    @ load character and incr
      BIC   R3, #0x20       @ kill the lower-case bit
      STRB  R3, [R1], #1    @ store character
      CMP   R3, #0          @ stop on hitting a null
      BNE   loop       @ loop if character isn't null
      SUB   R0, R1, R2 @ get the length by subtracting
.ENDM

_start:
      toupper    instr, outstr

@ Set up the parameters to print our hex number
@ and then call Linux to do it.
      MOV   R2,R0 @ return code is the string len

      MOV   R0, #1           @ 1 = StdOut
      LDR   R1, =outstr @ string to print
      MOV   R7, #4           @ linux write system call
      SVC   0         @ Call linux to print the string

@ Set up the parameters to exit the program
@ and then call Linux to do it.
      MOV   R0, #0     @ Use 0 return code
      MOV   R7, #1     @ command code 1 terminates
      SVC   0         @ Call linux to terminate

.data
instr:  .asciz  "ThisIsRatherALargeVariableNameAaZz@[`{\n"
      .align 4
outstr:     .fill 255, 1, 0
```

This file contains the _start entry point and print Linux calls, so no main.s is needed. Here is the output of building and running this version:

```
pi@raspberrypi:~/asm/Chapter 13 $ make
as -mfpu=neon-vfpv4    upper3.s -o upper3.o
ld -o upper3 upper3.o
pi@raspberrypi:~/asm/Chapter 13 $ ./upper3
THISISRATHERALARGEVARIABLENAMEAAZZ@[@[
pi@raspberrypi:~/asm/Chapter 13 $
```

There are a few special characters at the end of the string to show how some are converted correctly and some aren't.

Besides using this **BIC** instruction to eliminate all conditional processing, we implement the toupper routine as a macro to eliminate the overhead of calling a function. We change the register usage, so we only use the first four registers in the macro, so we don't need to save any registers around the call.

This is a quick and dirty conversion routine, showing how we can save instructions if we narrow our problem domain, in this case, to just working on alphabetic characters rather than all ASCII characters.

Using Parallelism with SIMD

In Chapter 12, "NEON Coprocessor," we looked at performing operations in parallel and mentioned that this coprocessor can process characters, as well as integers and floats. Let's see if we can use NEON instructions to process 16 characters at a time—16 characters fit in a **Q** register.

First let's look at the code in upper4.s shown in Listing 13-5.

Note   This code won't run until we make an adjustment to main.s at the end of this section in Listing 13-6.

Listing 13-5. Uppercase routine using the NEON coprocessor

```
@
@ Assembler program to convert a string to
@ all uppercase.
@
@ R0 - address of input string
@ R1 - address of output string
@ Q0 - 8 characters to be processed
@ Q1 - contains all a's for comparison
@ Q2 - result of comparison with 'a's
@ Q3 - all 25's for comp
@ Q8 - spaces for bic operation

.global toupper     @ Allow other files to call

      .EQU  N, 4
toupper:
      LDR   R3, =aaas
      VLDM    R3, {Q1} @ Load Q1 with all a's
      LDR   R3, =endch
      VLDM  R3, {Q3}    @ Load Q3 with all 25's
      LDR   R3, =spaces
      VLDM  R3, {Q8}    @ Load Q8 with all spaces
      MOV   R3, #N
@ The loop is until byte pointed to by R1 is non-zero
loop: VLDM R0!, {Q0}    @ load 16 characters and incr
      VSUB.U8    Q2, Q0, Q1 @ Subtract 'a's
      VCLE.U8    Q2, Q2, Q3 @ compare chars to 25's
      VAND.U8    Q2, Q2, Q8 @ and result with spaces
      VBIC.U8    Q0, Q0, Q2 @ kill the bit that makes it lower
                             case
      VSTM R1!, {Q0} @ store character to output str
```

```
        SUBS  R3, #1      @ decrement loop counter and set flags
        BNE   loop        @ loop if character isn't null
        MOV   R0, #(N*16)    @ Set the length
        BX    LR          @ Return to caller
.data
aaas:    .fill 16, 1, 'a'   @ 16 a's
endch:   .fill 16, 1, 25  @ after shift chars are 0-25
spaces: .fill 16, 1, 0x20  @ spaces for bic
.align 4
```

This routine uses the **Q** registers to process 16 characters at a time. There are more instructions than some of our previous routines, but the parallelism makes it worthwhile. We start by loading our constants into registers. You can't use immediate constants with NEON instructions, so these must be in registers. Additionally, they need to be duplicated 16 times, so there is one for each of our 16 lanes.

We then load 16 characters to process into **Q0** with a **VLDM** instruction.

Note   The **!** performs a writeback to move the pointer to the next set of characters for when we loop.

Figure 13-1 shows the processing through the NEON coprocessor for the first four lanes. We use VBIC, but we could have just as easily used **VSUB** to do the conversion. We test that the character is lowercase alphabetic before doing this, so it is correct for all ASCII characters.

Lane	1	2	3	4	
Q0	T	h	i	s	
Q1	a	a	a	a	

VSUB.U8   Q2, Q0, Q1

	1	2	3	4	
Q2	T-a	h-a	i-a	s-a	
Q3	25	25	25	25	'z' - 'a'

VCLE.U8   Q2, Q2, Q3

	1	2	3	4	
Q2	0	0xff	0xff	0xff	
Q8	0x20	0x20	0x20	0x20	Spaces

VAND.U8   Q2, Q2,Q8

	1	2	3	4
Q2	0	0x20	0x20	0x20

VBIC.U8   Q0, Q0, Q2

	1	2	3	4
Q0	T	H	I	S

Figure 13-1. *The parallel processing steps to convert to uppercase*

The **VCLE** is our first encounter with a NEON comparison instruction. It compares all 16 lanes at once. It places all 1s in the destination lane if the comparison is true, otherwise 0. All 1s is 0xFF hex. This is convenient since we can **VAND** it with a register full of 0x20s. Any lanes that don't have a lowercase alphabetic character will result in zero.

This means lanes with 0, there are no bits for **VBIC** to clear. Then the lanes that still have 0x20 will clear that 1 bit doing the conversion.

For this routine to work, we need to make a change to main.s. We need to add a ".**align 4**" between the two strings. This is because we can only load or store NEON data to word aligned memory locations. If we don't do this, we will get a "Bus Error" when the program runs. The updated code is shown in Listing 13-6.

Listing 13-6. Changes required in main.s

```
instr:  .asciz  "This is our Test String that we will convert.
            AaZz@[`{\n"
     .align 4
outstr:     .fill 255, 1, 0
```

I also added edge case characters to the end of the string; this ensures we don't have any off-by-one errors in our code.

This code runs fine, but that is partly because of the way our .data section is set up. Notice there is no test for the string NULL terminator. This routine just converts fixed length strings, and we have set the fixed length at 4*16 by making the loop perform four iterations. The NEON processor has no easy way to detect a NULL terminator. If we looped through the characters outside of the NEON processor to look for the NULL, we do nearly as much work as our last toupper routine. If we are going to do string processing in the NEON coprocessor, here are some notes:

- Don't use NULL-terminated strings. Use a length field followed by the string. Or use fixed length strings, for instance, every string is just 256 characters and contains spaces beyond the last character.

- Pad all strings so they use data storage in multiples of 16. This way you won't ever have to worry about NEON processing past the end of your buffer.

- Make sure all the strings are word aligned.

Summary

In this chapter, we looked at how to add condition codes to any instruction and why and when we should do this. We noted that this isn't supported in the 64-bit ARM instruction set and that newer ARM processor pipelines make this technique less useful than it was in the early days of ARM.

We then performed several optimizations on our toupper function. We looked at simplifying range comparisons, using conditional instructions, bit manipulations, and finally the NEON coprocessor.

In Chapter 14, "Reading and Understanding Code," we will examine how the C compiler generates code and talk about understanding compiled programs.

CHAPTER 14

Reading and Understanding Code

We've now learned quite a bit of ARM 32-bit Assembly language; one of the things we can do is read another programmer's code. Reading other programmer's code is a great way to add to our toolkit of tips and tricks and improve our own coding. We'll review some places where you can find Assembly source code for the ARM32. Then we'll look at how the GNU C compiler writes Assembly code and how we can analyze it. We'll look at the NSA's Ghidra hacking tool that can convert Assembly code back into C code—at least approximately.

We'll use our uppercase program to see how the C compiler writes Assembly code and then examine how Ghidra can take that code and reconstitute the C code. We'll also look at how the C compiler deals with the lack of an integer division instruction in older ARM processors.

Raspbian and GCC

One of the many nice things about working with the Raspberry Pi and GNU Compiler Collection is that they are open source. That means you can browse through the source code and peruse the Assembly parts contained there.

© Stephen Smith 2019
S. Smith, *Raspberry Pi Assembly Language Programming*,
https://doi.org/10.1007/978-1-4842-5287-1_14

They are available in the following Github repositories:

- **Raspbian Linux kernel**: https://github.com/
  raspberrypi/linux

- **GCC source code**: https://github.com/gcc-mirror/gcc

Clicking the "Clone or download" button and choosing "Download ZIP" is the easiest way to obtain it. Within all this source code, a couple of good folders to peruse ARM 32-bit Assembly source code are

- Raspbian Linux kernel:

  - arch/arm/common

  - arch/arm/kernel

  - arch/arm/crypto

- GCC:

  - libgcc/config/arm

Note   The arch/arm/crypto has several cryptographic routines implemented on the NEON coprocessor.

The Assembly source code for these are in ∗.S files (note the uppercase S). Raspbian is based on Debian Linux. Both Debian Linux and GCC support dozens of processor architectures, so when looking for Assembly source code, make sure you look for ∗.S files in an arm folder. If you are interested, you could compare the ARM 32-bit Assembly files to the files for other processors.

The source code for these use both GNU Assembler directives like .**MACRO** and C preprocessor directives like **#define** and **#ifdef**. If you are going to read this source code, it helps to brush up on the C preprocessor.

The GNU compiler supports older ARM processors than contained in any Raspberry Pi, as well as configurations of the ARM processor that the Raspberry foundation never used. For instance, there is a library to implement IEEE 754 floating-point for ARM processors without an FPU. However, all Raspberry Pis do have an FPU, so this isn't used.

Division Revisited

In Chapter 10, "Multiply, Divide, and Accumulate," we assumed we had a newer Raspberry Pi and used the newer ARM processor's **SDIV** or **UDIV** instructions. We just left a comment that if you wanted to divide on older Pi, then use the FPU or roll your own. We never covered how to roll our own. Another approach is to see what the C compiler does. Consider Listing 14-1, the simple C program.

Listing 14-1. Simple C program that divides two numbers

```
#include <stdio.h>

int main()
{
        int x = 100;
        int y = 25;
        int z;

        z = x / y;
        printf("%d / %d = %d\n", x, y, z);

        return(0);
}
```

We can compile this with

```
gcc -o div div.c
```

Note   We can't use any of the -O flag options, because any optimization will remove the expression and the compiler will just plug 4 in for z.

We can look at the generated Assembly code with

`objdump -d div`

Because we didn't compile with an -O option, there is a lot of code, but in the middle of the main routine, we see

```
10454:  e51b100c  ldr   r1, [fp, #-12]
10458:  e51b0008  ldr   r0, [fp, #-8]
1045c:  eb00000b  bl    10490 <__divsi3>
10460:  e1a03000  mov   r3, r0
```

which sets up and calls a division routine called **_divsi3**. The Assembly for the _divsi3 routine is also present in the output from objdump. It is very long and contains code like

```
104e0:  e1530f81  cmp   r3, r1, lsl #31
104e4:  e0a00000  adc   r0, r0, r0
104e8:  20433f81  subcs r3, r3, r1, lsl #31
```

and repeated 32 times. What's going on here? Since we can download the source code for **gcc** and all its libraries, we can look at the source code. If we search for the definition of _divsi3, we will find it in libgcc/config/arm/lib1funcs.S. This source code is confusing, because it contains versions of its routines for different generations of ARM, as well as having versions that use thumb code. We'll cover thumb code in Chapter 15, "Thumb Code," but until then we can ignore those parts.

Listing 14-2 is the main part of the division routine.

Listing 14-2. Main part of the gcclib division routine

```
        ARM_FUNC_START divsi3
        ARM_FUNC_ALIAS aeabi_idiv divsi3

        cmp    r1, #0
        beq    LSYM(Ldiv0)
LSYM(divsi3_skip_div0_test):
        eor    ip, r0, r1  @ save the sign of the result.
        do_it mi
        rsbmi r1, r1, #0   @ loops below use unsigned.
        subs   r2, r1, #1  @ division by 1 or -1 ?
        beq    10f
        movs   r3, r0
        do_it mi
        rsbmi r3, r0, #0              @ positive dividend value
        cmp    r3, r1
        bls    11f
        tst    r1, r2               @ divisor is power of 2?
        beq    12f

        ARM_DIV_BODY r3, r1, r0, r2

        cmp    ip, #0
        do_it mi
        rsbmi r0, r0, #0
        RET
```

The routine starts by checking for division by 0, which is an error. It then looks for the easy cases of division by 1 or –1, then the other cases of dividing by a power of 2. It also saves the sign bits so the answer can be set properly at the end.

There are a lot of macros used in this code. Listing 14-3 is the one that generates the actual division is ARM_DIV_BODY.

Listing 14-3. Main body of the division routine

```
.macro ARM_DIV_BODY dividend, divisor, result, curbit
     clz   \curbit, \dividend
     clz   \result, \divisor
     sub   \curbit, \result, \curbit
     rsbs  \curbit, \curbit, #31
     addne \curbit, \curbit, \curbit, lsl #1
     mov   \result, #0
     addne pc, pc, \curbit, lsl #2
     nop
     .set  shift, 32
     .rept 32
     .set  shift, shift - 1
     cmp   \dividend, \divisor, lsl #shift
     adc   \result, \result, \result
     subcs \dividend, \dividend, \divisor, lsl #shift
     .endr
.endm
```

Within this macro is

```
.set  shift, 32
     .rept 32
     .set  shift, shift - 1
     cmp   \dividend, \divisor, lsl #shift
     adc   \result, \result, \result
     subcs \dividend, \dividend, \divisor, lsl #shift
     .endr
```

which generates the repetitive code we see. This is a form of optimization
called **loop unrolling**, where if a loop executes a fixed number of times,
we just duplicate the code that many times. This saves us an expensive
branch instruction, as well as the arithmetic calculating the loop index.

Division will be used often enough that we want the code as fast as possible, and we can spare the extra code space to achieve this.

The algorithm for this division is basically the same long division algorithm you learned in elementary school. It is just a bit simpler in binary since there can only be two answers at each step, whether to put a 1 in the result or not.

Note   If we included the -march="armv8-a" compiler switch, then the compiler would use a **SDIV** instruction instead of this function call. GCC will use advanced ARM features if it knows they are available.

Sadly, the Assembly source code contained in **gcc** and Linux isn't always as well documented as we would like, but it does give us quite a bit of source code to ponder and learn from.

You might want to look at ieee754-sf.S and ieee754-df.S in the same folder as lib1funcs.S, gcc/libgcc/config/arm. These are the implementations of floating-point in single and double precision for ARM processors that don't have an FPU. It's interesting to see all the work the FPU does for us.

Code Created by GCC

In the last section, we looked at some code generated by **gcc** to see how it handles the lack of a **SDIV** instruction. Let's look at how **gcc** would write our code. We'll code our uppercase routine in C and compare the generated code to what we wrote. For this example, we want **gcc** to do as good a job as possible, so we will use the -O3 option to get maximal optimization.

We create upper.c from Listing 14-4.

Listing 14-4. C implementation of our mytoupper routine

```c
#include <stdio.h>

int mytoupper(char *instr, char *outstr)
{
    char cur;
    char *orig_outstr = outstr;

    do
    {
        cur = *instr;
        if ((cur >= 'a') && (cur <='z'))
        {
            cur = cur - ('a'-'A');
        }
        *outstr++ = cur;
        instr++;
    } while (cur != '\0');
    return( outstr - orig_outstr );
}

#define BUFFERSIZE 250

char *tstStr = "This is a test!";
char outStr[BUFFERSIZE];

int main()
{
    mytoupper(tstStr, outStr);
    printf("Input: %s\nOutput: %s\n", tstStr, outStr);

    return(0);
}
```

We can compile this with

```
gcc -O3 -o upper upper.c
```

then run objdump to see the generated code

```
objdump -d upper >od.txt
```

We get Listing 14-5.

Listing 14-5. Assembly code generated by the C compiler for our
uppercase function

```
00010318 <main>:
   10318:   e59f2048 ldr    r2, [pc, #72]   ; 10368 <main+0x50>
   1031c:   e59f3048 ldr    r3, [pc, #72]   ; 1036c <main+0x54>
   10320:   e92d4010 push   {r4, lr}
   10324:   e5921000 ldr    r1, [r2]
   10328:   e1a02001 mov    r2, r1
   1032c:   e4d24001 ldrb   r4, [r2], #1
   10330:   e2833001 add    r3, r3, #1
   10334:   e2440061 sub    r0, r4, #97      ; 0x61
   10338:   e3500019 cmp    r0, #25
   1033c:   e2440020 sub    r0, r4, #32
   10340:   95430001 strbls r0, [r3, #-1]
   10344:   9afffff8 bls    1032c <main+0x14>
   10348:   e3540000 cmp    r4, #0
   1034c:   e5434001 strb   r4, [r3, #-1]
   10350:   1afffff5 bne    1032c <main+0x14>
   10354:   e59f2010 ldr    r2, [pc, #16]   ; 1036c <main+0x54>
   10358:   e59f0010 ldr    r0, [pc, #16]   ; 10370 <main+0x58>
   1035c:   ebffffe1 bl     102e8 <printf@plt>
   10360:   e1a00004 mov    r0, r4
   10364:   e8bd8010 pop    {r4, pc}
```

```
10368:    00021028 .word    0x00021028
1036c:    00021030 .word    0x00021030
10370:    0001050c .word    0x0001050c
```

A few things to notice about this listing are as follows:

- The compiler automatically inlined the mytoupper function like our macro version.

- The compiler knows about the range optimization and shifted the range, so it only does one comparison.

- The compiler made good use of the registers and didn't create a stack frame. It only uses five registers, so it only needs to push/pop R4.

- The compiler knows how to use conditional instructions.

- The compiler took a slightly different approach to adding the conditional, putting it on a store instruction, so the converted character is only stored if the character is lowercase. It then jumps to loop since it knows if it's lowercase, it can't be NULL. Otherwise, it falls through, stores the unconverted character, checks for NULL, and loops if it isn't.

Overall, the compiler did a good job of compiling our code, just taking a couple extra instructions over what we wrote in the last chapter. GCC has supported the ARM processor for 20 years now. ARM Holdings has made major contributions to GCC to improve the ARM support. All the work over this time has led to a robust and performant system, and the best part is that it is all open source.

This is why many Assembly language programmers start with C code, then only recode in Assembly if the C code isn't efficient. This usually happens when the complexity is higher and the need for speed is greater, such as the code in the **gcclib** for floating-point arithmetic and division, where speed is crucial, and pure Assembler is better at bit-level manipulations than C.

In Chapter 8, "Programming GPIO Pins," we looked at programming the GPIO pins using the GPIO controller's memory registers. This sort of code will confuse the optimizer. Often it needs to be turned off, or it optimizes away the code that accesses these locations. This is because we write to memory locations and never read them and read memory we never set. There are keywords to help the optimizer, but in the end, Assembler can result in quite a bit better code, because you are working against the C optimizer, that doesn't know what the GPIO controller is doing with this memory.

Reverse Engineering and Ghidra

In the Raspbian world, most of the programs you encounter are open source that you can easily download the source code and study it. There is documentation on how it works, and you are actively encouraged to contribute to the program, perhaps fix bugs or add a new feature.

Suppose we encounter a program that we don't have the source code for, and we want to know how it works. Perhaps we want to study it to see if it contains malware. It might be the case that we are worried about privacy concerns and want to know what information the program sends on the Internet. Maybe it's a game, and we want to know if there is a secret code we can enter to go into God mode. What is the best way to go about this?

We can examine the Assembly code of any Linux executable using **objdump** or **gdb**. We know enough about Assembly that we can make sense of the instructions we encounter. However, this doesn't help us form a big picture of how the program is structured and it's time-consuming.

There are tools to help with this. Until recently there were only expensive commercial products available; however, the NSA, yes, that NSA, released a version of the tool that their hackers use to analyze code. It is called Ghidra, named after the three-headed monster that Godzilla fights. This tool lets you analyze compiled programs and includes the ability to decompile a program back into C code. It includes tools to show you the graphs of function calls and the ability to make annotations as you learn things.

Sadly, Ghidra doesn't run properly on the Raspberry Pi anymore, even though it is written in Java. The NSA states that Ghidra won't be supported running on 32-bit operating systems anymore. However, Ghidra still supports analyzing 32-bit programs. It also has full support for the ARM processor. This means we need to transfer our executable file to a computer running a 64-bit operating system, whether it is Linux, macOS, or Windows.

You can download Ghidra from `https://ghidra-sre.org/`. To install it, you unzip it, then run the **ghidraRun** script if you are on Linux. Ghidra requires the Java runtime; if you don't have this already installed, you will need to install it for your operating system.

Decompiling an optimized C program is difficult. As we saw in the last section, the GCC optimizer does some major rewriting of our original code as part of converting it to Assembly language. Let's take the upper program that we compiled from C in the last section, give it to Ghidra to decompile, and see whether the result is like our starting source code.

If we create a project in Ghidra, import our upper program, then run the code browser we get the window shown in Figure 14-1.

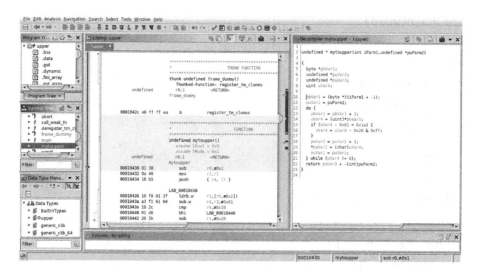

Figure 14-1. *Ghidra analyzing our upper program*

Listing 14-6 is the C code that Ghidra generated. I added the lines above the definition of the main routine, so the program will compile and run.

Listing 14-6. C code created by Ghidra for our upper C program

```
#include <stdio.h>

#define BUFFERSIZE 250

char *tstStr = "This is a test!";
char outStr[BUFFERSIZE];

typedef unsigned int uint;
typedef unsigned char byte;
typedef void undefined;

#define true 1
```

```
uint main(void)
{
  byte bVar1;
  undefined *puVar2;
  byte *pbVar3;
  byte *pbVar4;

  puVar2 = tstStr;
  pbVar3 = tstStr;
  pbVar4 = outStr;
  do {
    while( true ) {
      bVar1 = *pbVar3;
      if (0x19 < (uint)bVar1 - 0x61) break;
      *pbVar4 = bVar1 - 0x20;
      pbVar3 = pbVar3 + 1;
      pbVar4 = pbVar4 + 1;
    }
    *pbVar4 = bVar1;
    pbVar3 = pbVar3 + 1;
    pbVar4 = pbVar4 + 1;
  } while (bVar1 != 0);
  printf("Input: %s\nOutput: %s\n",puVar2,outStr);
  return (uint)bVar1;
}
```

If we run the program, we get the expected output:

```
pi@raspberrypi:~/asm/Chapter 14 $ make
gcc -O3 -o upperghidra upperghidra.c
pi@raspberrypi:~/asm/Chapter 14 $ ./upperghidra
Input: This is a test!
Output: THIS IS A TEST!
pi@raspberrypi:~/asm/Chapter 14 $
```

The code produced isn't pretty. The variable names are generated. It knows tstStr and outStr, because these are global variables. The logic is in smaller steps, often each C statement being the equivalent of a single Assembly instruction. When trying to figure out a program you don't have the source code for, having a couple of different viewpoints is a great help.

Note   This technique only works for true compiled languages like C, Fortran, or C++. It does not work for interpreted languages like Python or JavaScript; it also doesn't work for partially compiled languages that use a virtual machine architecture like Java or C#. There are other tools for these and often these are much more effective, since the compile step doesn't do as much.

Summary

In this chapter, we reviewed where we can find some sample Assembly source code in the Raspbian Linux kernel and the GCC runtime library. We looked at how GCC compiles the division operator from C and what happens when the ARM processor doesn't support a division instruction. We wrote a C version of our uppercase program, so we could compare the Assembly code that the C compiler produces and compare it to what we have written.

We then looked at the sophisticated Ghidra program for decompiling programs to reverse the process and see what it produces. Although it produces working C code from Assembly code, it isn't that easy to read.

In Chapter 15, "Thumb Code," we'll look at thumb code where we reduce the Assembly instruction size from 32 bits to 16 bits.

CHAPTER 15

Thumb Code

The Assembly code we've been developing produces compact code compared to high-level languages due to not needing a runtime and each instruction only taking 32 bits. However, in the early days of the ARM processor, there were a lot of complaints that this was too large. People used ARMs in small embeddable devices with very limited RAM and needed more compact programs. Others created systems with a 16-bit memory bus that allowed 64K of memory—tiny by today's standards and took two memory cycles to load each 32-bit instruction slowing down the processor.

ARM took these concerns and applications seriously and developed a 16-bit version of the instruction set, called **thumb code**. The original thumb code was expanded, and we'll be looking at the slightly newer Thumb-2 code available on the Raspberry Pis. The smallest Raspberry Pi has 512 MB of memory and a 32-bit bus. However, there is a lot of thumb code around; it is supported by **GCC** and provides smaller programs.

Thumb code is implemented in the ARM processor as part of the instruction load and decode part of the pipeline. The ARM instruction decoder converts each 16-bit instruction into a 32-bit counterpart in the CPU, so the execution unit doesn't know the difference.

In this chapter, we will look at the basics of Thumb-2 code, how we get useful 16-bit instructions, and how we can interoperate between Thumb and normal code.

© Stephen Smith 2019
S. Smith, *Raspberry Pi Assembly Language Programming*,
https://doi.org/10.1007/978-1-4842-5287-1_15

Note   In the 64-bit instruction world, there is no similar concept. There is no 32-bit Thumb mode. In the 64-bit instruction world, all instructions are 32 bits long without exception.

16-Bit Instruction Format

We've battled with how ARM packs information into 32 bits, giving us problems loading registers with immediate values; we often need two instructions to load a 32-bit value. Won't this just get worse in 16-bit instructions? The big savings to reduce the number of instruction bits are

- Eliminate conditional instructions; this saves 4 bits. There is a way to do conditional instructions in some cases using the **IT** instruction.

- Only access to the lower eight registers. This reduces each register encoding from 4 to 3 bits.

- Reduce the number of registers in an instruction.

- Reduce the size of immediate constants, usually to whatever is left over; it can be as small as 3 bits.

- Eliminate all the pre- and post-indexing addressing modes. You must do this in separate instructions.

- The **S** suffix to say whether an instruction updates the CPSR is fixed either on or off.

Let's look at three forms of the 16-bit **ADD** instruction:

- ADDS Rd, Rn, #imm
  @ imm can be 0–7

- ADDS Rd, #imm
  @ imm can be 0–255

- ADDS Rd, Rn, Rm

In the first example, if we add an immediate to a register and put it in a separate destination register, then there are only 3 bits left for the immediate code, so it must be in the range 0–7.

The second example is adding an immediate to a register; since there is one less register, there are more bits available for the immediate operand, allowing it to be in the range 0–255.

The registers in all these three examples have to be in the range **R0–R7**, though there are forms of the **ADD** instruction for adding to **SP** and adding an immediate constant to **PC**.

Note   All three examples have the **S** flag set; it is not optional.

Calling Thumb Code

In Chapter 4, "Controlling Program Flow," we noted that the **CPSR** contained a bit that indicates if the processor is running in **Thumb** mode. The ARM processor supports running some code in Thumb mode and some as the normal ARM 32-bit instructions we've been studying up until now.

In Chapter 6, "Functions and the Stack," we mentioned that the **BX** instruction can switch between processor states when it executes. If we want to return from a function written with Thumb instruction to one that isn't, then we must use the **BX** instruction; we can't just **POP** the return address into **PC**—if we do, we'll get an "Illegal Instruction" exception.

There is a matching **BLX** instruction to call between ARM32 and Thumb code. Both these instructions can go either way between Thumb and ARM32 instructions.

How do the **BLX** and **BX** instructions know whether they are branching to Thumb or ARM32 code? The ARM processor uses a trick. All ARM32 instructions must be word aligned, and all Thumb instructions have to be aligned to a 16-bit boundary. That means any address pointing to an instruction must be even, which means the low-order bit isn't used.

The ARM processor uses the low-order bit of an instruction address to indicate if the pointer is to an ARM32 or a Thumb instruction.

This means if you are going to call **BLX** to call Thumb code, you need to add one to the address. When you do this, **LR** will be set with the correct address for **BX** to do the right thing when it returns. This is a bit of a hack, but the ARM processor works hard to get functionality out of every bit.

This holds if you pass these instructions as a register. If you use the form of **BLX** where you pass a label, then **BLX** will always change modes, whether from Thumb to ARM32 or vice versa. This is partly because the label is represented by an offset from the **PC** in words, so the even/odd trick won't work.

To see how the Assembler helps us, consider the following code:

```
@ ARM Code
_start:
l1:  LDR    R0, =myfunc
     BLX    R0
...
.thumb_func
myfunc:
L2:  ADDS  R2, R1, #2
...
```

The ARM code will compile as

```
00010054 <_start>:
   10054:  e59f001c    ldr    r0, [pc, #28]    ; 10078 <L4+0x6>
   10058:  e12fff30    blx    r0
...
00010068 <myfunc>:
   10068:  1c8a        adds   r2, r1, #2
...
   10078:    00010069    .word 0x00010069
```

We see that the **LDR** instruction loads 0x00010069 from the location pc+28 (0x10078) which is the address of myfunc (00010068) plus 1.

Thumb-2 Is More than 16 Bits

The original Thumb instruction set was limited to 16-bit instructions except for a handful of exceptions. The newer Thumb-2 variant allows many 32-bit instructions, so you can do much more in Thumb mode. It also adds a new IT instruction which provided limited conditional execution.

Within Thumb code if we want to force an instruction to be 32 bits, we can add a **.W** suffix, for wide, or if we want to force the instruction to be 16 bits, we can add a **.N** suffix, for narrow. There are still limitations on these **.W** instructions compared to what we have done, like no conditional instructions without an **IT** instruction.

To enable this syntax, we start our source file with a

```
.syntax unified
```

Assembler directive.

This tells the Assembler this file is using all the Thumb-2 features. If we wanted only the old Thumb-1 instructions, then we would start the file with a **.Thumb** directive.

IT Blocks

Thumb code doesn't support conditional execution; however, with Thumb-2 it was considered important enough to add a new instruction If-Then (**IT**) to make the following instruction conditional, for example:

```
IT    EQ
ADDEQ R2, R1
```

Instructions in Thumb-2 are only allowed condition codes when following an **IT** instruction, and the conditions in the two instructions must be the same.

Note   Originally **IT** supported IF-THEN-ELSE and allowed up to four following instructions. This functionality is deprecated, meaning it may not be supported in future generations of the ARM processor, so we won't mention it.

The 16-bit version of the **ADD** instruction is either **ADDS** or **ADD**<condition code>. Other versions will generate a 32-bit instruction.

Uppercase in Thumb-2

How this all works will become clearer with an example. Let's convert our upper2.s file from Chapter 13, "Conditional Instructions and Optimizing Code," to Thumb code. The way we do this is add the Assembly directives to the top of the file. We add ".syntax unified", then ".thumb_func" after the .global directive. The ".thumb_func" directive tells the Assembler that the following function is in Thumb code, so assemble it accordingly. It also handles the details of switching between Thumb-2 and ARM32 mode, so we don't have to.

If we do this to the original upper2.s and compile, we get the error message

```
pi@raspberrypi:~/asm/Chapter 15 $ make
as -march="armv8-a" -mfpu=neon-vfpv4   upper2.s -o upper2.o
upper2.s: Assembler messages:
upper2.s:27: Error: thumb conditional instruction should be in
IT block -- `subls R5,#(97-65)'
```

```
make: *** [makefile:14: upper2.o] Error 1
pi@raspberrypi:~/asm/Chapter 15 $
```

This is expected since we know Thumb code doesn't support conditional execution. If we add

```
    IT   LS
```

before the SUBLS instruction, then it will compile. Listing 15-1 is our first attempt at Thumb code.

Listing 15-1. Our first attempt at converting upper2.s to Thumb code

```
@
@ Assembler program to convert a string to
@ all uppercase.
@
@ R1 - address of output string
@ R0 - address of input string
@ R4 - original output string for length calc.
@ R5 - current character being processed
@ R6 - minus 'a' to compare < 26.
@

.syntax unified

.global toupper    @ Allow other files to call this

.thumb_func
toupper:   PUSH  {R4-R6}    @ Save the registers
      MOV   R4, R1
@ The loop is until byte pointed to by R1 is non-zero
loop: LDRB  R5, [R0], #1    @ load character
@ Want to know if 'a' <= R5 <= 'z'
```

```
@ First subtract 'a'
      SUB   R6, R5, #'a'
@ Now want to know if R6 <= 25
      CMP   R6, #25      @ chars are 0-25 after shift
@ if we got here then the letter is
@ lowercase, so convert it.
      IT    LS
      SUBLS R5, #('a'-'A')
      STRB  R5, [R1], #1    @ store character
      CMP   R5, #0          @ stop on hitting a null
      BNE   loop       @ loop if character isn't null
      SUB   R0, R1, R4 @ get the length
      POP   {R4-R6}         @ Restore the registers
      BX    LR         @ Return to caller
```

We have to make one modification to main.s; we have to change

```
      BL    toupper
```

to

```
      BLX   toupper
```

Because we placed ".thumb_func" in front of the definition calling, it will be handled correctly by the Assembler.

Now we can compile and run the program, then get the expected output

```
pi@raspberrypi:~/asm/Chapter 15 $ make
as -march="armv8-a" -mfpu=neon-vfpv4   upper2.s -o upper2.o
ld -o upper2 main.o upper2.o
pi@raspberrypi:~/asm/Chapter 15 $ ./upper2
THIS IS OUR TEST STRING THAT WE WILL CONVERT. AAZZ@[`{
pi@raspberrypi:~/asm/Chapter 15 $
```

That was too easy. Listing 15-2 is the generated Assembly code using objdump.

Listing 15-2. Objdump output of our uppercase program

```
Disassembly of section .text:

00010074 <_start>:
   10074:   e59f002c ·  ldr    r0, [pc, #44]    ; 100a8 <_start+0x34>
   10078:   e59f102c    ldr    r1, [pc, #44]    ; 100ac <_start+0x38>
   1007c:   e3a0400c    mov    r4, #12
   10080:   e3a0500d    mov    r5, #13
   10084:   fa000009    blx    100b0 <toupper>
   10088:   e1a02000    mov    r2, r0
   1008c:   e3a00001    mov    r0, #1
   10090:   e59f1014    ldr    r1, [pc, #20]    ; 100ac <_start+0x38>
   10094:   e3a07004    mov    r7, #4
   10098:   ef000000    svc    0x00000000
   1009c:   e3a00000    mov    r0, #0
   100a0:   e3a07001    mov    r7, #1
   100a4:   ef000000    svc    0x00000000
   100a8:   000200e0    .word  0x000200e0
   100ac:   00020120    .word  0x00020120

000100b0 <toupper>:
   100b0:   b470        push   {r4, r5, r6}
   100b2:   460c        mov    r4, r1

000100b4 <loop>:
   100b4:   f810 5b01   ldrb.w    r5, [r0], #1
   100b8:   f1a5 0661   sub.w  r6, r5, #97      ; 0x61
   100bc:   2e19        cmp    r6, #25
   100be:   bf98        it     ls
   100c0:   3d20        subls  r5, #32
   100c2:   f801 5b01   strb.w    r5, [r1], #1
```

```
100c6:  2d00        cmp    r5, #0
100c8:  d1f4        bne.n 100b4 <loop>
100ca:  eba1 0004   sub.w r0, r1, r4
100ce:  bc70        pop    {r4, r5, r6}
100d0:  4770        bx     lr
```

We see the main program at _start contains normal 32-bit code. The only change from the Chapter 13 version is calling **BLX** instead of **BL**. The call to **BLX** will change the processor from ARM32 mode to Thumb mode.

If we look at the toupper part of the program, we see that nine instructions are 16 bits, but four instructions are 32 bits. As a result, we saved 18 bytes over the Chapter 13 version, but it seems we can do better.

There are two **SUB** instructions that are 32 bits; they look simple enough, but why are they 32 bits? The reason is that **ADD** and **SUB** instructions can either have the **S** suffix or be part of an **IT** block. If we add the S to these instructions, they will become 16 bits and won't affect the operation of this routine.

The **LDRB** and **STRB** instructions are wide because Thumb mode doesn't support post-index updates. We have to move these to separate **ADDS** instructions. The result is two 16-bit instructions rather than one 32-bit instruction, so we go from one instruction to two instructions, but use the same space. We will make this change to show we can make toupper all 16 bits. When we go to force

```
SUB    R6, R5, #'a'
```

to be 16 bits, we run into the problem that the immediate constant is limited to 3 bits so 'a' doesn't fit. To get around this, we add

```
MOVS   R7, #'a'
```

near the top and subtract **R7** instead. Since we had to break this instruction into two, we don't save any space here. The **S** is required to keep this **MOV** instruction 16 bits.

If we make these changes, we get upper3.s, shown in Listing 15-3.

Listing 15-3. Modified toupper routine that is all 16-bit instructions

```
@
@ Assembler program to convert a string to
@ all uppercase.
@
@ R1 - address of output string
@ R0 - address of input string
@ R4 - original output string for length calc.
@ R5 - current character being processed
@ R6 - minus 'a' to compare < 26.
@

.syntax unified

.global toupper     @ Allow main.s to call.

.thumb_func
toupper:    PUSH   {R4-R7}    @ Save the registers
       MOV    R4, R1
       MOVS   R7, #'a'
@ The loop is until byte pointed to by R1 is non-zero
loop: LDRB   R5, [R0]  @ load character
       ADDS   R0, #1    @ increment pointer
@ Want to know if 'a' <= R5 <= 'z'
@ First subtract 'a'
       SUBS   R6, R5, R7
@ Now want to know if R6 <= 25
       CMP    R6, #25    @ chars are 0-25 after shift
@ if we got here then the letter is
@ lowercase, so convert it.
       IT     LS
```

```
SUBLS R5, #('a'-'A')

STRB   R5, [R1]      @ store character to output str
ADDS   R1, #1        @ increment output pointer
CMP    R5, #0        @ stop on hitting a null
BNE    loop          @ loop if character isn't null
SUBS   R0, R1, R4    @ get the length
POP    {R4-R7}       @ Restore the registers we use.
BX     LR            @ Return to caller
```

To prove it is all 16-bit instructions, we run objdump to get Listing 15-4.

Listing 15-4. Objdump output of our fully 16-bit toupper function

```
000100b0 <toupper>:
  100b0:   b4f0      push   {r4, r5, r6, r7}
  100b2:   460c      mov    r4, r1
  100b4:   2761      movs   r7, #97     ; 0x61

000100b6 <loop>:
  100b6:   7805      ldrb   r5, [r0, #0]
  100b8:   3001      adds   r0, #1
  100ba:   1bee      subs   r6, r5, r7
  100bc:   2e19      cmp    r6, #25
  100be:   bf98      it     ls
  100c0:   3d20      subls  r5, #32
  100c2:   700d      strb   r5, [r1, #0]
  100c4:   3101      adds   r1, #1
  100c6:   2d00      cmp    r5, #0
  100c8:   d1f5      bne.n  100b6 <loop>
  100ca:   1b08      subs   r0, r1, r4
  100cc:   bcf0      pop    {r4, r5, r6, r7}
  100ce:   4770      bx     lr
```

In summary, the sizes of our various toupper functions are given in Table 15-1.

Table 15-1. *Comparison of the sizes of our three toupper routines*

Function version	Size (bytes)
Original 32 bits	48
Quick port	34
All 16 bits	32

Overall, we made the routine about a third smaller, which is what you typically attain using Thumb mode code.

Use the C Compiler

The GNU C compiler can generate Thumb code. There is a switch:

```
-mthumb
```

to generate thumb code when compiling. If you switch this on, you will get an error message because the C runtime uses the FPU by default and Thumb-1 instructions don't have the ability to access the FPU. We need to add the switch

```
-march="armv8-a"
```

or at least v6 to have the ability to use Thumb-2 instructions. When we do this, we can compile our C program from Listing 14-4 and compare the code sizes. The code generated by the C compiler is different based on the optimization levels. Table 15-2 is a comparison of the code size of the toupper routine under different compiler options, no optimization, optimized for speed, and optimized for size.

Table 15-2. *Sizes of toupper routine generated by the C compiler*

Instruction set	Optimization	Size (bytes)
ARM	None	148
	-03	56
	-0s	48
Thumb-2	None	78
	-03	44
	-0s	36

We see that the thumb code saves us memory. In the 16-bit optimized for size case, the compiler could save another 2 bytes; it does the following:

```
subs    r3, #32
uxtb    r3, r3
```

UXTB is zero extend byte. The compiler is worried the **SUBS** instruction results in a negative number, so it zeros the upper 3 bytes in **R3** to keep it as an unsigned byte. However, this can't happen since we only execute the subtraction if **R3** is between 'a' and 'z'.

The code generation is interesting. Unoptimized, almost all the Thumb instructions are 16 bits, but as you turn up the optimization level, more 32-bit instructions creep in. I won't include the generated Assembly code here, but you can easily change the compile options on the Chapter 14 code to see the results.

Summary

This chapter was a quick overview of the ARM processor's Thumb mode. This mode allows extremely compact code for devices with limited memory. Raspberry Pi have lots of memory compared to embedded devices; still saving memory is always worthwhile. You can generate Thumb code from either Assembly or C source code. The new Thumb-2 instruction set lets you do almost anything you can do in ARM32 code.

Keep in mind that most instructions execute in one cycle whether 16 or 32 bits. This means each 16-bit instruction takes less memory but uses the same processing time as matching 32-bit instructions that can do more in a single instruction.

CHAPTER 16

64 Bits

The ARM processors used in the Raspberry Pi have supported a 64-bit mode of operation since the Raspberry Pi 2. Raspbian, the official supported version of Linux for the Raspberry Pi, is a 32-bit operating system and cannot run 64-bit programs. You cannot switch to 64-bit mode, like you can switch to Thumb mode. If you boot the chip into 64-bit mode, run a 64-bit operating system, then you can run either 32-bit or 64-bit programs, but the switch between the modes can only be performed by the operating system.

The Raspberry Pi foundation's public statement is that they are only going to support one operating system for all their products. The Raspberry Pi 1 and Raspberry Pi Zero cannot support 64-bit operation, and since these are still manufactured and supported, the Raspberry Pi foundation says they will keep the entire ecosystem at 32 bits. Therefore, the majority of this book is dedicated to 32-bit ARM Assembly programming.

Ubuntu MATE

But all is not lost; there are other operating systems available for the Raspberry Pi. One of these is Ubuntu MATE, which has separate 32-bit and 64-bit version available. In this chapter, we will work with the 64-bit version of Ubuntu MATE on a Raspberry Pi 3 to see what is involved with 64-bit ARM Assembly language programming. The good news is that most of the concepts we've been dealing with up until this point still

© Stephen Smith 2019
S. Smith, *Raspberry Pi Assembly Language Programming*,
https://doi.org/10.1007/978-1-4842-5287-1_16

directly apply in the 64-bit world. Ubuntu MATE works fine, but it isn't as refined and adapted to the Raspberry Pi as Raspbian, largely because the community contributing to it isn't as large.

About 64 Bits

The key limitation of 32 bits is memory addressing. In the 32-bit world, our program uses 32-bit registers to address memory; this gives us a limitation of addressing 4 GB or memory in our program. Typically, operating systems use some of this memory space for its own purposes, so realistically you only have 2 GB of memory available to your program. The operating system can physically access more memory and allow different parts of memory to be swapped in and out of the virtual address space, but this comes with the cost of having programs needing to do this with Linux system calls. Modern computers usually contain 4 GB or more of memory, and managing this with 64-bit addresses is far easier and more efficient.

A downside of 64-bit operating systems is that they take more memory, since all memory addresses now take 64 bits of memory. All the registers become 64 bits in size, so there is a temptation to make all integers 64 bits, and now storing these are all twice as large as in 32 bits. Before the Raspberry Pi 4, all Raspberry contained either 512MB or 1Gig of RAM. This memory isn't enough to run 64-bit Linux kernels, then a selection of 64-bit programs. To have a 64-bit Linux run well, you need 4 GB of memory.

In 64-bit mode, instructions are still 32 bits in length. In 64-bit mode, the ARM engineers used the same tricks they used in 32-bit mode to pack as much information into those 32 bits as possible. This is good, since we've studied these and much of what we've done will be similar, usually only differing in the number of bits dedicated to an operand.

One goal of the ARM 64-bit instruction set is to make life easier for compiler developers. Generating code with conditional instructions, constructing operand2's, and dealing with overlapping registers all make their jobs harder. A lot of the changes that you see in the ARM 64-bit instruction set are designed to make it easier for compilers to generate efficient code.

Another goal is to make it easier for the ARM hardware engineers to create a more efficient execution pipeline—to greatly reduce pipeline execution stalls and to allow more instructions to be executed in parallel. Many of the "features" that were removed are to accomplish this goal.

More and Bigger Registers

Not only are the registers each 64 bits in size, but now we have 31 general purpose registers labeled **X0–X30**. You can access the lower 32 bits of each of these registers with **W0–W30**. Whenever you use an instruction that writes to one of these, the upper 32 bits of the same **X** register is set to zero.

Note   In 64 bits, the idea of multiple registers overlapping a larger register goes away. There is no **W** register that maps to the upper 32 bits.

X30 is the Link Register (**LR**), and the same rules apply as to the **LR** in 32 bits.

The Program Counter (**PC**) is not part of this register set. It is separate and not accessible like the other registers. Only certain instructions can alter it. This greatly simplifies optimization of the execution pipeline to prevent stalling.

SP and Zero Register

Register **X31** is the Stack Pointer (**SP**). However, the number of instructions that can access **SP** is greatly restricted. The following instructions can access **SP**:

- All loads and stores can use **SP** as the base register.

- AND, OR, and EOR (with immediate and without the **S** suffix) can use **SP** as the destination.

- ADD/SUB with immediate can use **SP** as the destination.

- ADD/SUB extend can use **SP** as destination or first operand.

All other instructions will see **X31** as the zero register. This register will always read zero, and if you write to it, nothing happens. You refer to the zero register as either **XZR** or **WZR**. Using **X31** as the name will result in an error.

The zero register doesn't benefit programmers that much, but it lets the ARM designers squish a bit more information in each 32-bit instruction. For example, in 64 bits

```
CMP    X1, X2
```

is really an alias for

```
SUBS   XZR, X1, X2
```

since writing to the zero register doesn't do anything. This saves an opcode.

Function Call Interface

With more registers there are more registers available for function parameters. Here is the function of each register at a function call boundary and who is responsible for saving it:

- **X0-X7**: Up to eight parameters passed in these registers, any additional parameters are passed on the stack.

- **X0**: For returning a single 64-bit result.

- **X0-X1**: For returning a 128-bit result in **X1:X0**.

- **X8**: Referred to as **XR**, used to pass a pointer to a structure that will contain the results.

- **X0-X18**: Corruptible registers that a function is free to use without saving. If a caller needs these, then it is responsible for saving them.

- **X19-X30**: These are callee saved, so must be pushed to the stack if used in a function.

- **X29**: The frame pointer (**FP**). Has the same purpose as the **FP** in 32 bits.

- **X30**: The Link Register (**LR**). Has the same rules as in 32 bits.

Note   The stack pointer must always be 16-byte aligned.

In 32 bits we could return from a function using any of

- MOV   PC, LR

- POP   {PC}

- BX   LR

This made it hard for the execution pipeline to know what the next instruction will be and would cause the pipeline to stall, wasting precious cycles. In the 64-bit world, access to the **PC** is greatly reduced. To return from a function, you use

RET

This way the execution pipeline knows to look in **LR** to see where the next instruction is, and the function return won't stall the execution pipeline.

Push and Pop Are Gone

The **PUSH** and **POP** instructions are replaced with the Load Pair (**LDP**) and Store Pair (**STP**) instructions. These aren't as handy as **PUSH** and **POP** as they will only process a pair of registers at a time. Table 16-1 shows the equivalent instructions in 32 bits vs. 64 bits.

Table 16-1. *Comparison of the PUSH/POP to STP/LDP instructions*

A32	A64
PUSH {R0–R1}	STP X0, X1, [SP, #-16]!
POP {R0–R1}	LDP X0, X1, [SP], #16

Note   Not only are they restricted to two registers at a time, but you must put in the correct **SP** processing, which leaves room for bugs to be introduced. I suggest using macros for these.

It is best to always process pairs of **X** registers, even if you need to add one that doesn't need to be saved. The hardware requires **SP** maintain 128-bit alignment, and this is the easiest way to do it.

Calling Linux Services

Since all programs need to be recompiled for 64 bits and some porting is required, Linux took the opportunity to clean up its system services. This affects us, since all the Linux system service numbers are different. You can check them out at

```
/usr/include/asm-generic/unistd.h
```

The services are grouped together by category, and many of the duplicates are removed.

Note   In Ubuntu MATE, you need to install these. You do this with

---

```
sudo apt-get install build-essential
```

Note   To exit a program is now service 93 and writing to a file is service 64.

They also took advantage of the additional registers. You now place the service number in register **X8** (in 32 bits it was **R7**) and can use registers **X0-X7** for passing parameters before you need to use the stack.

Porting from 32 Bits to 64 Bits

The GNU Assembler contains quite a few differences between 32 bits and 64 bits. Here are a few notes:

- You cannot use "@" as a comment character. You must use C style comments:

  - // meaning ignore everything to the end of the line

  - /* ... */ to comment out everything between them

- The error messages are mostly better, but some are misleading.

- You can't omit redundant registers. For instance, we could say "SUB R1, #2" in 32 bits, but we must say "SUB R1, R1, #2" in 64 bits.

- You need to change all **R** registers to **X** or **W** registers:

  - Addresses are 64 bits and must be in an **X** register.

  - Integers can go in either, but if you don't need 64 bits, you should use a **W** register.

- **PUSH** and **POP** instructions need to be converted to **STP** and **LDP** instructions.

- Function returns must be changed to use the **RET** instruction.

- If function parameters spill to the stack, some can now go in registers.

- The integer divide instruction is standard in 64 bits.

- The use of shift operations in operands is greatly reduced, and in fact eliminated in many cases. This might require some code rework with larger immediate constants.

- If you use tricks like adding constants to the **PC**, this won't work anymore and will need to be rewritten.

Porting Uppercase to 64 Bits

We apply all these notes and rules to our uppercase program from Chapter 13, "Conditional Instructions and Optimizing Code," and convert it to 64 bits. Listing 16-1 is main.s.

Listing 16-1. 64-bit version of our uppercase main.s file

```
//
// Assembler program to convert a string to
// all uppercase by calling a function.
//
// X0-X2 - parameters to linux function services
// X1 - address of output string
// X0 - address of input string
// W5 - current character being processed
// X8 - linux function number
//

.global _start     // Provide program starting address

_start: LDR X0, =instr // start of input string
        LDR   X1, =outstr // address of output string

        BL    toupper

// Set up the parameters to print our hex number
// and then call Linux to do it.
        MOV   W2, W0       // return code is the length

        MOV   W0, #1          // 1 = StdOut
        LDR   X1, =outstr // string to print
        MOV   X8, #64         // linux write system call
        SVC   0           // Call linux to output

// Set up the parameters to exit the program
// and then call Linux to do it.
        MOV   W0, #0       // Use 0 return code
// Service command code 93 terminates this program
        MOV   X8, #93
        SVC   0           // Call linux to terminate
```

```
.data
instr:  .asciz  "This is our Test String that we will convert.
AaZz@[`{\n"
        .align 4
outstr:     .fill 255, 1, 0
```

This code should look quite familiar. We use **X** registers for addresses and then **W** registers for everything else. The big changes are the global search and replace of "@" to "//" and then changing the register names. Notice the changes of the Linux service numbers.

Listing 16-2 is the upper.s file.

Listing 16-2. The toupper function in 64 bits

```
//
// Assembler program to convert a string to
// all uppercase.
//
// X1 - address of output string
// X0 - address of input string
// X4 - original output string for length calc.
// W5 - current character being processed
// W6 - minus 'a' to compare < 26.
//

.global toupper             // Allow other files to call this
                            // routine

toupper:
      MOV   X4, X1
// The loop is until byte pointed to
// by R1 is non-zero
loop: LDRB  W5, [X0], #1    // load character
// Want to know if 'a' <= R5 <= 'z'
```

```
// First subtract 'a'
     SUB   W6, W5, #'a'
// Now want to know if R6 <= 25
     CMP   W6, #25          // chars are 0-25 after shift
     BHI   cont
// if we got here then the letter is
// lowercase, so convert it.
     SUB   W5, W5, #('a'-'A')
cont: // end if
     STRB  W5, [X1], #1     // store character
     CMP   W5, #0           // stop on hitting a null character
     BNE   loop       // loop if character isn't null
// get the length by subtracting the pointers
     SUB   X0, X1, X4
     RET             // Return to caller
```

Notice the **RET** instruction at the end and that we had to change

```
     SUB   W5, #('a'-'A')
```

to

```
     SUB   W5, W5, #('a'-'A')
```

We used **X** register for the addresses and then **W** registers for manipulating the characters. Besides this, the code is all the same.

The makefile is shown in Listing 16-3.

Listing 16-3. The makefile for our uppercase program

```
UPPEROBJS = main.o upper.o

ifdef DEBUG
DEBUGFLGS = -g
else
DEBUGFLGS =
```

```
endif
LSTFLGS =

all: upper

%.o : %.s
        as $(DEBUGFLGS) $(LSTFLGS) $< -o $@

upper: $(UPPEROBJS)
        ld -o upper $(UPPEROBJS)
```

Note   **make** isn't installed by Ubuntu MATE by default so you need to install either build essentials as mentioned previously or install make separately using

---

```
sudo apt-get install make
```

Moving this program to 64 bits was painless and shows that almost all of what we learned for 32 bits applies in the 64-bit world.

Conditional Instructions

In 32 bits, we could add a condition code to any instruction, and in Thumb-2 mode, we could use the **IT** instruction. These all saved us using branch instructions. Besides the problem with branches interrupting the execution pipeline, littering our code with branches makes it harder to read. In 64 bits, neither of these previous methods are supported, but the ARM64 instruction set does include a couple of instructions to help us out. First consider conditional select:

- CSEL   Xd, Xn, Xm, cond

This statement implements

```
IF cond is true then
     Xd = Xn
else
     Xd = Xm
```

This is like the C conditional operator which is

```
Xd = cond ? Xn : Xm
```

Note   You can use either **W** or **X** registers with the **CSEL** instruction, but all the registers must be the same type.

There are a few variations on this instruction; a typical one is conditional select increment

- CSINC Xd, Xn, Xm, cond

which implements

```
IF condition is true then
     Xd = Xn
else
     Xd = Xm + 1
```

Example with CSEL

Listing 16-4 is our upper2.s file from Chapter 13, "Conditional Instructions and Optimizing Code," modified to use a **CSEL** instruction in place of the conditional subtraction.

Listing 16-4. Toupper function using a conditional CSEL instruction

```
//
// Assembly program to convert a string to
// all uppercase.
//
// X1 - address of output string
// X0 - address of input string
// X4 - original output string for length calc.
// W5 - current character being processed
// W6 - minus 'a' to compare < 26.
// W6 - char minus 0x20, potentially uppercased
//

.global toupper       // Allow other files to call

toupper:
      MOV   X4, X1
// The loop is until byte pointed to by R1 is zero
loop: LDRB  W5, [X0], #1    // load character
// Want to know if 'a' <= W5 <= 'z'
// First subtract 'a'
      SUB   W6, W5, #'a'
// Now want to know if W6 <= 25
      CMP   W6, #25    // chars are 0-25 after shift
// perform lower case conversion to W6
      SUB   W6, W5, #('a'-'A')
// Use W6 if lower case, otherwise
// use original character in W5
      CSEL  W5, W6, W5, LS
      STRB  W5, [X1], #1    // store character
      CMP   W5, #0          // stop on hitting a null
```

```
BNE    loop           // loop if character isn't null
SUB    X0, X1, X4     // get the length
RET                   // Return to caller
```

In this example, we perform

```
SUB    W6, W5, #('a'-'A')
```

into a different result register **W6**. Now, we have the original character in **W5** and the converted character in **W6**. We perform

```
CSEL   W5, W6, W5, LS
```

This places **W6** into **W5** if the **LS** condition is true—the character is an alphabetic lowercase character; else, it puts **W5** into **W5**—the original character.

This code is more structured; it isn't a spaghetti of branch instructions; once you are used to using these operators, following the logic is easier. This sequence is easier on the execution pipeline, since branch prediction isn't required to keep things moving.

FPU and the NEON Coprocessors

Both the FPU and NEON SIMD processor become integral parts of the CPU in the 64-bit world. They aren't optional coprocessors anymore. This allows much tighter integration with the instruction set.

Registers

These processing units still share their own set of registers, but now there are 32 128-bit registers. If you are treating these as integer registers, then you refer to them as **Q0–Q31**. If you are referring to them as floating-point, then they are **V0–V31**. There are 32 64-bit **D** registers for double-precision floating-point operations and 32 32-bit **S** registers for single-precision floating-point.

However, these registers don't overlap like they did in the 32-bit world. Compiler developers complained about the complexity of the 32-bit scheme, so it's simplified in the 64-bit world. Now, it's like how the **W** registers are just half of the matching **X** registers. This means that **D0** is half of **V0**, and **D1** is half of **V1** all the way up to **D31** being half of **V31**. Similarly, **S0** is half of **D0**, or a quarter of **V0**, then all the way up to **S31** being half of **D31**, or a quarter of **V31**. Both the FPU and NEON units see all these registers, so we don't have the strange dichotomy we had in 32 bits, where the FPU can see one set and NEON a slightly different set.

Figure 16-1 shows how the registers share the space in the 64-bit world.

	V15
	Q15
Unused	D15
Unused	S15

Figure 16-1. *How register V15 can be used for 128-, 64-, or 32-bit values*

There are **H** and **B** registers for 16-bit and 8-bit values, respectively, but these are used for conversions and not by FPU calculations.

With the instruction sets integrated into the main CPU, we can load and store these registers with our standard **LDR** and **STR** instruction, which means we can use all the supported addressing modes.

Instructions

With the instruction sets unified, we can now use the same instruction mnemonics as we use for integer instructions, so for floating-point, we can use

- ADD   D2, D1, D0

- ADD   S2, S1, S0

This simplifies our coding for floating-point operations. For NEON SIMD versions, we need to specify the size of the lanes; we do this by specifying the number of lanes for each operand. For instance:

```
ADD    V2.16B, V0.16B, V1.16B
```

will treat the registers as 16 lanes and separately add all the lanes in **V0** and **V1** putting the results in **V2**. The valid values for the lane type specifier are 8B, 16B, 4H, 8H, 2S, 4S, or 2D. This is represented graphically in Figure 16-2.

V1																	
D								D									V1.2D
S				S				S				S					V1.4S
H		H		H		H		H		H		H		H			V1.8H
B	B	B	B	B	B	B	B	B	B	B	B	B	B	B	B		V1.16B

Figure 16-2. *The lane configurations for register V1*

Comparisons

The FPU and NEON instructions now update the **CPSR** directly. This means we no longer need to copy the **FPSR** over manually to the **CPSR**.

This makes life easier, but beware the set of comparison operators is different between 32 bits and 64 bits. This can be a nuisance porting our programs as we shall see shortly.

Example Using NEON

Listing 16-5 is the NEON version of our uppercase program from Chapter 13, "Conditional Instructions and Optimizing Code," ported to 64 bits. This is the upper4.s file.

Listing 16-5. 64-bit NEON version of our toupper function

```
//
// Assembler program to convert a string to
// all uppercase.
//
// X0 - address of input string
// X1 - address of output string
// X2 - use as indirection to load data
// Q0 - 8 characters to be processed
// Q1 - contains all a's for comparison
// Q2 - result of comparison with 'a's
// Q3 - all 25's for comp
// Q8 - spaces for bic operation

.global toupper        // Allow other files to call

        .EQU  N, 4
toupper:
        LDR X2, =aaas
        LDR  Q1, [X2]    // Load Q1 with all as
        LDR X2, =endch
        LDR  Q3, [X2]   // Load Q3 with all 25's
        LDR X2, =spaces
        LDR  Q8, [X2] // Load Q8 with all spaces
        MOV  W3, #N
// The loop is until byte pointed to by R1 is zero
// load 16 characters and increment pointer
loop: LDR Q0, [X0], #16
        SUB   V2.16B, V0.16B, V1.16B // Subtract 'a's
// compare chars to 25's
        CMHI  V2.16B, V2.16B, V3.16B
```

```
// no CMLO so need to not
    NOT     V2.16B, V2.16B
// and result with spaces
    AND V2.16B, V2.16B, V8.16B
// kill the bit that makes it lowercase
    BIC  V0.16B, V0.16B, V2.16B
    STR  Q0, [X1], #16       // store character
// decrement loop counter and set flags
    SUBS  W3, W3, #1
    BNE   loop       // loop if character isn't null
    MOV   X0, #(N*16)       // return length
    RET              // Return to caller

.data
aaas:   .fill  16, 1, 'a'    // 16 a's
endch:  .fill  16, 1, 25     // after shift, chars are 0-25
spaces: .fill  16, 1, 0x20   // spaces for bic
```

Notice that we now load and store the NEON registers like any others. The instructions that operate on the lanes use the regular mnemonics, but have the lane specifiers on each operand. There is no **CMLS** instruction to compare the registers the way we want. Rather than rework the algorithm, I used a **CMHI** comparator, followed by a **NOT** operator to get the same result. Otherwise, this was a straightforward port of our 32-bit code.

Summary

This chapter gave a quick overview of the ARM 64-bit Assembly instruction set, along with how it is like the ARM 32-bit world. There are quite a few differences and we covered a selection of these.

If you've read this far, you should have a good idea of how to write 32-bit Assembly programs for your Raspberry Pi under Raspbian. You know how to write basic programs, as well as use the FPU and the advanced NEON processor to execute SIMD instructions. You are aware of what will work in the 64-bit world and know how to write your Assembly code with the future in mind.

Now it's up to you to go forth and experiment. The only way to learn programming is by doing. Think up your own Assembly language projects—perhaps controlling a robot connected to the GPIO pins. You could optimize an AI object recognition algorithm with Assembly code, even using the NEON processor. You could contribute to the ARM-specific parts of the Linux kernel to improve the operating system's performance or enhance GCC to generate more efficient ARM code. Or think of something original that might be the next great thing, the next killer application.

APPENDIX A

The ARM Instruction Set

This appendix lists the core ARM 32-bit instruction set, with a brief description of each instruction.

Instruction	Description
ADC, ADD	Add with Carry, Add
ADR	Load program or register-relative address (short range)
AND	Logical AND
ASR	Arithmetic Shift Right
B	Branch
BFC, BFI	Bit Field Clear and Insert
BIC	Bit Clear
BKPT	Software breakpoint
BL	Branch with Link
BLX	Branch with Link, change instruction set
BLXNS	Branch with Link and Exchange (Non-secure)
BX	Branch, change instruction set
BXNS	Branch and Exchange (Non-secure)

(continued)

© Stephen Smith 2019
S. Smith, *Raspberry Pi Assembly Language Programming,*
https://doi.org/10.1007/978-1-4842-5287-1

Instruction	Description
CBZ, CBNZ	Compare and Branch if {Non}Zero
CDP	Coprocessor Data Processing operation
CDP2	Coprocessor Data Processing operation
CLREX	Clear Exclusive
CLZ	Count leading zeros
CMN, CMP	Compare Negative, Compare
CPS	Change Processor State
CRC32	Cyclic Redundancy Check 32
CRC32C	Cyclic Redundancy Check 32C
CSDB	Consumption of Speculative Data Barrier
DBG	Debug
DCPS1	Debug switch to exception level 1
DCPS2	Debug switch to exception level 2
DCPS3	Debug switch to exception level 3
DMB, DSB	Data Memory Barrier, Data Synchronization Barrier
DSB	Data Synchronization Barrier
EOR	Exclusive OR
ERET	Exception Return
ESB	Error Synchronization Barrier
HLT	Halting breakpoint
HVC	Hypervisor Call
ISB	Instruction Synchronization Barrier
IT	If-Then

(continued)

Instruction	Description
LDAEX, LDAEXB	Load-Acquire Register Exclusive Word, Byte
LDAEXH	Load-Acquire Register Exclusive Halfword
LDAEXD	Load-Acquire Register Exclusive Doubleword
LDC, LDC2	Load Coprocessor
LDM	Load Multiple registers
LDR	Load Register with word
LDA, LDAB	Load-Acquire Register Word, Byte
LDAH	Load-Acquire Register Halfword
LDRB	Load Register with Byte
LDRBT	Load Register with Byte, user mode
LDRD	Load Registers with two words
LDREX, LDREXB	Load Register Exclusive Word, Byte
LDREXH	Load Register Exclusive Halfword
LDREXD	Load Register Exclusive Doubleword
LDRH	Load Register with Halfword
LDRHT	Load Register with Halfword, user mode
LDRSB	Load Register with Signed Byte
LDRSBT	Load Register with Signed Byte, user mode
LDRSH	Load Register with Signed Halfword
LDRSHT	Load Register with Signed Halfword, user mode
LDRT	Load Register with word, user mode
LSL, LSR	Logical Shift Left, Logical Shift Right
MCR	Move to Coprocessor from Register

(continued)

319

Instruction	Description
MCRR	Move to Coprocessor from Registers
MLA	Multiply Accumulate
MLS	Multiply and Subtract
MOV	Move
MOVT	Move Top
MRC	Move from Coprocessor to Register
MRRC	Move from Coprocessor to Registers
MRS	Move from PSR to Register
MSR	Move from Register to PSR
MUL	Multiply
MVN	Move Not
NOP	No Operation
ORN	Logical OR NOT
ORR	Logical OR
PKHBT, PKHTB	Pack Halfwords
PLD	Preload Data
PLDW	Preload Data with intent to Write
PLI	Preload Instruction
PUSH, POP	PUSH registers to stack, POP registers from stack
QADD, QDADD	Saturating arithmetic
QDSUB, QSUB	Saturating arithmetic
QADD8	Parallel signed saturating arithmetic
QADD16, QASX	Parallel signed saturating arithmetic

(continued)

Instruction	Description
QSUB8	Parallel signed saturating arithmetic
QSUB16	Parallel signed saturating arithmetic
QSAX	Parallel signed saturating arithmetic
RBIT	Reverse Bits
REV, REV16	Reverse byte order
REVSH	Reverse byte order
RFE	Return from Exception
ROR	Rotate Right Register
RRX	Rotate Right with Extend
RSB	Reverse Subtract
RSC	Reverse Subtract with Carry
SADD8, SADD16	Parallel Signed arithmetic
SASX	Parallel Signed arithmetic
SBC	Subtract with Carry
SBFX, UBFX	Signed, Unsigned Bit Field eXtract
SDIV	Signed Divide
SEL	Select bytes according to APSR GE flags
SETEND	Set Endianness for memory accesses
SETPAN	Set Privileged Access Never
SEV	Set Event
SEVL	Set Event Locally
SG	Secure Gateway
SHADD8	Parallel Signed Halving arithmetic

(*continued*)

Instruction	Description
SHADD16	Parallel Signed Halving arithmetic
SHASX, SHSUB8	Parallel Signed Halving arithmetic
SHSUB16	Parallel Signed Halving arithmetic
SHSAX	Parallel Signed Halving arithmetic
SMC	Secure Monitor Call
SMLAxy	Signed Multiply with Accumulate
SMLAD	Dual Signed Multiply Accumulate
SMLAWy	Signed Multiply with Accumulate
SMLSD	Dual Signed Multiply Subtract Accumulate
SMLSLD	Dual Signed Multiply Subtract Accumulate Long
SMMLA	Signed top word Multiply with Accumulate
SMMLS	Signed top word Multiply with Subtract
SMMUL	Signed top word Multiply
SMUAD	Dual Signed Multiply, and Add products
SMUSD	Dual Signed Multiply, and Subtract products
SMULxy	Signed Multiply
SMULL	Signed Multiply
SMULWy	Signed Multiply
SRS	Store Return State
SSAT	Signed Saturate
SSAT16	Signed Saturate, parallel halfwords
SSUB8, SSUB16	Parallel Signed arithmetic
SSAX	Parallel Signed arithmetic

(continued)

Instruction	Description
STC	Store Coprocessor
STM	Store Multiple registers
STR	Store Register with word
STRB	Store Register with Byte
STRBT	Store Register with Byte, user mode
STRD	Store Registers with two words
STREX, STREXB	Store Register Exclusive Word, Byte
STREXH,STREXD	Store Register Exclusive Halfword, Doubleword
STRH	Store Register with Halfword
STRHT	Store Register with Halfword, user mode
STL, STLB, STLH	Store-Release Word, Byte, Halfword
STLEX, STLEXB	Store-Release Exclusive Word, Byte
STLEXH, STLEXD	Store-Release Exclusive Halfword, Doubleword
STRT	Store Register with word, user mode
SUB	Subtract
SUBS pc, lr	Exception return, no stack
SVC	Supervisor Call
SXTAB	Signed extend, with Addition
SXTAB16	Signed extend, with Addition
SXTAH	Signed extend, with Addition
SXTB, SXTH	Signed extend
SXTB16	Signed extend
SYS	Execute System coprocessor instruction

(*continued*)

Instruction	Description
TBB, TBH	Table Branch Byte, Halfword
TEQ	Test Equivalence
TST	Test
TT, TTT, TTA	Test Target (Alternate Domain, Unprivileged)
TTAT	Test Target (Alternate Domain, Unprivileged)
UADD8	Parallel Unsigned arithmetic
UADD16, UASX	Parallel Unsigned arithmetic
UDF	Permanently Undefined
UDIV	Unsigned Divide
UHADD8	Parallel Unsigned Halving arithmetic
UHADD16	Parallel Unsigned Halving arithmetic
UHASX	Parallel Unsigned Halving arithmetic
UHSUB8	Parallel Unsigned Halving arithmetic
UHSUB16	Parallel Unsigned Halving arithmetic
UHSAX	Parallel Unsigned Halving arithmetic
UMAAL	Unsigned Multiply Accumulate Long
UMLAL, UMULL	Unsigned Multiply Accumulate, Unsigned Multiply
UQADD8	Parallel Unsigned Saturating arithmetic
UQADD16	Parallel Unsigned Saturating arithmetic
UQASX	Parallel Unsigned Saturating arithmetic
UQSUB8	Parallel Unsigned Saturating arithmetic
UQSUB16	Parallel Unsigned Saturating arithmetic
UQSAX	Parallel Unsigned Saturating arithmetic

(continued)

Instruction	Description
USAD8	Unsigned Sum of Absolute Differences
USADA8	Accumulate Unsigned Sum of Absolute Differences
USAT	Unsigned Saturate
USAT16	Unsigned Saturate, parallel halfwords
USUB8	Parallel Unsigned arithmetic
USUB16, USAX	Parallel Unsigned arithmetic
UXTAB	Unsigned extend with Addition
UXTAB16	Unsigned extend with Addition
UXTAH	Unsigned extend with Addition
UXTB, UXTH	Unsigned extend
UXTB16	Unsigned extend
V*	Advanced FPU or SIMD Instructions
WFE, WFI	Wait For Event, Wait For Interrupt
YIELD	Yield

APPENDIX B

Linux System Calls

This appendix lists the system call numbers for all Raspbian's Linux system services and the error codes that they could return. This is a listing of unistd.s from the source code that accompanies this book.

Linux System Call Numbers

```
@
@ Defines for the Linux system calls.
@ This list is from Raspbian Buster
@

.EQU sys_restart_syscall,   0  @ restart a system call
.EQU sys_exit,              1  @ cause normal process termination
.EQU sys_fork,             2  @ create a child process
.EQU sys_read,             3  @ read from a file descriptor
.EQU sys_write,            4  @ write to a file descriptor
.EQU sys_open,             5  @ open and possibly create a file
.EQU sys_close,            6  @ close a file descriptor
.EQU sys_creat,            8  @ create a new file
.EQU sys_link,             9  @ make a new name for a file
.EQU sys_unlink,          10  @ delete a name and the file it
                              refers to
.EQU sys_execve,          11  @ execute program
```

© Stephen Smith 2019
S. Smith, *Raspberry Pi Assembly Language Programming*,
https://doi.org/10.1007/978-1-4842-5287-1

```
.EQU sys_chdir,          12  @ change working directory
.EQU sys_mknod,          14  @ create a special or ordinary file
.EQU sys_chmod,          15  @ change file mode bits
.EQU sys_lchown,         16  @ change the owner/group of a
                             symbolic link

.EQU sys_lseek,          19  @ reposition read/write file offset
.EQU sys_getpid,         20  @ get process identification
.EQU sys_mount,          21  @ mount filesystem
.EQU sys_setuid,         23  @ set user identity
.EQU sys_getuid,         24  @ get user identity
.EQU sys_ptrace,         26  @ process trace
.EQU sys_pause,          29  @ wait for signal
.EQU sys_access,         33  @ check user's permissions for a file
.EQU sys_nice,           34  @ change process priority
.EQU sys_sync,           36  @ commit filesystem caches to disk
.EQU sys_kill,           37  @ send signal to a process
.EQU sys_rename,         38  @ change the name or location of a
                             file

.EQU sys_mkdir,          39  @ create a directory
.EQU sys_rmdir,          40  @ delete a directory
.EQU sys_dup,            41  @ duplicate a file descriptor
.EQU sys_pipe,           42  @ create pipe
.EQU sys_times,          43  @ get process times
.EQU sys_brk,            45  @ change data segment size
.EQU sys_setgid,         46  @ set group identity
.EQU sys_getgid,         47  @ get group identity
.EQU sys_geteuid,        49  @ get user identity
.EQU sys_getegid,        50  @ get group identity
.EQU sys_acct,           51  @ switch process accounting on or off
.EQU sys_umount2,        52  @ unmount filesystem
.EQU sys_ioctl,          54  @ control device
```

```
.EQU sys_fcntl,          55   @ manipulate file descriptor
.EQU sys_setpgid,        57   @ set process group
.EQU sys_umask,          60   @ set file mode creation mask
.EQU sys_chroot,         61   @ change root directory
.EQU sys_ustat,          62   @ get filesystem statistics
.EQU sys_dup2,           63   @ duplicate a file descriptor
.EQU sys_getppid,        64   @ get the parent process ID
.EQU sys_getpgrp,        65   @ get process group
.EQU sys_setsid,         66   @ Sets the process group ID
.EQU sys_sigaction,      67   @ examine and change a signal action
.EQU sys_setreuid,       70   @ set real and/or effective user ID
.EQU sys_setregid,       71   @ set real and/or effective group ID
.EQU sys_sigsuspend,     72   @ wait for a signal
.EQU sys_sigpending,     73   @ examine pending signals
.EQU sys_sethostname,    74   @ set hostname
.EQU sys_setrlimit,      75   @ control maximum resource consumption
.EQU sys_getrusage,      77   @ get resource usage
.EQU sys_gettimeofday,   78   @ get time
.EQU sys_settimeofday,   79   @ set time
.EQU sys_getgroups,      80   @ get list of supplementary group IDs
.EQU sys_setgroups,      81   @ set list of supplementary group IDs
.EQU sys_symlink,        83   @ make a new name for a file
.EQU sys_readlink,       85   @ read value of a symbolic link
.EQU sys_uselib,         86   @load shared library
.EQU sys_swapon,         87   @ start swapping to file/device
.EQU sys_reboot,         88   @ reboot
.EQU sys_munmap,         91   @ unmap files or devices into memory
.EQU sys_truncate,       92   @ truncate a file to a specified
                                length

.EQU sys_ftruncate,      93   @ truncate a file to a specified
                                length
```

```
.EQU sys_fchmod,          94    @ change permissions of a file
.EQU sys_fchown,          95    @ change ownership of a file
.EQU sys_getpriority,     96    @ get program scheduling priority
.EQU sys_setpriority,     97    @ set program scheduling priority
.EQU sys_statfs,          99    @ get filesystem statistics
.EQU sys_fstatfs,         100   @ get filesystem statistics
.EQU sys_syslog,          103   @ read/clear kernel message ring
                                  buffer

.EQU sys_setitimer,       104   @ set value of an interval timer
.EQU sys_getitimer,       105   @ get value of an interval timer
.EQU sys_stat,            106   @ get file status
.EQU sys_lstat,           107   @ get file status
.EQU sys_fstat,           108   @ get file status
.EQU sys_vhangup,         111   @ virtually hang up the current
                                  terminal

.EQU sys_wait4,           114   @ wait for process to change state
.EQU sys_swapoff,         115   @ stop swapping to file/device
.EQU sys_sysinfo,         116   @ return system information
.EQU sys_fsync,           118   @ synch a file's in-core state with
                                  storage

.EQU sys_sigreturn,       119   @ return  from  signal handler
.EQU sys_clone,           120   @ create a child process
.EQU sys_setdomainname,   121   @ set NIS domain name
.EQU sys_uname,           122   @ get name and info about current
                                  kernel

.EQU sys_adjtimex,        124   @ tune kernel clock
.EQU sys_mprotect,        125   @ set protection on a region of
                                  memory

.EQU sys_sigprocmask,     126   @ examine and change blocked signals
.EQU sys_init_module,     128   @ load a kernel module
.EQU sys_delete_module,   129   @ unload a kernel module
```

```
.EQU sys_quotactl,          131   @ manipulate disk quotas
.EQU sys_getpgid,           132   @ get process group
.EQU sys_fchdir,            133   @ change working directory
.EQU sys_bdflush,           134   @ start, flush, or tune
                                    buffer-dirty-flush
.EQU sys_sysfs,             135   @ get filesystem type information
.EQU sys_personality,       136   @ set the process execution domain
.EQU sys_setfsuid,          138   @ set user identity used for filesys
                                    checks
.EQU sys_setfsgid,          139   @ set group ident used for filesys
                                    checks
.EQU sys__llseek,           140   @ reposition read/write file offset
.EQU sys_getdents,          141   @ get directory entries
.EQU sys__newselect,        142   @ synchronous I/O multiplexing
.EQU sys_flock,             143   @ apply an advisory lock on an
                                    open file
.EQU sys_msync,             144   @ synchronize a file with a memory map
.EQU sys_readv,             145   @ read data into multiple buffers
.EQU sys_writev,            146   @ write data into multiple buffers
.EQU sys_getsid,            147   @ get session ID
.EQU sys_fdatasync,         148   @ sync a file's in-core state with
                                    storage
.EQU sys__sysctl,           149   @ read/write system parameters
.EQU sys_mlock,             150   @ lock memory
.EQU sys_munlock,           151   @ unlock memory
.EQU sys_mlockall,          152   @ lock memory
.EQU sys_munlockall,        153   @ unlock memory
.EQU sys_sched_setparam,    154   @ set scheduling parameters
.EQU sys_sched_getparam,    155   @ get scheduling parameters
.EQU sys_sched_setscheduler, 156 @ set scheduling policy/params
.EQU sys_sched_getscheduler, 157 @ get scheduling policy/params
```

```
.EQU sys_sched_yield,          158  @ yield the processor
.EQU sys_sched_get_priority_max, 159 @ get static priority max
.EQU sys_sched_get_priority_min, 160 @ get static priority min
.EQU sys_sched_rr_get_interval, 161 @ get  the  SCHED_RR  interval
.EQU sys_nanosleep,            162  @ high-resolution sleep
.EQU sys_mremap,               163  @ remap a virtual memory address
.EQU sys_setresuid,            164  @ set real, effective and
                                      saved user ID
.EQU sys_getresuid,            165  @ get real, effective and
                                      saved user ID
.EQU sys_poll,                 168  @ wait for some event on a file
                                      descriptor
.EQU sys_nfsservctl,           169  @ syscall interface to kernel nfs
                                      daemon
.EQU sys_setresgid,            170  @ set real, effective and
                                      saved group ID
.EQU sys_getresgid,            171  @ get real, effective and
                                      saved group ID
.EQU sys_prctl,                172  @ operations on a process
.EQU sys_rt_sigreturn,         173  @ return  from  signal and
                                      cleanup stack
.EQU sys_rt_sigaction,         174  @ examine and change a signal action
.EQU sys_rt_sigprocmask,       175  @ examine and change blocked
                                      signals
.EQU sys_rt_sigpending,        176  @ examine pending signals
.EQU sys_rt_sigtimedwait,      177  @ synchronously wait for
                                      queued signals
.EQU sys_rt_sigqueueinfo,      178  @ queue a signal and data
.EQU sys_rt_sigsuspend,        179  @ wait for a signal
.EQU sys_pread64,              180  @ read from a file desc at a
                                      given offset
```

.EQU sys_pwrite64,	181	@ write to a file descriptor at a given offset
.EQU sys_chown,	182	@ change ownership of a file
.EQU sys_getcwd,	183	@ get current working directory
.EQU sys_capget,	184	@ get capabilities of thread(s)
.EQU sys_capset,	185	@ set capabilities of thread(s)
.EQU sys_sigaltstack,	186	@ set and/or get signal stack context
.EQU sys_sendfile,	187	@ transfer data between file descriptors
.EQU sys_vfork,	190	@ create a child process and block parent
.EQU sys_ugetrlimit,	191	@ get resource limits
.EQU sys_mmap2,	192	@ map files or devices into memory
.EQU sys_truncate64,	193	@ truncate a file to a specified length
.EQU sys_ftruncate64,	194	@ truncate a file to a specified length
.EQU sys_stat64,	195	@ get file status
.EQU sys_lstat64,	196	@ get file status
.EQU sys_fstat64,	197	@ get file status
.EQU sys_lchown32,	198	@ change ownership of a file
.EQU sys_getuid32,	199	@ get user identity
.EQU sys_getgid32,	200	@ get group identity
.EQU sys_geteuid32,	201	@ get user identity
.EQU sys_getegid32,	202	@ get group identity
.EQU sys_setreuid32,	203	@ set real and/or effective user ID
.EQU sys_setregid32,	204	@ set real and/or effective group ID
.EQU sys_getgroups32,	205	@ get list of supplementary group IDs
.EQU sys_setgroups32,	206	@ set list of supplementary group IDs
.EQU sys_fchown32,	207	@ change ownership of a file

```
.EQU sys_setresuid32,    208   @ set real, effective and
                                 saved user ID
.EQU sys_getresuid32,    209   @ get real, effective and
                                 saved user ID
.EQU sys_setresgid32,    210   @ set real, effective and
                                 saved group ID
.EQU sys_getresgid32,    211   @ get real, effective and
                                 saved group ID
.EQU sys_chown32,        212   @ change ownership of a file
.EQU sys_setuid32,       213   @ set user identity
.EQU sys_setgid32,       214   @ set group identity
.EQU sys_setfsuid32,     215   @ set user ident used for
                                 filesystem checks
.EQU sys_setfsgid32,     216   @ set group ident used for
                                 filesys checks
.EQU sys_getdents64,     217   @ get directory entries
.EQU sys_pivot_root,     218   @ change the root filesystem
.EQU sys_mincore,        219   @ whether pages are resident
                                 in memory
.EQU sys_madvise,        220   @ give advice about use of memory
.EQU sys_fcntl64,        221   @ manipulate file descriptor
.EQU sys_gettid,         224   @ get thread identification
.EQU sys_readahead,      225   @ initiate file readahead into
                                 page cache
.EQU sys_setxattr,       226   @ set an extended attribute value
.EQU sys_lsetxattr,      227   @ set an extended attribute value
.EQU sys_fsetxattr,      228   @ set an extended attribute value
.EQU sys_getxattr,       229   @ retrieve an extended attribute
value
.EQU sys_lgetxattr,      230   @ retrieve an extended attribute value
```

334

```
.EQU sys_fgetxattr,       231   @ retrieve an extended attribute
                                  value
.EQU sys_listxattr,       232   @ list extended attribute names
.EQU sys_llistxattr,      233   @ list extended attribute names
.EQU sys_flistxattr,      234   @ list extended attribute names
.EQU sys_removexattr,     235   @ remove  an  extended attribute
.EQU sys_lremovexattr,    236   @ remove  an  extended attribute
.EQU sys_fremovexattr,    237   @ remove  an  extended attribute
.EQU sys_tkill,           238   @ send a signal to a thread
.EQU sys_sendfile64,      239   @ transfer data between file
                                  descriptors
.EQU sys_futex,           240   @ fast user-space locking
.EQU sys_sched_setaffinity, 241 @ set a thread's CPU affinity mask
.EQU sys_sched_getaffinity, 242 @ get a thread's CPU affinity mask
.EQU sys_io_setup,        243   @ create an asynchronous I/O context
.EQU sys_io_destroy,      244   @ destroy an asynchronous I/O context
.EQU sys_io_getevents,    245   @ read async I/O events from compl
                                  queue
.EQU sys_io_submit,       246   @ submit async I/O blocks for
                                  processing
.EQU sys_io_cancel,       247   @ cancel an outstanding async I/O
                                  operation
.EQU sys_exit_group,      248   @ exit all threads in a process
.EQU sys_lookup_dcookie,  249   @ return a directory entry's path
.EQU sys_epoll_create,    250   @ open an epoll file descriptor
.EQU sys_epoll_ctl,       251   @ control interface for an epoll
                                  file desc
.EQU sys_epoll_wait,      252   @ wait  for  an I/O event on an
                                  epoll fd
.EQU sys_remap_file_pages, 253 @ create a nonlinear file mapping
.EQU sys_set_tid_address, 256 @ set pointer to thread ID
```

```
.EQU sys_timer_create,      257  @ create a POSIX per-process timer
.EQU sys_timer_settime,     258  @ arm/disarm state of per-process
                                   timer
.EQU sys_timer_gettime,     259  @ fetch state of POSIX per-process
                                   timer
.EQU sys_timer_getoverrun,  260  @ get overrun count for a per-proc
                                   timer
.EQU sys_timer_delete,      261  @ delete a POSIX per-process timer
.EQU sys_clock_settime,     262  @ clock and timer functions
.EQU sys_clock_gettime,     263  @ clock and timer functions
.EQU sys_clock_getres,      264  @ clock and timer functions
.EQU sys_clock_nanosleep,   265  @ high-res sleep with specifiable
                                   clock
.EQU sys_statfs64,          266  @ get filesystem statistics
.EQU sys_fstatfs64,         267  @ get filesystem statistics
.EQU sys_tgkill,            268  @ send a signal to a thread
.EQU sys_utimes,            269  @ change file last access and mod
                                   times
.EQU sys_arm_fadvise64_64,  270  @ predeclare access pattern for file
                                   data
.EQU sys_pciconfig_iobase,  271  @ pci device information handling
.EQU sys_pciconfig_read,    272  @ pci device information handling
.EQU sys_pciconfig_write,   273  @ pci device information handling
.EQU sys_mq_open,           274  @ open a message queue
.EQU sys_mq_unlink,         275  @ remove a message queue
.EQU sys_mq_timedsend,      276  @ send a message to a message queue
.EQU sys_mq_timedreceive,   277  @ receive a message from a message
                                   queue
.EQU sys_mq_notify,         278  @ reg for notif when a message is
                                   available
.EQU sys_mq_getsetattr,     279  @ get/set message queue attributes
```

.EQU sys_waitid,	280	@ wait for a child process to change state
.EQU sys_socket,	281	@ create an endpoint for communication
.EQU sys_bind,	282	@ bind a name to a socket
.EQU sys_connect,	283	@ initiate a connection on a socket
.EQU sys_listen,	284	@ listen for connections on a socket
.EQU sys_accept,	285	@ accept a connection on a socket
.EQU sys_getsockname,	286	@ get socket name
.EQU sys_getpeername,	287	@ get name of connected peer socket
.EQU sys_socketpair,	288	@ create a pair of connected sockets
.EQU sys_send,	289	@ send a message on a socket
.EQU sys_sendto,	290	@ send a message on a socket
.EQU sys_recv,	291	@ receive a message from a socket
.EQU sys_recvfrom,	292	@ receive a message from a socket
.EQU sys_shutdown,	293	@ shutdown part of a full-duplex connection
.EQU sys_setsockopt,	294	@ set options on sockets
.EQU sys_getsockopt,	295	@ get options on sockets
.EQU sys_sendmsg,	296	@ send msg on a socket using a msg struct
.EQU sys_recvmsg,	297	@ receive a message from a socket
.EQU sys_semop,	298	@ System V semaphore operations
.EQU sys_semget,	299	@ get a System V semaphore set identifier
.EQU sys_semctl,	300	@ System V semaphore control operations
.EQU sys_msgsnd,	301	@ XSI message send operation
.EQU sys_msgrcv,	302	@ XSI message receive operation
.EQU sys_msgget,	303	@ get a System V message queue identifier

```
.EQU sys_msgctl,             304   @ System V message control operations
.EQU sys_shmat,              305   @ XSI shared memory attach operation
.EQU sys_shmdt,              306   @ XSI shared memory detach operation
.EQU sys_shmget,             307   @ allocates a System V shared memory
                                     seg
.EQU sys_shmctl,             308   @ System V shared memory control
.EQU sys_add_key,            309   @ add key to kernel's key mngment
                                     facility
.EQU sys_request_key,        310   @ req key from kernel's key
                                     management fac
.EQU sys_keyctl,             311   @ manipulate kernel's key
                                     management fac
.EQU sys_semtimedop,         312   @ System V semaphore operations
.EQU sys_vserver,            313   @ Unimplemented
.EQU sys_ioprio_set,         314   @ set I/O scheduling class and
                                     priority
.EQU sys_ioprio_get,         315   @ get I/O scheduling class and
                                     priority
.EQU sys_inotify_init,       316   @ initialize an inotify instance
.EQU sys_inotify_add_watch, 317 @ add watch to initialized
                                     inotify inst
.EQU sys_inotify_rm_watch,  318 @ remove existing watch from
                                     inotify inst
.EQU sys_mbind,              319   @ set memory policy for a memory
                                     range
.EQU sys_get_mempolicy, 320 @ retrieve NUMA memory policy for
                                     a thread
.EQU sys_set_mempolicy, 321 @ set def NUMA memory policy for
                                     a thread
.EQU sys_openat,             322   @ open file relative to dir file
                                     descriptor
```

```
.EQU sys_mkdirat,         323    @ create a directory
.EQU sys_mknodat,         324    @ create a special or ordinary file
.EQU sys_fchownat,        325    @ change owner and grp of a file rel
                                   to dir
.EQU sys_futimesat,       326    @ change timestamps of file rel
                                   to a dir
.EQU sys_fstatat64,       327    @ get file status
.EQU sys_unlinkat,        328    @ del name and possibly the file it
                                   refs to
.EQU sys_renameat,        329    @ change the name or location
                                   of a file
.EQU sys_linkat,          330    @ make a new name for a file
.EQU sys_symlinkat,       331    @ make a new name for a file
.EQU sys_readlinkat,      332    @ read value of a symbolic link
.EQU sys_fchmodat,        333    @ change permissions of a file
.EQU sys_faccessat,       334    @ det accessibility of file relative
                                   to dir
.EQU sys_pselect6,        335    @ synchronous I/O multiplexing
.EQU sys_ppoll,           336    @ wait for some event on a file
                                   descriptor
.EQU sys_unshare,         337    @ run prog with namespace unshared
                                   from par
.EQU sys_set_robust_list, 338 @ set list of robust futexes
.EQU sys_get_robust_list, 339 @ get list of robust futexes
.EQU sys_splice,          340    @ splice data to/from a pipe
.EQU sys_arm_sync_file_range, 341 @ sync a file segment with disk
.EQU sys_tee,             342    @ duplicating pipe content
.EQU sys_vmsplice,        343    @ splice user pages to/from a pipe
.EQU sys_move_pages,      344    @ move ind pages of a proc to
                                   another node
.EQU sys_getcpu,          345    @ determine CPU and NUMA node
```

```
.EQU sys_epoll_pwait,      346    @ wait for I/O event on epoll file desc
.EQU sys_kexec_load,       347    @ load a new kernel for later execution
.EQU sys_utimensat,        348    @ chg file timestamps with nanosecond
                                    prec
.EQU sys_signalfd,         349    @ create a file desc for accepting
                                    signals
.EQU sys_timerfd_create, 350      @ timers that notify via file
                                    descriptors
.EQU sys_eventfd,          351    @ create a file descr for event notif
.EQU sys_fallocate,        352    @ manipulate file space
.EQU sys_timerfd_settime, 353     @ timers that notify via file
                                    descriptors
.EQU sys_timerfd_gettime, 354     @ timers that notify via file
                                    descriptors
.EQU sys_signalfd4,        355    @ create a file desc for accepting
                                    signals
.EQU sys_eventfd2,         356    @ create a file desc for event
                                    notification
.EQU sys_epoll_create1,    357    @ open an epoll file descriptor
.EQU sys_dup3,             358    @ duplicate a file descriptor
.EQU sys_pipe2,            359    @ create pipe
.EQU sys_inotify_init1,    360    @ initialize an inotify instance
.EQU sys_preadv,           361    @ read data into multiple buffers
.EQU sys_pwritev,          362    @ write data into multiple buffers
.EQU sys_rt_tgsigqueueinfo, 363 @ queue a signal and data
.EQU sys_perf_event_open, 364     @ set up performance monitoring
.EQU sys_recvmmsg,         365    @ receive multiple messages on a
                                    socket
.EQU sys_accept4,          366    @ accept a connection on a socket
.EQU sys_fanotify_init, 367       @ create and initialize fanotify group
.EQU sys_fanotify_mark, 368       @ add, remove, or modify fanotify mark
```

```
.EQU sys_prlimit64,       369   @ get/set resource limits
.EQU sys_name_to_handle_at, 370 @ obtain handle for a pathname
.EQU sys_open_by_handle_at, 371 @ open file via a handle
.EQU sys_clock_adjtime,   372   @ tune kernel clock
.EQU sys_syncfs,          373   @ commit filesystem caches to disk
.EQU sys_sendmmsg,        374   @ send multiple messages on a socket
.EQU sys_setns,           375   @ reassociate thread with a
                                  namespace
.EQU sys_process_vm_readv, 376  @ trans data betwn process address
                                  spaces
.EQU sys_process_vm_writev, 377 @ trans data between proc address
                                  spaces
.EQU sys_kcmp,            378   @ comp 2 procs to det if share kern
                                  res
.EQU sys_finit_module,    379   @ load a kernel module
.EQU sys_sched_setattr,   380   @ set scheduling policy and
                                  attributes
.EQU sys_sched_getattr,   381   @ get scheduling policy and
                                  attributes
.EQU sys_renameat2,       382   @ change the name or location of a
                                  file
.EQU sys_seccomp,         383   @ operate on Secure Computing state
.EQU sys_getrandom,       384   @ obtain a series of random bytes
.EQU sys_memfd_create,    385   @ create an anonymous file
.EQU sys_bpf,             386   @ perform a command on an extended
                                  BPF map
.EQU sys_execveat,        387   @ execute program relative to a dir fd
.EQU sys_userfaultfd,     388   @ create fd for handling page faults
.EQU sys_membarrier,      389   @ issue memory barriers on a set of
                                  threads
.EQU sys_mlock2,          390   @ lock memory
```

```
.EQU sys_copy_file_range, 391    @ Copy rng of data frm one file to
                                   another
.EQU sys_preadv2,         392    @ read data into multiple buffers
.EQU sys_pwritev2,        393    @ write data into multiple buffers
.EQU sys_pkey_mprotect,   394    @ set protection on a region of
                                   memory
.EQU sys_pkey_alloc,      395    @ allocate a protection key
.EQU sys_pkey_free,       396    @ free a protection key
.EQU sys_statx,           397    @ get file status (extended)
.EQU sys_rseq,            398    @ restartable sequences
```

Linux System Call Error Codes

```
@
@ Assembler version of the C errno.h files.
@ All the Linux error codes for the Raspbian Buster release.
@
.EQU  EPERM,       1    @ Operation not permitted
.EQU  ENOENT,      2    @ No such file or directory
.EQU  ESRCH,       3    @ No such process
.EQU  EINTR,       4    @ Interrupted system call
.EQU  EIO,         5    @ I/O error
.EQU  ENXIO,       6    @ No such device or address
.EQU  E2BIG,       7    @ Argument list too long
.EQU  ENOEXEC,     8    @ Exec format error
.EQU  EBADF,       9    @ Bad file number
.EQU  ECHILD,     10    @ No child processes
.EQU  EAGAIN,     11    @ Try again
.EQU  ENOMEM,     12    @ Out of memory
.EQU  EACCES,     13    @ Permission denied
```

```
.EQU  EFAULT,        14   @ Bad address
.EQU  ENOTBLK,       15   @ Block device required
.EQU  EBUSY,         16   @ Device or resource busy
.EQU  EEXIST,        17   @ File exists
.EQU  EXDEV,         18   @ Cross-device link
.EQU  ENODEV,        19   @ No such device
.EQU  ENOTDIR,       20   @ Not a directory
.EQU  EISDIR,        21   @ Is a directory
.EQU  EINVAL,        22   @ Invalid argument
.EQU  ENFILE,        23   @ File table overflow
.EQU  EMFILE,        24   @ Too many open files
.EQU  ENOTTY,        25   @ Not a typewriter
.EQU  ETXTBSY,       26   @ Text file busy
.EQU  EFBIG,         27   @ File too large
.EQU  ENOSPC,        28   @ No space left on device
.EQU  ESPIPE,        29   @ Illegal seek
.EQU  EROFS,         30   @ Read-only filesystem
.EQU  EMLINK,        31   @ Too many links
.EQU  EPIPE,         32   @ Broken pipe
.EQU  EDOM,          33   @ Math argument out of domain of func
.EQU  ERANGE,        34   @ Math result not representable
.EQU  EDEADLK,       35   @ Resource deadlock would occur
.EQU  ENAMETOOLONG,  36   @ File name too long
.EQU  ENOLCK,        37   @ No record locks available
.EQU  ENOSYS,        38   @ Invalid system call number
.EQU  ENOTEMPTY,     39   @ Directory not empty
.EQU  ELOOP,         40   @ Too many symbolic links encountered
.EQU  ENOMSG,        42   @ No message of desired type
.EQU  EIDRM,         43   @ Identifier removed
.EQU  ECHRNG,        44   @ Channel number out of range
.EQU  EL2NSYNC,      45   @ Level 2 not synchronized
```

```
.EQU  EL3HLT,      46   @ Level 3 halted
.EQU  EL3RST,      47   @ Level 3 reset
.EQU  ELNRNG,      48   @ Link number out of range
.EQU  EUNATCH,     49   @ Protocol driver not attached
.EQU  ENOCSI,      50   @ No CSI structure available
.EQU  EL2HLT,      51   @ Level 2 halted
.EQU  EBADE,       52   @ Invalid exchange
.EQU  EBADR,       53   @ Invalid request descriptor
.EQU  EXFULL,      54   @ Exchange full
.EQU  ENOANO,      55   @ No anode
.EQU  EBADRQC,     56   @ Invalid request code
.EQU  EBADSLT,     57   @ Invalid slot
.EQU  EBFONT,      59   @ Bad font file format
.EQU  ENOSTR,      60   @ Device not a stream
.EQU  ENODATA,     61   @ No data available
.EQU  ETIME,       62   @ Timer expired
.EQU  ENOSR,       63   @ Out of streams resources
.EQU  ENONET,      64   @ Machine is not on the network
.EQU  ENOPKG,      65   @ Package not installed
.EQU  EREMOTE,     66   @ Object is remote
.EQU  ENOLINK,     67   @ Link has been severed
.EQU  EADV,        68   @ Advertise error
.EQU  ESRMNT,      69   @ Srmount error
.EQU  ECOMM,       70   @ Communication error on send
.EQU  EPROTO,      71   @ Protocol error
.EQU  EMULTIHOP,   72   @ Multihop attempted
.EQU  EDOTDOT,     73   @ RFS specific error
.EQU  EBADMSG,     74   @ Not a data message
.EQU  EOVERFLOW,   75   @ Value too large for defined data type
.EQU  ENOTUNIQ,    76   @ Name not unique on network
.EQU  EBADFD,      77   @ File descriptor in bad state
```

```
.EQU  EREMCHG,         78   @ Remote address changed
.EQU  ELIBACC,         79   @ Cannot access a needed shared library
.EQU  ELIBBAD,         80   @ Accessing a corrupted shared library
.EQU  ELIBSCN,         81   @ .lib section in a.out corrupted
.EQU  ELIBMAX,         82   @ Attempting to link too many shared
                              libs
.EQU  ELIBEXEC,        83   @ Cannot exec a shared library directly
.EQU  EILSEQ,          84   @ Illegal byte sequence
.EQU  ERESTART,        85   @ Interrupted sys call should be
                              restarted
.EQU  ESTRPIPE,        86   @ Streams pipe error
.EQU  EUSERS,          87   @ Too many users
.EQU  ENOTSOCK,        88   @ Socket operation on non-socket
.EQU  EDESTADDRREQ,    89   @ Destination address required
.EQU  EMSGSIZE,        90   @ Message too long
.EQU  EPROTOTYPE,      91   @ Protocol wrong type for socket
.EQU  ENOPROTOOPT,     92   @ Protocol not available
.EQU  EPROTONOSUPPORT, 93   @ Protocol not supported
.EQU  ESOCKTNOSUPPORT, 94   @ Socket type not supported
.EQU  EOPNOTSUPP,      95   @ Operation not sup on transport
                              endpoint
.EQU  EPFNOSUPPORT,    96   @ Protocol family not supported
.EQU  EAFNOSUPPORT,    97   @ Address family not supported by
                              protocol
.EQU  EADDRINUSE,      98   @ Address already in use
.EQU  EADDRNOTAVAIL,   99   @ Cannot assign requested address
.EQU  ENETDOWN,        100  @ Network is down
.EQU  ENETUNREACH,     101  @ Network is unreachable
.EQU  ENETRESET,       102  @ Network dropped conn because of reset
.EQU  ECONNABORTED,    103  @ Software caused connection abort
.EQU  ECONNRESET,      104  @ Connection reset by peer
```

```
.EQU  ENOBUFS,        105  @ No buffer space available
.EQU  EISCONN,        106  @ Transport endpoint is already
                              connected
.EQU  ENOTCONN,       107  @ Transport endpoint is not connected
.EQU  ESHUTDOWN,      108  @ Cannot send after trans endpoint
                              shutdown
.EQU  ETOOMANYREFS,   109  @ Too many references: cannot splice
.EQU  ETIMEDOUT,      110  @ Connection timed out
.EQU  ECONNREFUSED,   111  @ Connection refused
.EQU  EHOSTDOWN,      112  @ Host is down
.EQU  EHOSTUNREACH,   113  @ No route to host
.EQU  EALREADY,       114  @ Operation already in progress
.EQU  EINPROGRESS,    115  @ Operation now in progress
.EQU  ESTALE,         116  @ Stale file handle
.EQU  EUCLEAN,        117  @ Structure needs cleaning
.EQU  ENOTNAM,        118  @ Not a XENIX named type file
.EQU  ENAVAIL,        119  @ No XENIX semaphores available
.EQU  EISNAM,         120  @ Is a named type file
.EQU  EREMOTEIO,      121  @ Remote I/O error
.EQU  EDQUOT,         122  @ Quota exceeded
.EQU  ENOMEDIUM,      123  @ No medium found
.EQU  EMEDIUMTYPE,    124  @ Wrong medium type
.EQU  ECANCELED,      125  @ Operation Canceled
.EQU  ENOKEY,         126  @ Required key not available
.EQU  EKEYEXPIRED,    127  @ Key has expired
.EQU  EKEYREVOKED,    128  @ Key has been revoked
.EQU  EKEYREJECTED,   129  @ Key was rejected by service
.EQU  EOWNERDEAD,     130  @ Owner died
.EQU  ENOTRECOVERABLE, 131 @ State not recoverable
.EQU  ERFKILL,        132  @ Operation not possible due to RF-kill
.EQU  EHWPOISON,      133  @ Memory page has hardware error
```

APPENDIX C

Binary Formats

This appendix describes the basic characteristics of the data types we have been working with.

Integers

The following table provides the basic integer data types we have used. Signed integers are represented in two's complement form.

Table C-1. *Size, alignment, range, and C type for the basic integer types*

Size	Type	Alignment in bytes	Range	C type
8	Signed	1	−128 to 127	signed char
8	Unsigned	1	0 to 255	char
16	Signed	2	−32,768 to 32,767	short
16	Unsigned	2	0 to 65,535	unsigned short
32	Signed	4	−2,147,483,648 to 2,147,483,647	int
32	Unsigned	4	0 to 4,294,967,295	unsigned int
64	Signed	8	−9,223,372,036,854,775,808 to 9,223,372,036,854,775,807	long long
64	Unsigned	8	0 to 18,446,744,073,709,551,615	unsigned long long

© Stephen Smith 2019
S. Smith, *Raspberry Pi Assembly Language Programming*,
https://doi.org/10.1007/978-1-4842-5287-1

Note   In 32-bit mode, only the NEON processor can process 64-bit integers. However, you can process them yourself as we indicated with instructions like **ADDS** followed by **ADDC**.

Floating-Point

The ARM floating-point and NEON coprocessors use the IEEE 754 standard for representing floating-point numbers. All floating-point numbers are signed.

Note   The ARM implementation of 16-bit half precision floating-point differs from the standard by not supporting infinity or NaNs.

Table C-2.   *Size, alignment, positive range, and C type for floating-point numbers*

Size	Alignment in bytes	Range	C type
16	2	0.000061035 to 65504	half
32	4	1.175494351e-38 to 3.40282347e+38	Float
64	8	2.22507385850720138e-308 to 1.79769313486231571e+308	double

Note   Not all C compilers support 16-bit floating-point numbers.

These ranges are for normalized values; the ARM processor will allow floats to become unnormalized to avoid underflow.

Addresses

All addresses or pointers are 32 bits. They point to memory in the processes' virtual address space. They do not point directly to physical memory.

Table C-3. *Size, alignment, range, and C type of a pointer*

Size	Alignment in bytes	Range	C type
32	4	0 to 4,294,967,295	void $*$

64 Bits

The two differences in 64 bits are

1. All addresses (pointers) are 64 bits and must be 64-bit aligned.

2. The C long data type is 64 bits, and the main CPU can perform 64-bit arithmetic.

Assembler Directives

This appendix lists a useful selection of GNU Assembler directives. It includes all the directives used in this book, and a few more that are commonly used.

Directive	Description
.align	Pads the location counter to a particular storage boundary
.ascii	Defines memory for an ASCII string with no NULL terminator
.asciz	Defines memory for an ASCII string and adds a NULL terminator
.byte	Defines memory for bytes
.data	Assembles following code to the end of the data subsection
.double	Defines memory for double floating-point data
.else	Part of conditional assembly
.elseif	Part of conditional assembly
.endif	Part of conditional assembly
.endm	End of a macro definition
.endr	End of a repeat block
.equ	Defines values for symbols
.fill	Defines and fills some memory
.float	Defines memory for single-precision floating-point data

(*continued*)

© Stephen Smith 2019
S. Smith, *Raspberry Pi Assembly Language Programming,*
https://doi.org/10.1007/978-1-4842-5287-1

Directive	Description
.global	Makes a symbol global, needed if reference from other files
.hword	Defines memory for 16-bit integers
.if	Marks the beginning of code to be conditionally assembled
.include	Merges a file into the current file
.int	Defines storage for 32-bit integers
.long	Defines storage for 32-bit integers (same as .int)
.macro	Defines a macro
.octa	Defines storage for 64-bit integers
.quad	Same as .octa
.rept	Repeats a block of code multiple times
.set	Sets the value of a symbol to an expression
.short	Same as .hword
.single	Same as .float
.text	Generates following instructions into the code section
.word	Same as .int

ASCII Character Set

Here is the ASCII Character Set. The characters from 0 to 127 are standard. The characters from 128 to 255 are taken from code page 437, which is the character set of the original IBM PC.

Dec	Hex	Char	Description
0	00	NUL	Null
1	01	SOH	Start of Header
2	02	STX	Start of Text
3	03	ETX	End of Text
4	04	EOT	End of Transmission
5	05	ENQ	Enquiry
6	06	ACK	Acknowledge
7	07	BEL	Bell
8	08	BS	Backspace
9	09	HT	Horizontal Tab
10	0A	LF	Line Feed
11	0B	VT	Vertical Tab
12	0C	FF	Form Feed

(continued)

© Stephen Smith 2019
S. Smith, *Raspberry Pi Assembly Language Programming*,
https://doi.org/10.1007/978-1-4842-5287-1

Dec	Hex	Char	Description
13	0D	CR	Carriage Return
14	0E	SO	Shift Out
15	0F	SI	Shift In
16	10	DLE	Data Link Escape
17	11	DC1	Device Control 1
18	12	DC2	Device Control 2
19	13	DC3	Device Control 3
20	14	DC4	Device Control 4
21	15	NAK	Negative Acknowledge
22	16	SYN	Synchronize
23	17	ETB	End of Transmission Block
24	18	CAN	Cancel
25	19	EM	End of Medium
26	1A	SUB	Substitute
27	1B	ESC	Escape
28	1C	FS	File Separator
29	1D	GS	Group Separator
30	1E	RS	Record Separator
31	1F	US	Unit Separator
32	20	space	Space
33	21	!	Exclamation mark
34	22	"	Double quote

(continued)

Dec	Hex	Char	Description
35	23	#	Number
36	24	$	Dollar sign
37	25	%	Percent
38	26	&	Ampersand
39	27	'	Single quote
40	28	(	Left parenthesis
41	29	)	Right parenthesis
42	2A	*	Asterisk
43	2B	+	Plus
44	2C	,	Comma
45	2D	-	Minus
46	2E	.	Period
47	2F	/	Slash
48	30	0	Zero
49	31	1	One
50	32	2	Two
51	33	3	Three
52	34	4	Four
53	35	5	Five
54	36	6	Six
55	37	7	Seven
56	38	8	Eight
57	39	9	Nine

(continued)

Dec	Hex	Char	Description
58	3A	:	Colon
59	3B	;	Semicolon
60	3C	<	Less than
61	3D	=	Equality sign
62	3E	>	Greater than
63	3F	?	Question mark
64	40	@	At sign
65	41	A	Capital A
66	42	B	Capital B
67	43	C	Capital C
68	44	D	Capital D
69	45	E	Capital E
70	46	F	Capital F
71	47	G	Capital G
72	48	H	Capital H
73	49	I	Capital I
74	4A	J	Capital J
75	4B	K	Capital K
76	4C	L	Capital L
77	4D	M	Capital M
78	4E	N	Capital N
79	4F	O	Capital O

(*continued*)

Dec	Hex	Char	Description
80	50	P	Capital P
81	51	Q	Capital Q
82	52	R	Capital R
83	53	S	Capital S
84	54	T	Capital T
85	55	U	Capital U
86	56	V	Capital V
87	57	W	Capital W
88	58	X	Capital X
89	59	Y	Capital Y
90	5A	Z	Capital Z
91	5B	[	Left square bracket
92	5C	\	Backslash
93	5D	]	Right square bracket
94	5E	^	Caret/circumflex
95	5F	_	Underscore
96	60	`	Grave/accent
97	61	a	Small a
98	62	b	Small b
99	63	c	Small c
100	64	d	Small d
101	65	e	Small e

(*continued*)

Dec	Hex	Char	Description
102	66	f	Small f
103	67	g	Small g
104	68	h	Small h
105	69	i	Small i
106	6A	j	Small j
107	6B	k	Small k
108	6C	l	Small l
109	6D	m	Small m
110	6E	n	Small n
111	6F	o	Small o
112	70	p	Small p
113	71	q	Small q
114	72	r	Small r
115	73	s	Small s
116	74	t	Small t
117	75	u	Small u
118	76	v	Small v
119	77	w	Small w
120	78	x	Small x
121	79	y	Small y
122	7A	z	Small z
123	7B	{	Left curly bracket
124	7C			Vertical bar

(continued)

Dec	Hex	Char	Description
125	7D	}	Right curly bracket
126	7E	~	Tilde
127	7F	DEL	Delete
128	80	Ç	
129	81	ü	
130	82	é	
131	83	â	
132	84	ä	
133	85	à	
134	86	å	
135	87	ç	
136	88	ê	
137	89	ë	
138	8A	è	
139	8B	ï	
140	8C	î	
141	8D	ì	
142	8E	Ä	
143	8F	Å	
144	90	É	
145	91	æ	
146	92	Æ	
147	93	ô	

(continued)

Dec	Hex	Char	Description
148	94	ö	
149	95	ò	
150	96	û	
151	97	ù	
152	98	ÿ	
153	99	Ö	
154	9A	Ü	
155	9B	¢	
156	9C	£	
157	9D	¥	
158	9E	Pts	
159	9F	ƒ	
160	A0	á	
161	A1	í	
162	A2	ó	
163	A3	ú	
164	A4	ñ	
165	A5	Ñ	
166	A6	ª	
167	A7	º	
168	A8	¿	
169	A9	⌐	

(continued)

Dec	Hex	Char	Description
170	AA	¬	
171	AB	½	
172	AC	¼	
173	AD	¡	
174	AE	«	
175	AF	»	
176	B0	▓	
177	B1	▒	
178	B2	█	
179	B3	│	
180	B4	┤	
181	B5	╡	
182	B6	╢	
183	B7	╖	
184	B8	╕	
185	B9	╣	
186	BA	║	
187	BB	╗	
188	BC	╝	
189	BD	╜	
190	BE	╛	
191	BF	┐	

(*continued*)

Dec	Hex	Char	Description
192	C0	└	
193	C1	⊥	
194	C2	⊤	
195	C3	├	
196	C4	—	
197	C5	+	
198	C6	╞	
199	C7	╟	
200	C8	╚	
201	C9	╔	
202	CA	╩	
203	CB	╦	
204	CC	╠	
205	CD	=	
206	CE	╬	
207	CF	╧	
208	D0	╨	
209	D1	╤	
210	D2	╥	
211	D3	╙	
212	D4	╘	
213	D5	╒	

(*continued*)

Dec	Hex	Char	Description
214	D6	π	
215	D7	$\#$	
216	D8	$\ddagger$	
217	D9	$\lrcorner$	
218	DA	$\ulcorner$	
219	DB	■	
220	DC	▬	
221	DD	▌	
222	DE	▐	
223	DF	▀	
224	E0	α	
225	E1	β	
226	E2	Γ	
227	E3	π	
228	E4	Σ	
229	E5	σ	
230	E6	μ	
231	E7	τ	
232	E8	Φ	
233	E9	Θ	
234	EA	Ω	
235	EB	δ	

(*continued*)

Dec	Hex	Char	Description
236	EC	∞	
237	ED	φ	
238	EE	ε	
239	EF	∩	
240	F0	≡	
241	F1	±	
242	F2	≥	
243	F3	≤	
244	F4	⌠	
245	F5	⌡	
246	F6	÷	
247	F7	≈	
248	F8	°	
249	F9	•	
250	FA	·	
251	FB	√	
252	FC	ⁿ	
253	FD	²	
254	FE	■	
255	FF		

References

Arm Limited. (2018). *Arm® Instruction Set Reference Guide Version 1.0.*
Retrieved from `https://developer.arm.com/docs/100076/latest`.

Arm Limited. (2006–2010). *ARMv7-M Architecture Reference Manual.*
Retrieved from `https://developer.arm.com/docs/ddi0403/e/armv7-m-`
`architecture-reference-manual`.

Arm Limited. (2006–2010). *ARM ® Cortex ®-A72 MPCore Processor*
Technical Reference Manual. Retrieved from `https://developer.arm.com/`
`docs/100400/latest`.

Arm Limited. (2015*). Cortex®-A72 Software Optimization Guide.*
Retrieved from `http://infocenter.arm.com/help/index.jsp?topic=/`
`com.arm.doc.uan0016a/index.html`.

Arm Limited. (2013). *NEON Programmer's Guide.* Retrieved from
`https://developer.arm.com/docs/den0018/latest`.

Arm Limited. (2015). *ARM Cortex -A Series Programmer's Guide for*
ARMv8-A. Retrieved from `https://developer.arm.com/docs/den0024/a`.

Arm Limited. (2015). *Procedure Call Standard for the ARM*
Architecture. Retrieved from `https://developer.arm.com/docs/ihi0042/`
`latest`.

Broadcom. (2012). *BCM2835 ARM Peripherals.* Retrieved from `www.`
`raspberrypi.org/app/uploads/2012/02/BCM2835-ARM-Peripherals.pdf`.

Elsner, Dean and Fenlason Jay. (1991–2010). *Using as The GNU*
Assembler. Retrieved from `https://web.eecs.umich.edu/~prabal/`
`teaching/resources/eecs373/Assembler.pdf`.

Shore, Chris. (2014). *Porting to 64-bit Arm – White Paper.* Retrieved
from `https://community.arm.com/developer/ip-products/`
`processors/b/processors-ip-blog/posts/porting-to-arm-64-bit`.

© Stephen Smith 2019
S. Smith, *Raspberry Pi Assembly Language Programming,*
https://doi.org/10.1007/978-1-4842-5287-1

Index

A

Accumulate operation
  accumulate
    instructions, 199, 200
  dual multiply/accumulate,
    201, 207, 209
  LDR, 210
  multiply 3x3 matrices
  matrix elements, 205
  matrix
    multiplication, 201–204
  registers, 206
  SMLAL instruction, 206
  Ra operand, 200
  .short Assembler directive, 206
ADC instruction, 45–50, 68, 173
ADD instructions, 45–50
ADDS instruction, 68, 71, 173
Advanced RISC Machine (ARM)
    processor, 1, 2, 13, 190, 281
Arithmetic Logic Unit (ALU), 34
ARM Assembly Instructions
  clock cycle, 15
  CPU Registers, 12, 13
  instruction format, 13, 14
  memory, 15, 16
  RISC, 11

ARM32 bit instruction set, 317–325
ASCII character set, 353–364
.asciz directive, 173
asm statement, 183, 184
Assembly language, 1
  CPU registers, 5
  memory addressing, 5
  usage, 5, 7

B

Barrel shifter, 34
Bi-endian, 32
Big-endian, 31
Binary formats
  integers, 347
  floating-point, 348–349
Bit Clear (BIC) operation, 76–77, 256
BLX instruction, 283
Branch and Exchange (BX)
    instruction, 111, 283
Branch instruction, 70
  condition codes, 70, 71
  performance, 83, 84
Branch prediction, 251
Branch with Link (BL)
    instruction, 111

C

Carry flag, 33, 68
Closed loop branch instruction, 68
CMP instruction, 71, 84–85
Code, pack
  shared library, 179–181
  static library, 178, 179
Computers
  byte, 9
  decimal number, 9
  hexadecimal numbers, 11
Conditional instructions, 64-bit, 250
Conditional statements, 46, 48
Condition code, 24, 70, 251
Condition flags, 68
Coprocessors
  comparison, 313
  instruction, 312
  NEON version, 313, 315
  registers, 311, 312
C routines
  add with carry, 173, 175
  Assembly function
    compile and run, 177
    parameters, 177
    toupper function, 176
  embedding Assembly code
    asm statement, 183, 184
    GNU C compiler, 182
    registers, 184
  inputs and outputs, print, 174
  ld command, 170
  print debug information

call Printf, 172
  printf function, 170, 171
  string, 173
  _start label, 169
CSEL instruction, 309–311
Current Program Status Register
  (CPSR)
  bits, 68
  condition flags, 68
  interrupt flags, 69

D

Design patterns, 77, 78
Division
  ARM Cortex-A53
    processors, 194
  GNU Compiler Collection, 196
  instructions, 194, 195
  SDIV and UDIV
    instructions, 195, 196
Division routine, 270

E

.ENDM directive, 128
.EQU Assembler directive, 124

F

File to uppercase, conversion
  case conversion
    program, 137, 138
  error checking

.asciz, 141
  error message, 141, 142
  error module, 142
  looping, 142
  MOVS instruction, 141
  strlen() function, 141
file I/O library, 135
  Linux open service, 140
  makefile, 139
  read and write files, 135, 136
Flashing LEDs
  .EQU directive, 166, 167
  GPIO pins, control, 149, 150
  main program, 151, 152
  mapped memory, 159–163
  pin direction, 165, 166
  resistors, 148
  root access, 164
  table lookup, 164
Floating-Point comparison
  maincomp.s, 228–230
  makefile, 230
  rounding error, 231
  routine, tolerance, 227, 228
  VCMP instruction, 226
  VMRS instruction, 226
Floating-Point conversions
  from integer, 224
  rounding method, 225
  to integer, 225
  VCVT, 224
Floating-point coprocessor
  (FPU), 3, 211
Floating-point numbers

arithmetic operations, 218, 219
coprocessor instructions, 216
defined, 212, 214
distance function, 220–222
gcc, 217
IEEE 754 standard, 212
NaNs, 212
normalization, 213
protocol, 216, 217
rounding errors, 213, 214
VLDM instruction, 223
VMOV instruction, 223
Floating-Point Status Control
  Register (FPSCR), 225
for loop, 72, 73
FPU registers, 214, 215
  load and save, 217, 218
Frame Pointer (FP), 122, 123
Functions, 109
  branch with link, 111, 112
  call algorithm, 115, 116
  parameters and return
    values, 114
  uppercase, 116, 118–120

G

GCC Assembler, 16, 17
General Purpose I/O
  (GPIO) pins
  GPIO controller, 153
  libraries, control, 147
  Linux device driver, 146
  memory

General Purpose I/O
    (GPIO) pins (*cont.*)
    ARM32 instruction, 154
    locations, 155
    registers, 154
    overview, 145, 146
    Raspberry Pi 4 RAM, 154
    registers (*see* Registers in bits)
    virtual memory, 153
Ghidra, 276
    C code, 277
    upper program, 277
Git, 63, 64
Gnome programmer's
    calculator, 29, 30
GNU Assembler, 53, 110
GNU Assembler directives, 351–352
GNU C compiler, 182
    Thumb code, 293
GNU compiler collection
    (GCC), 7, 266, 271, 274
    Assembly code, 274
    C code, 275
    code creation, 271
GNU Debugger (GDB), 7, 43, 51, 56
    breakpoint command, 59
    commands, 63
    debug flag, 57
    delete command, 61
    HelloWorld program, 56
    info breakpoints, 61
    info registers, 60
    makefile, 57
    movexamps program, 58

step command, 60
x /Nfu addr format, 61, 62
GNU Make
    Hello World makefile, 54, 55
    Linux utility, 53
    rebuilding file, 54
    .s file, rule, 54, 55
    variables defining, 55, 56
goto statement, 67, 84
Graphics processing unit (GPU), 3

H

Hello World
    .ascii statement, 22
    assembly instructions, 21
    bash-x, 18
    .data, 22
    disassembly, 23
    LDR instruction, 25
    Linux system, 22, 23
    MOV instruction, 24, 25
    objdump command-line, 23
    program, 17, 18
    _start, 21
    starting comment, 20
    terminal command, 18

I

If/Then/Else statements, 67, 74, 75
If-Then (IT) blocks, 285–286
Instruction set flags, 69
Integers to ASCII conversion

decimal, 83
expressions, 82
pseudo-code, print register, 79
register, printing, 79–81
register to memory, storing, 82
Interrupt flags, 69

J, K

Jenkins, 64–65

L

LIFO (last in first out) queue, 110
Link Register (LR), 111
Linux Gnome calculator, 10, 11
Linux linker/loader, 53
Linux open service, 140
Linux system call error
    codes, 341–346
Linux system call numbers, 327–342
Linux system services, 131, 132, 303
    calling convention
        file descriptor, 133
        structures, 133, 134
        system calls, 132, 133
    file to uppercase (*see* File to
        Uppercase, conversion)
    GNU Assembler's macro, 134
    wrappers, 134
Little-endian format, 31, 32
Load Multiple (LDM), 110
Load Pair (LDP) instructions, 302
Load register with byte (LDRB)
    instructions, 290, 319

Logical operators
    AND, 75
    BIC, 76
    EOR, 76
    NOT, 40
    ORR, 76
Loops, 46
    for loop, 72, 73
    unrolling, 270
    while, 73

M

.MACRO directive, 128
Macros
    BX branch to return, 130
    definition, 128
    directive, 128
    labels, 129
    performance, 130
    toupper function, 125–127
Matrix 3x3 multiplication
    NEON-enabled, 245–247
    scalar, 248
    vector calculations, 244, 245
Move Not (MVN) instruction,
    40, 46, 47
MOV instructions, 39, 41–43, 45,
    46, 48, 112, 290
MOV/MOVT pair, 40, 41
MOVT instruction, 36–37
Multiplication
    ARM multiply instructions, 189
    examples, 192, 193

Multiplication (*cont.*)
multiply instructions, 190
SMULL instructions, 191
SMULW instructions, 191
32-bit instruction, 189
MVT, 40, 41

N

Negative numbers
Gnome programmer's
calculator, 29, 30
one's complement, 30
two's complement, 27, 28
NEON coprocessor, 263
arithmetic operations, 237, 238
4D vector distance
calculation, 239, 240
distance function, 240, 241
makefile, 241
operations flow, 242, 243
VMUL.F32 instruction, 242
FPU registers, 233
lanes, 236, 237
SIMD, 233
VADD instruction, 237
NEON registers, 234–236
Nesting function calls, 112, 113

O

Operand2
register and shift, 38
small number and rotation, 38, 39

P, Q

Program counter (PC) register, 16
Pulse-position modulation
(PPM), 146
Pulse width modulation (PWM), 146
Python
ASCII characters, 186
CDLL function, 186
C functions, 185
shared library, 185, 186
Thonny IDE, 186, 187

R

Raspberry Pi models, 4
Raspberry Pi's memory
ASCII strings, 88
assembler directives, 90
byte statement, 88
double register, 108
escape character
sequences, 91
indexing from memory
computing address, 99
using LDR, 97
using register, 98
write back, 99
loading register, 92
from memory, 95, 96
operators, 89
PC relative addressing
ARM32 instruction set, 94, 95
LDR instruction, 92
load/store instructions, 93

post-indexed addressing
conversion to
uppercase, 100–107
examples, 100
Store Register, 107
Reduced Instruction Set Computer
(RISC), 11, 197
Register destination (Rd), 46
Registers, 114, 115
Registers in bits
GPIO controller, 155
GPSEL0–GPSEL5, 156, 157
GP set and clear pin, 158
protocol, 156
Register to register MOV, 37

S

SDIV/UDIV instructions, 267
-shared command-line
parameter, 179
Shared libraries, 179–181
Shifting and rotating
arithmetic shift right, 35
logical shift left, 35
logical shift right, 35
rotate right, 35
rotate right extend, 36
Single Instruction Multiple Data
(SIMD), 233, 259
16-bit instructions
ADD, 282
IT, 282
64-bit mode

conditional instructions, 308
instructions, 298
memory addressing, 298
registers, 299
uppercase program,
304, 306
SMULL instruction, 190, 322
Source Register (Rs), 46
Stack frames
.data section, 121
define symbols, 124
FP, 123
LIFO protocol, 122
optimization, 124
skeletal function, 123, 124
Stack pointer (SP), 110, 120
execution pipeline, 302
function call, 301
instructions, 300
Stacks, 109
pop, 110
push, 110
Raspbian, 110, 111
Store Byte (STRB)
instruction, 82
Store Multiple (STM), 110, 323
Store Pair (STP)
instructions, 302, 304
STP/LDP instructions, 302
STRB instructions,
104, 290, 323
strlen() function, 141
SUB instructions, 290
SUBS instruction, 71, 294

T

32-bit instructions, 285
32 bits *vs.* 64 bits, 303, 304
Thumb code, 268
    ARM processor, 281, 283
    definition, 281
Thumb-2 variant, 285, 286

U

Ubuntu MATE, 297–298
UMULL instruction, 190, 324
Unconditional branch, 67–68
Uppercase function, 116, 118–120
Uppercase routine
    conditional instruction, 255, 256
    NEON instructions, 259
    parallel processing steps, 262

problem domain, 256, 257, 259
pseudo-code, 251
simplify range
    comparisons, 252–254
VLDM instruction, 261

V

Vector floating-point (VFP), 211
Vectors
    ARM processor, 199
    defined, 198
    dot product, 198
    matrix multiplication, 198, 199
    matrix size, 199

W, X, Y, Z

While loops, 73

Printed in the United States
By Bookmasters